About the Nutritional Information

Nutritional information is provided for each recipe in this book. When there is a choice of two ingredients, such as "salt-free or regular tomato sauce," the breakdown is based on the first one mentioned. It is important to note that the nutritional analysis may vary slightly depending on the brands of food that are used. If a recipe contains a "trace" of a particular item (less than 1/2 gram of protein, total fat, saturated fat, or carbohydrate, or less than 1/2 milligram of sodium or cholesterol), the number will be listed as zero.

Important

This book is not intended as a promotion or recommendation for any specific diet, nor as a substitute for your physician's advice. Its purpose is to show you how you can enjoy a balanced diet, which is low in fat and rich in fruits, vegetables, grains, and legumes.

Bobbie Hinman
"The Meatless Gourmet"

Bobbie Hinman, a pioneer in the field of lowfat cooking, has been preparing healthful meals for her family for over twenty years. Aware of a hereditary cholesterol problem, and determined to raise her family on a lowfat diet, Bobbie has learned to make healthful meals that are also tasty meals. Her transition to a vegetarian diet came over a period of several years and seemed a "natural progression" in her quest to master the art of healthful cooking and, at the same time, provide delicious meals for herself and her family. Called "The Meatless Gourmet," Bobbie has developed an amazing ability to transform high-fat, meat-laden meals into healthful, meatless meals.

Bobbie is constantly in demand as a speaker and cooking teacher and has been a guest on numerous television and radio shows, including "The Regis Philbin Show" and "The Low Cholesterol Gourmet." She also completed a media tour for General Mills, where she discussed the benefits of eating a lowfat, high-fiber diet. Bobbie is the co-author of the *Lean and Luscious* series, bestselling books filled with easy lowfat recipes. She is the author of *The Meatless Gourmet: Favorite Recipes from Around the World, Oat Cuisine*, a unique book of tasty high-fiber recipes, and *Burgers 'n Fries 'n Cinnamon Buns*, a collection of lowfat, meatless recipes for fast food favorites. In addition to writing cooking columns for several monthly publications, Bobbie is a frequent contributor to *The Vegetarian Journal*. She also travels extensively, teaching classes and speaking to hospital groups, cardiac centers, weight management centers, colleges, and private organizations.

Even with her busy schedule, Bobbie still finds time to read as many health publications as possible and consult with doctors, dietitians, and other health professionals. Her goal is to keep abreast of the latest advances in food and health issues so that she can continue to help people enjoy the benefits of healthful eating.

Bobbie resides in Delaware with her husband Harry. They have four grown children and an ever-widening circle of magnificent grandchildren.

Contents

Introduction

Basics of Meatless Meals

This book is not only for vegetarians. It's for the ever-growing number of health-conscious people who want to enjoy meatless meals, whether occasionally or every day. More and more people are becoming increasingly aware of the health benefits of meatless meals.

Scientific studies have consistently shown that the higher the consumption of meat and high-fat dairy products, the higher the risk of heart disease, certain types of cancer, and possibly other diseases as well. On the other hand, studies have shown that the frequency of heart disease and cancer *decrease* as the consumption of fruits and vegetables *increases*.

Meatless meals are also a good source of carbohydrates, the "fuel" that gives our bodies energy. In countries where high-carbohydrate diets, based on fruits, vegetables, grains, and beans, are the norm, there are lower incidences of the diseases that appear to be linked to high-fat foods. The old way of thinking was that foods such as pasta and potatoes were "fattening." Now we know that these foods are high in energy-producing carbohydrates, and the only fattening part of the foods was what we put on them!

What Are the Main Components of Meatless Meals?

People always ask me "But what *do* you eat?" It's very simple: fruits, vegetables, grains, and beans (legumes). But, like any other meal, meatless meals should be balanced and consist of a wide variety of different foods. Simply eliminating the meat from your diet is not enough. The rest of your foods should be fresh and wholesome, with as few packaged or processed foods as possible. In other words, if you give up the steak, but the rest of the meal consists of high-fat, nutritionally poor foods such as fried potatoes, iceberg lettuce, donuts, and beer, you are definitely on the wrong track!

Consume ample portions each day of:

Fruits   All types, preferably fresh

Vegetables   Green vegetables such as broccoli, kale, spinach, cabbage, and romaine lettuce, and yellow vegetables such as carrots, squash, sweet potatoes, and pumpkin

Grains   Whole grains such as brown rice, corn, millet, oats, bulgur, barley, buckwheat, and wheat (including breads, pasta, and cereals)

Legumes   Lentils, split peas, soy beans (including tofu), and beans of all types (navy, kidney, pinto, lima, black, etc.)

But Will I Get Enough Protein?

Most people are unaware that there is high-quality protein in vegetables, grains, nuts, seeds, and legumes. So you can get the protein (and the fiber) without all the fat and cholesterol that comes from meat. Also, contrary to what we once believed, it is not necessary to combine proteins at each meal. The answer is to eat a balanced diet and include a variety of protein-rich foods each day. For instance, the protein from oatmeal for breakfast, peanut butter on whole wheat bread for lunch, and lentil casserole and broccoli for dinner will all "find each other" and combine so that your body can utilize them.

Fat and Cholesterol

This is often a very confusing subject. Many people do not realize that fat and cholesterol are *not* the same thing.

What Is the Difference Between Fat and Cholesterol?

Cholesterol is a substance that is produced by the body and is used in the production of body tissues. We also get cholesterol from consuming foods that contain cholesterol. When faced with more cholesterol than the body can handle, the response is often to "store" the excess cholesterol in the arteries. Health professionals feel that this is a major factor in the development of heart disease.

No plant contains cholesterol. It is only found in animal foods. However, some plant foods are relatively high in fat so, while large amounts of them do not actually contain cholesterol, they still contribute too much fat to the diet and this, too, may raise the levels of cholesterol in the blood. These high-fat foods should be consumed in moderation. They include nuts, peanut butter, coconut, olives, margarine, and vegetable oils. Be sure to read labels carefully and be aware that some advertisers may tout the advantages of their products as being *cholesterol-free* and fail to mention the possible *high fat* content of the other ingredients.

Which Foods Contain Cholesterol?

Remember that *only animal products contain cholesterol.* This includes meat, poultry, seafood, dairy products, and egg yolks (the egg white contains no cholesterol), and also animal fats such as butter, chicken fat, suet, and lard. However, remember that any food with a high percentage of saturated fat can also potentially raise your blood cholesterol level. Vegetable sources with a high percentage of saturated fat include palm kernel oil, coconut, and coconut oil.

What Is the Difference Between Saturated and Unsaturated Fat?

The simple answer is that different fats affect the body in different ways. Saturated fats are thicker fats that are solid at room temperature. They tend to elevate blood cholesterol levels. Unsaturated fats are liquid at room temperature and it is believed that they generally do not raise blood cholesterol levels. Many health professionals recommend that we use the fats that contain the lowest amounts of *saturated* fat and the highest amount of *monounsaturated* fat. The better choices include olive oil and canola oil. (In all of my recipes that call for vegetable oil, I have used canola oil.) But remember that these are still all fat and should be consumed in moderation.

How Much Fat Should I Eat?

Many health professionals recommend that we get less than 30 percent of our total daily calories from fat. Still others feel that we should go as low as 10 percent. Most, however, are somewhere in the middle. Of the total number, most of this should come from unsaturated fat. No one is suggesting that you keep a calculator nearby whenever you eat. However, it is a good idea to keep track of your fat grams for a few days and see what you are actually consuming. You may be surprised. Many unsuspected foods contain hidden fats that can really add up if you are not careful. (See below.)

To figure your own daily fat allowance, multiply your daily calorie intake by 0.3 (to find 30 percent of calories) or by 0.2 (to find 20 percent of calories). Then divide your answer by 9 for the number of fat grams that you would be allowed each day.

For example: 1500 calories × 0.30 = 450 ÷ 9 = 50 grams of fat daily

Total Daily Calories	Number of Fat Grams Daily 30% of Calories from Fat	Number of Fat Grams Daily 20% of Calories from Fat
1200	40	27
1500	50	33
2000	67	44
2500	83	56

Remember that it is figured *by the day*, not the individual food, so if you eat a little more fat in one meal, you can compensate by eating less fat in the other meals. Ideally, the formula should be used to evaluate your daily or weekly diet, rather than single foods.

Which Foods Contain the Most Fat?

The foods that are highest in saturated fat are butter, whole-milk dairy products, meat, poultry, and eggs, and also the recipes and products that contain them. This includes mayonnaise, cheese, puddings, and chocolate products.

Many people are surprised to learn that foods such as crackers may contain very high amounts of (often saturated) fat. Other potential sources of fat are some cereals (usually the granola-types), nondairy coffee creamers, whipped toppings, snack foods, and even the seemingly innocent foods such as packaged popcorn and dry bread crumbs. The answer here is to *always read the labels and ingredients carefully*.

What About Dairy Products?

When choosing dairy products, always choose those that are lowest in fat and cholesterol. Choose skim milk, nonfat yogurt, evaporated skim milk, buttermilk, nonfat dry milk, and nonfat or reduced-fat cheeses. If you want "meltability," the reduced-fat cheeses seem to melt better than the nonfat ones.

Many people either choose not to, or are unable to, eat dairy products for a variety of reasons. Fortunately, there are many new reduced-fat soy and rice-based substitutes on the market today, including milk and cheese. I have found these to work in any recipe that calls for dairy products. They can be substituted in equal amounts.

What About Eggs?

In baked goods that call for eggs, two egg whites can be substituted for each whole egg, thereby eliminating the cholesterol (found only in the yolk) and lowering the fat content of the recipe. Commercial egg substitutes will also work (these are made from egg whites and you may want to compare the price to that of regular egg whites). If you want to eliminate the eggs completely, a three-ounce piece of tofu, blended until smooth, can be substituted for one whole egg (or two egg whites) in baked goods. There are also several completely egg-free egg substitutes available in health food stores.

What About Sugar?

Whatever your choice of sweetener, whether it's sugar, honey, molasses, or maple syrup, the nutritional values are not significantly different. When our well-meaning mothers told us that foods such as chocolate, cakes, and pastries were "fattening," we all assumed that the sugar was causing the bulges. Now we know that it was really the fat in these products. The main goal is to reduce the total amounts called for in a recipe, remembering that moderation is the key.

What About Calories?

It's a hard concept to "swallow," but counting calories is out! It's the fat that's clogging our arteries, not the calories. While no one is saying that you can eat everything in sight without regard to calories, it is wise to pay attention to the amount of fat in foods and make sure that, in your daily diet, you consume no more than 20 percent to 30 percent of your calories from fat. If you do this and plan your diet around fresh fruits and vegetables, along with whole grains and beans, you will automatically eat fewer calories. Isn't it nice that most of the *foods that are low in fat are also low in calories?*

Fiber

Fiber is the flip side of the coin. We always think of cutting back, but here is something that we actually need more of. Isn't it convenient that most of the foods that are *low in fat are also high in fiber?*

What Is Fiber?

In recent years, there has been quite a lot of publicity surrounding fiber. The reason for this is that studies have shown that a high-fiber diet may be our first line of defense against heart disease and several forms of cancer. (The word "fiber" refers to the indigestible parts of plant food, such as pectin, cellulose, and bran.) One particular type of fiber—water soluble fiber—may significantly lower blood cholesterol levels. This type of fiber is abundant in many plant foods including oats, apples, figs, prunes, carrots, plums, squash, barley, kidney beans, split peas, and chickpeas. The other type of fiber—insoluble fiber—is found in whole grains such as cornmeal and whole wheat flour (especially wheat bran) and in fruits and vegetables such as broccoli, cabbage, raspberries, and strawberries. This type of fiber seems to improve intestinal function, and many researchers feel that it may aid in preventing some types of cancer. It is important to have both types of fiber in our diet. (Our grandmothers were right about fiber. They called it roughage and *knew* it was good for us.)

Remember that *fiber is only found in plant foods.* No animal food contains this important nutrient.

How Much Fiber Do I Need?

Many health professionals recommend that we boost our intake of fiber-rich foods, preferably to 25 to 30 grams a day. Remember that fresh fruits and vegetables, as well as whole grains and legumes, are our main sources of fiber and we need to have several servings of each of these foods every day. *Meat and dairy products contain no fiber.*

How Can I Add Fiber to My Meals?

Here are some quick and easy ways to add fiber to your meals:

- Choose whole grain breads, crackers, and pasta.
- Choose breakfast cereals made from whole grains.
- Make your own bread crumbs from toasted whole grain bread.
- Add peas, beans, and lentils to soups, stews, and salads.
- Leave the skin on fruits and vegetables whenever possible.
- Add grated vegetables to sauces and casseroles.
- Use puréed vegetables to thicken soups and stews.
- Make tossed salads using vegetables of all colors.
- Eat fresh or dried fruit for snacks and desserts.
- Use brown rice in place of white rice and try other whole grains, such as oats, millet, barley, and bulgur.
- Add cooked grains to soups and casseroles.
- Replace at least half the flour in baked goods with whole wheat flour.

Sodium

We also hear a lot about sodium. Here are some frequently asked questions.

What Is Sodium?

Sodium is a mineral that occurs naturally in many foods. Most of the sodium in the American diet, however, comes from table salt and from sodium that is added to processed foods and beverages. It is added for flavor and as a preservative and sometimes appears under different names, such as sodium citrate, sodium nitrate, and sodium phosphate.

The problem is that too much sodium can contribute to high blood pressure. Although some sodium is essential to our health, the recommendation from many health professionals is that we limit our daily sodium intake to 2,400 to 3,000 milligrams, or about 1 to 1 1/2 teaspoons of salt. (Sounds easy until you read the ingredients and labels on packaged foods!) *Most plant foods are relatively low in sodium,* making them especially healthful for blood pressure.

Here are some helpful hints for reducing sodium in your diet:

- Use herbs and spices in place of salt.
- Always taste food before adding salt.
- Choose reduced-sodium or salt-free canned foods whenever available.
- Rinse canned foods, such as beans, to remove salt.
- Choose reduced-sodium soy sauce and other condiments.
- Don't add salt to boiling water when cooking pasta.
- Read labels carefully.

Basic Substitutions

Instead of:	Try:
Whole eggs	Two egg whites in place of each egg, or egg substitutes (in cakes and muffins, a 3-ounce piece of tofu will also work in place of 1 egg).
Whole milk	Skim milk or lowfat soy or other nondairy milk
Cream	Evaporated skim milk or plain nonfat yogurt
Sour cream	Plain nonfat yogurt (for a cooked sauce, blend 1 tablespoon of cornstarch into each cup of yogurt before heating; do not boil)
Ice cream	Reduced-fat or fat-free ice cream, yogurt, soy-based, or other nondairy frozen desserts
Whipped cream (as a dessert topping)	Vanilla nonfat yogurt
Chicken or beef broth	Vegetable broth or water mixed with Vegetable Broth Mix (page 34)
Mayonnaise	Half reduced-calorie mayonnaise and half plain nonfat yogurt
Butter	Margarine that lists a liquid oil as the first ingredient, or vegetable oil (however, all are high in fat and should be used sparingly)
Vegetable oil	An oil with a high amount of monounsaturated fat, such as olive oil or canola oil
Oil in baked goods	Replace 3/4 of the oil with applesauce or nonfat yogurt

Instead of:	Try:
Salad dressings with lots of oil	Replace 1/2 the oil with water or fruit juice
Cheese	Reduced-fat cheese or reduced-fat soy or other nondairy cheese (many fat-free cheeses are still relatively high in fat and sodium and should be used sparingly; many are also loaded with chemicals and don't melt or even taste like cheese)
Sugar	Use *half* the amount called for (this works in most recipes, except cookies)
White rice	Brown rice or other whole grains
All-purpose flour	Replace half with whole wheat flour
French fries	Baked potatoes (with a lowfat topping such as nonfat yogurt and chopped chives)
Frying	Grilling, baking, roasting, broiling

Time-Saving Tips for Quicker Meals

While many of the recipes in this collection take only minutes to prepare, others may take a little longer. My goal is to eliminate extra steps and, using healthful ingredients, prepare the quickest and easiest meals possible. Here are some hints to guide you:

- Assemble all of your ingredients before you begin to cook. Then, put each one away as you finish using it. This is especially helpful when making stir-fried dishes.
- Always start preparations with the food that takes the longest to cook. For example, if the brown rice takes 40 minutes and the bean dish takes only 15 minutes, the rice can cook while you prepare the beans.
- Clean up as you cook. Saving all the cleaning for last makes a lot more work.
- When cooking brown rice, always cook more than you need. Freeze the leftovers in small containers and defrost by placing them in a strainer and pouring boiling water over them.
- For a quick salad, toss any leftover grain with a lowfat or fat-free vinaigrette and serve cold.
- Choose angel hair pasta when you're in a rush. It cooks in just a few minutes.

- It *is* more expensive, but you can buy precut vegetables at most grocery store salad bars. It's such a luxury to have someone else do the washing and chopping!
- Soups and stews that often take a bit longer to prepare can be made ahead on weekends or when there is a little more time, then enjoyed all week.
- Plan ahead and, while you're chopping vegetables, chop for the next day's dinner also.
- Whenever you chop onions or green peppers, chop a few extras and keep them in the freezer. They're perfect for cooking.
- Whenever you grate orange or lemon peel, grate a few extras and store the peel in the freezer in airtight containers. It can be added to recipes without thawing.

Hints for Organizing Your Kitchen

A well-organized kitchen can cut preparation times in half. Try these easy strategies:

- Keep all of your measuring cups and spoons handy and in one place.
- Make sure your knives are sharp. Nothing slows down chopping like a dull knife. A sharpening stone is a good tool to have.
- Keep frequently used appliances such as the blender handy, preferably right on the kitchen counter.
- Store mixing spoons and spatulas on the counter within easy reach.
- Keep clutter to a minimum by storing less frequently used items inside cabinets.
- Keep spices on narrow shelves or small turntables to make it easy to locate the ones you need.
- Always label and date jars and containers as soon as you transfer items into them.
- Store like items together, such as baking supplies, grains, pastas, etc.

The Well-Stocked Lowfat Pantry

If you keep your pantry well stocked, you will always be able to put together a meal in less time than it takes to run to the nearest fast food restaurant. You'll save lots of fat that way, too, and you'll always have healthful snacks available when the "munchies" strike.

Fruits

Dried fruits   A selection of raisins, dates, figs, prunes, apricots, and
   any other favorites
Canned fruits   Unsweetened applesauce and fruits packed in juice,
   such as crushed pineapple, peaches, and apricots

Vegetables

Canned tomato products   Salt-free or regular (according to tastes and
   dietary needs) canned whole tomatoes, crushed tomatoes, tomato
   sauce and tomato paste
Canned pumpkin
Chopped green chilies
Black olives
Canned vegetable broth (or dry broth mix)

Pasta and Pasta Sauces

Pasta   A variety of shapes and sizes, including angel hair, elbows,
   and orzo
Yolk-free noodles
Jars of reduced-fat, meatless pasta sauces
Pizza sauce

Grains

Rolled oats
Brown rice   Quick-cooking and long-grain
Basmati rice
Other grains   A selection, such as couscous, bulgur, millet, barley,
   cornmeal, oat bran (store the grains in jars and keep the cornmeal
   and oat bran in the refrigerator)

Legumes

Canned beans   A variety, such as pinto, kidney, black, Great North-
   ern, and chickpeas (garbanzos)
Dried split peas, lentils, and red lentils
Vegetarian baked beans

Baking Supplies

Honey
Molasses
Brown sugar
Granulated sugar
Cocoa (unsweetened) or carob powder
Cornstarch
All-purpose and whole wheat flour   (although listed here, whole wheat
    flour keeps longer and stays fresher when kept in the refrigerator)
Baking powder and baking soda
Nonfat dry milk or powdered soy milk
Evaporated skim milk
Vegetable oils   Canola oil and extra-virgin olive oil
Nonstick cooking spray

Spices and Extracts

Always keep dried herbs and spices in airtight containers away
from heat and light. Buy in small quantities, as packaged spices lose
quality if stored for a long period of time, and be sure to buy from
stores that have a good turnover. Try not to keep dried spices for
longer than six months to one year.

A good basic selection consists of basil, bay leaves, chili powder,
ground cinnamon, chives, ground cloves, ground cumin, curry
powder, dill weed, garlic powder, ground ginger, dry mustard,
onion powder, oregano, salt, paprika, pepper, and thyme.

Extracts   Pure vanilla, almond, coconut, lemon, mint, orange
Vegetable Broth Mix (page 34)

Condiments

Many of these condiments need to be refrigerated after opening.
Be sure to read the labels carefully.

Soy sauce (reduced-sodium or regular)
Barbecue sauce
Vinegar (white, red wine, and cider vinegar)
Pure fruit jams and spreads

Mustard (yellow and Dijon)
Ketchup
Salsa

Miscellaneous

Fat-free crackers
Peanut butter   (without added sugar or oil)
Bread   (if you buy whole grain breads or breads made without
    preservatives, store them in the refrigerator)

In the Refrigerator

Fresh fruits and vegetables
Fruit juice
Skim milk
Reduced-fat or fat-free cheese
Eggs or egg substitute
Tub-style margarine
Reduced-fat mayonnaise
Grated Parmesan cheese
Nonfat plain and vanilla yogurt

In the Freezer

   If you buy frozen fruits and vegetables in bags, rather than boxes,
you will have the option to use part of a package.

Frozen strawberries, blueberries, and cranberries
Frozen vegetables
Lowfat or fat-free ice cream or frozen yogurt
Chopped onion   To avoid having the vegetables clump together,
    spread the onions on a cookie sheet in a single layer, place in the
    freezer just until frozen, then store them in plastic bags.
Chopped green bell pepper   Prepared the same way as the onions.
Corn tortillas and flour tortillas
Shredded reduced-fat Cheddar and mozzarella cheeses
Juice concentrate
Bread, English muffins, bagels, burger buns

Snack Foods to Have Handy

Popcorn (hot-air type, with no added fat)
Baked potato chips
Pretzels
Baked tortilla chips

All About Beans

Legumes, the dried seeds of certain pod-bearing plants, are known simply as "beans." These little nutrition powerhouses are high in protein, minerals, fiber, and B vitamins and are low in fat and sodium. They also have the added advantage of being very low in cost. Dried beans come in many shapes, colors, flavors, and textures.

About Dried Beans

Dried legumes are available all year and are usually sold in clear plastic bags. Choose beans with a uniform size and color, without a lot of cracking or holes. One pound of dried beans equals 2 cups and will yield approximately 6 cups of cooked beans.

How to Store Beans

Stored in tightly covered containers in a cool, dry place, legumes can be kept for six to nine months. Cooked beans can be refrigerated for a week and they can also be frozen. They thaw quickly and are ready for use.

About Canned Beans

Canned beans are already cooked and ready to use. However, they usually contain salt and should be rinsed well and drained before using. In most of the recipes, I refer to 1-pound cans. However, can sizes do vary and, as long as they are close to 1 pound, the recipes will not be affected. A 1-pound can contains approximately 2 cups of beans.

Avoid Stomach Upset

Often, people complain of gastric distress after eating beans. Sometimes the problem is not as much from the beans as it is from simply eating too much fiber without allowing time for your body to become accustomed to a new type of diet. The good news is that with most people the distress is temporary and disappears as their bodies become used to a high-fiber diet. You may want to start by eating small portions of beans and gradually increase the serving size as your body becomes accustomed to them. It sometimes helps to start with canned beans which are cooked longer and tend to cause fewer stomach problems. It's also important to always chew your food thoroughly.

Preparation Tips for Dried Beans

- Always pick over dried beans first and remove any stones, dirt, or discolored beans.
- The beans should be rinsed before using.
- With the exception of split peas and lentils, all dried beans need to be soaked before cooking.
- Legumes should always be simmered; rapid boiling will break them apart.
- Keep the lid of the pot partially open to keep the beans from boiling over.
- Stir beans occasionally while cooking and add additional water if necessary.

How to Cook Beans

Before cooking, beans need to be soaked in order to restore the water lost in drying. (This does not hold true for split peas and lentils, which do not require soaking.)

Soak the beans first, using either of the two following methods. Then, using 2 to 3 cups of water for each cup of beans, bring the water to a boil and add beans. (There should be enough water to cover the beans by 1 inch.) Reduce heat to low, cover partially, and simmer for the amount of time specified, or until beans are tender. Cooking times may vary with the size, quality, and freshness of the legumes.

Quick-Soaking Method Place beans in a pot and add enough water to cover beans by 3 inches. Bring to a boil over medium heat. Boil 2 minutes. Remove from heat, cover, and let stand 2 hours. Drain and cook as directed.

Overnight Soaking Method   Place beans in a bowl and add
enough water to cover beans by 3 inches. Soak overnight, drain, and
cook as directed.

Cooking Times for Legumes

Black beans	1 to 2 hours
Black-eyed peas	30 to 45 minutes
Garbanzo beans	2 to 3 hours
Great Northern beans	1 to 1 1/2 hours
Kidney beans	1 1/2 to 2 hours
Lentils	30 to 45 minutes
Lima beans	1 to 1 1/2 hours
Navy beans	1 1/2 to 2 hours
Pinto beans	1 1/2 to 2 hours
Soy beans	2 to 3 hours
Split peas	30 to 45 minutes

* Cooking times are for soaked beans, except for split peas and lentils, which do not
require soaking.

All About Tofu

Tofu, also known as bean curd (both unfortunate names!), is a
protein food produced from soybeans. The process is similar to that
of making cheese: a coagulating agent is added to soy milk, causing
the milk to separate into curds (the tofu) and whey.

When adapting recipes to make them meatless and lower in fat,
tofu makes a wonderful replacement for meat. Being rather bland
and almost tasteless, it easily takes on the flavor of whatever it is
cooked with.

Nutritional Information

Tofu is a superior source of both protein and essential minerals
and vitamins. (The soybean is a complete protein.) Tofu is entirely
free of cholesterol, very low in saturated fat, and also low in calories.
Tofu is also a good source of calcium, iron, phosphorus, potassium,
sodium, essential B vitamins, and vitamin E. Clearly it is a nutritious
alternative protein source that contributes to a healthy diet.

Along with tofu's high nutritional profile, here's an added bonus—it's inexpensive. An entire meal consisting of tofu, vegetables, and whole grains can usually be prepared for a fraction of the cost of a meat-based meal.

Different Types of Tofu

Tofu is available in a variety of forms:

Medium tofu   It has a soft texture resembling that of cheesecake and can be used in casseroles and in tofu "cheesecakes."

Firm tofu   It is more solid and dense and is ideal for stir-frying.

Silken tofu   It has a smooth, custardy texture and is ideal for dips, sauces, and puddings. Many large grocery stores carry 10-ounce aseptic packages of silken tofu (Mori-Nu brand), which is available in a reduced-fat version that tastes just like the original.

How to Store Tofu

Prepackaged tofu is available in the produce section of most large grocery stores. Fresh tofu is also widely available in many health food stores. When buying packaged tofu, always check the date on the container to be sure the tofu is fresh. When you get home, open the package, drain the water, add fresh water, cover, and refrigerate. The water should be changed every one to two days, and the tofu can be kept up to ten days. (This is not true of the tofu in aseptic packages, which can be stored at room temperature and opened just before using. Once opened, it should be refrigerated, but adding water is not necessary.)

Freezing Tofu

Tofu can easily be frozen, however, the texture will change dramatically. Frozen tofu becomes slightly yellow in color, and the texture becomes somewhat chewy and more meat-like. While it can still be used in most recipes, the results will be different. To freeze tofu, remove it from the water and wrap it securely. To thaw, place the tofu in a heatproof bowl and cover it with boiling water. Drain after 10 minutes. If the tofu is still frozen, repeat the process. Gently press tofu between the palms of both hands to squeeze out the water before using. Tofu can also be thawed overnight in the refrigerator.

All About Grains

Grains are actually the seed kernels of certain plants. They add different tastes and textures, as well as fiber and important nutrients, to the diet. You may occasionally have to visit a specialty store to find a particular grain, but large grocery stores are meeting the demand and more and more of them are stocking large varieties of grains. Remember that grains are not just for dinner. Cooked grains topped with cinnamon and raisins, with added milk or orange juice, make a tasty, nutritious breakfast.

Nutritional Information

Whole grains have the bran and germ still intact and therefore contain more fiber and B vitamins than grains that have been *milled*, or *polished*. (An example is brown rice, which is more nutritious than white rice that has had the bran and germ removed by milling.)

Grains are an important source of carbohydrates that provide fuel and energy to our bodies. The fiber in whole grains is also believed by health professionals to help protect us from heart disease and possibly some forms of cancer. Ideally, we should add a variety of different grains to our diet, supplying not only different nutrients, but a delicious assortment of flavors and textures.

About Buying Grains

Grains are available all year and are usually found packaged or in bulk in health food stores and most large grocery stores. Health food stores also carry many unusual varieties, such as triticale, teff, quinoa, spelt, and Job's tears (I hope these names will pique your interest and you will seek them out!).

Forms of Grains

Whole grains   Called groats, these are the entire kernel with the bran and germ intact. Examples are brown rice, wheat berries, barley, and millet.

Cracked grains   The entire kernel is cracked into small pieces, allowing the grains to cook more quickly. They are minimally processed and contain most of their original vitamins. Examples are cracked wheat and steel-cut oats.

Flakes The entire kernel is flattened and steamed, allowing it to cook quickly. An example is rolled oats, however, wheat and barley are also available as flakes and make delicious breakfast cereals. The "quick" or "instant" varieties are further processed, which reduces their nutritional value.

Flour Most grains can be ground into flour. Whole wheat flour is made from the entire kernel, unlike all-purpose flour which is made from wheat that has been milled. *Stone-ground whole wheat flour* is the best nutritionally, because it is ground between heavy stones using water power and no artificial enrichment is added. It is a little heavier than commercial whole wheat flour. *Unbleached flour* is all-purpose flour that has been allowed to whiten naturally, rather than chemically bleached like all-purpose flour. It has a slightly higher protein content than all-purpose flour and contains more of the vitamin E that is lost during chemical whitening. Unbleached flour is available in health food stores and most large grocery stores and can be used wherever all-purpose flour is called for.

About Storing Grains

Whole grains contain the germ that is rich in oil, making them more susceptible to rancidity than milled grains. Cracked grains also become rancid quickly because the oily germ is exposed. Therefore, it is best to buy both of these types in small quantities and store them in airtight containers in the refrigerator, where they will keep for several months. It is also wise to buy from a store that you know has a rapid turnover.

Milled grains have a longer shelf life and can be stored in a cool, dry place in airtight containers for up to one year.

About Cooking Grains

Most packaged grains are clean, however, if you buy grains in bulk, you may find bits of chaff or weeds among the grains, so it is wise to pick over the grains before cooking.

Following are the cooking times for a selection of the most popular grains. Generally, unless stated otherwise, they are stirred into boiling water, then covered, the heat is reduced, and they are simmered until the grains are tender and most of the liquid has been absorbed. If the grain is not soft enough, add a small amount of hot liquid and cook a little longer. Grains can be cooked in water or broth.

It is important to remember that the cooking times are approximate and may vary slightly with the size and quality of the grains. Grains with similar cooking times can be combined and cooked together.

Grain	Amount	Water	Cooking Method	Cooking Time	Yield
Barley	1 cup	4 cups	Add to boiling water	45 minutes	3¹/2 cups
Bulgur	1 cup	2 cups	Add to boiling water	15 minutes	3 cups
Cornmeal	1 cup	3 cups	Add to boiling water	25 minutes	4 cups
Kasha	1 cup	3 cups	Toast in pan and add boiling water	15 minutes	3¹/2 cups
Millet	1 cup	2 cups	Add to boiling water	20 minutes	3 cups
Quinoa	1 cup	2 cups	Add to boiling water	15 minutes, then let stand 10 minutes	3 cups
Rolled oats	1 cup	2 cups	Stir into boiling water	5 to 8 minutes	1³/4 cups
Oats, steel-cut	1 cup	3¹/2 cups	Add to boiling water	20 minutes	3 cups
Rice, brown	1 cup	2¹/2 cups	Add to boiling water	45 minutes	3¹/2 cups
Wheat berries	1 cup	3¹/2 cups	Add to boiling water	40 to 60 minutes	3 cups

Cooking Brown Rice in the Microwave

It may not save a lot of time, but this is an easy way to cook brown rice. Be sure to use an extra-large microwave-safe casserole to prevent overflow (a 1³/4-quart bowl or casserole is ideal for 1 cup of uncooked rice) and *do not* cover the casserole.

Place 1 cup of uncooked brown rice in the casserole and add 2¹/2 cups of water or broth. Microwave on 100 percent power for 10 minutes, then 60 percent power for 20 minutes. Then cover rice and let stand 5 minutes. Fluff with a fork before serving.

Note: Cooking times may vary according to the power and type of microwave used and you may have to make adjustments to fit your particular oven.

All About Fruits and Vegetables

Eat Your Fruits and Vegetables

Health experts recommend that we eat at least five servings of fruits and vegetables each day. Think of it—they contain vitamins, minerals, fiber, and *almost no fat at all.* Most fruits can be eaten raw, and although most vegetables can be eaten either raw or cooked, generally, the longer vegetables are cooked, the more nutrients are lost. So remember one of my cardinal rules that says to "cook vegetables only until they are tender-crisp." Ideally, they should be steamed rather than boiled. Cooking texture is a big factor in whether or not people like vegetables, and nothing is less appealing than a plate of soggy veggies!

Wash Fruits and Vegetables

Always wash fruits and vegetables just before preparing, but do not soak them in water unless necessary, because this may draw out some of the valuable vitamins. Vegetables such as leeks and romaine lettuce are usually very sandy and should be washed well under running water to remove grit.

Leave the Skin On

Whenever possible, do not peel fruits or vegetables. There are valuable nutrients and fiber both in and under the skin that are lost in peeling. However, if you buy produce that has been waxed, such as apples or cucumbers, you *should* peel them.

Storage

In an ideal world, it would be nutritionally best to buy and eat freshly picked fruits and vegetables each day. However, for most of us this is quite impossible. It is best to use fruits and vegetables as soon as possible and to always store them in the refrigerator, preferably in the vegetable crisper. In addition, most vegetables will keep better if they are stored unwashed and then washed before preparing.

How to Select and Store Fruits and Vegetables

When shopping for vegetables, try to choose those that are bright in color and firm in texture. The healthy-looking vegetables that have deep, rich colors will contain more vitamins than the limp, pale ones.

Basic Steaming Directions for Vegetables

Steaming is a cooking method that preserves much of the flavor and texture of the vegetables and keeps vitamin loss to a minimum. (There *are* some vegetables that are usually boiled or baked, such as beets and potatoes, and many of the ones in the following list are also delicious stir-fried.) If you do choose to boil a vegetable, add just enough water to cover the vegetable, and be sure to save the cooking liquid to add to soups and sauces.

Always wash and trim vegetables before using (see descriptions following). Place a steamer basket or rack in the bottom of a saucepan and add water almost up to, but not touching, the rack. Bring the water to a boil and add the vegetables. Cover and cook just until vegetables are tender-crisp. Cooking times will depend on the freshness and variety of the vegetables.

A word of caution: When removing the cover from a steaming pot, always open it *away* from you.

Choosing, Storing, and Preparing Fresh Produce

Vegetables

Alfalfa sprouts   Look for sprouts that are fresh, crisp, and bright green with no signs of mold or stickiness. Refrigerate, unwashed, in a plastic bag and use within a few days.

Artichokes   Choose ones that are heavy and fairly compact with tightly closed leaves. Avoid ones with brown spots. To prevent drying, wrap unwashed artichokes in a damp towel and store in a plastic bag in the refrigerator for up to three days. Before cooking, cut off the stem close to the base, remove tough bottom leaves, and trim off leaf points with a pair of scissors. Wash the artichoke well.

The edible portions are the heart and the soft, moist inner flesh of the leaves. To cook: steam.

Asparagus Choose straight, firm stalks of uniform thickness with tightly closed tips. The stalks should be at least two-thirds green. Use asparagus as soon as possible, and if necessary to store, place a moist paper towel in a plastic bag with the asparagus to keep it from drying out and store it in the refrigerator. Wash asparagus well to remove dirt that may accumulate under the leafy parts of the tips. Before cooking, break off the tough woody ends. (Bend the stalks and break them where they snap easily.) To cook: steam or stir-fry.

Beans Green beans, also known as string beans, should be slender, firm, and smooth, and should snap easily. Wax beans are a similar, yellow bean. Avoid tough, rubbery beans and beans with signs of shriveling or drying. Store in plastic bags in the refrigerator for three or four days. Before cooking remove strings and brown tips. Many of today's beans are bred to be "stringless." To cook: steam, sauté, stir-fry, add to soups and stews.

Bean sprouts Choose firm, white sprouts without brown spots. Refrigerate in a plastic bag and use right away. Bean sprouts are also available canned, but tend to be salty and mushy. To cook: stir-fry.

Beets Often sold in bunches with their edible green tops attached, beets can vary in color, with the most common variety being a deep, rich red. Choose firm, smooth, round beets, avoiding soft or elongated ones with soft spots or scaly areas. The tops are very perishable, but the tubers (red parts) will keep in the refrigerator vegetable crisper for two weeks. Before refrigerating, cut off the green tops, leaving one to two inches intact. Peel beets before using. To cook: boil, bake.

Bell peppers Peppers may be either green, red, purple, orange, or yellow. Choose firm, bright peppers with tight, unwrinkled skin. Avoid those with dull, soft skins or soft spots. They will keep in the refrigerator crisper for a week. Remove the stalk, seeds, and inner white membranes before using. To cook: steam, stir-fry, grill, broil, bake, add to soups and stews.

Broccoli Choose broccoli with firm stalks, compact heads, and firm, tender, lighter green stalks. The color of the heads can range from green to purple, depending on the variety of the broccoli. Avoid those with open yellow buds. The stalks are edible, as well as the buds, however, they should be peeled before cooking as they tend to be tough. The heads cook more quickly than the stalks, so the

stalks should be split lengthwise and sliced just up to the heads before cooking. Wrap unwashed broccoli in plastic and refrigerate.
Use within five days. To cook: steam, stir-fry.

Brussels sprouts   Choose bright green Brussels sprouts with tightly
closed leaves. Avoid yellowing heads. Refrigerate unwashed
sprouts in a plastic bag and use within three days. Wash under
running water, removing any loose outer leaves. Cut an "x" into
the base of each one before cooking. To cook: steam.

Cabbage   The varieties include the smooth green, red, and white types,
the loose, crinkle-leafed savoy cabbage, and also bok choy and Chinese cabbage (also known as napa or celery cabbage). Choose firm
heads, heavy for their size, with well-colored leaves that are crisp
and fresh. Avoid any with yellowing, wilted leaves. Remove and
discard the coarse outer leaves and store heads in plastic bags in
the refrigerator. Green, white, and red cabbages keep as long as ten
days, but savoy and Chinese cabbage should be used within two
days. To cook: steam, braise, stir-fry, add to soups and stews.

Carrots   Select carrots that are firm, crisp, and brightly colored.
Avoid those with green or yellow areas at the top. Plastic-wrapped
carrots may be refrigerated for several weeks. If greens are attached, remove them before storing. Instead of peeling carrots,
scrub them with a vegetable brush. To cook: steam, braise, stir-fry,
add to soups and stews.

Cauliflower   Choose white, closely packed heads with fresh, green
leaves. (These leaves are edible and are delicious steamed.) Cauliflower can be broken into flowerets or steamed whole. Wrap unwashed cauliflower in plastic and use within five days. To cook:
steam, stir-fry.

Celery   Choose firm, crisp heads with healthy-looking green leaves.
Avoid celery with wilted, flabby branches or discolored areas.
Stored in a plastic bag in the refrigerator, celery will keep for seven
to ten days. To cook: stir-fry, braise, add to soups and stews.

Chives   Look for chives with fresh green, unwithered shoots. Wrap
unwashed chives in damp paper towels and store in a plastic bag
in the refrigerator. Wash just before using and use with a few days.
Chives are generally sprinkled on foods just before serving.

Corn   Choose corn that is as freshly picked as possible. Look for
fresh, green husks with no sign of decay in the silk ends. Refrigerate corn and use as soon as possible. To cook: steam, grill, add to
soups and stews.

Cucumber   Look for firm cucumbers with a strong green color and no
yellowing or shriveling. Choose relatively slender ones rather than

the overly mature larger ones. Refrigerate and use within a few
days. If the skins have been waxed, peel before using.

Eggplant Choose firm, glossy eggplant, heavy for its size, with a
deep purple color. (There are also white and black varieties.)
Avoid ones that are soft or shriveling. Refrigerate and use within
a week. To cook: broil, grill, bake, stir-fry.

Fennel Look for well-rounded white or light green stalks. Avoid
bulbs with brown spots. Store fennel in a plastic bag in the refrigerator and use within one week. Generally, the bulb is more tender
than the stalks, and both can be eaten raw or cooked. To cook:
steam, stir-fry, braise, grill, add to soups and stews.

Garlic Look for bulbs that are tightly closed, with unwrinkled skins
of pink, white, or purple. Store in a cool, dry, dark place. Garlic
will keep well for several weeks. To cook: bake, stir-fry, add to
soups and stews.

Ginger Also called ginger root, this tuber should be firm and plump
with a pale tan skin. Keep, loosely covered, in the refrigerator for
several weeks. It is usually minced or grated and does not need to
be peeled.

Green onions Look for ones with crisp, green, unwithered tops and
unblemished white bottoms. Store in the vegetable crisper and use
within a few days. To cook: stir-fry, add to soups and stews.

Kale Look for broad, crisp leaves of dark green. Avoid drooping or
yellowed leaves. Place in a plastic bag and refrigerate in the vegetable crisper. Use as soon as possible. Before using, wash kale and
cut away tough stems. To cook: steam.

Leeks Choose leeks with crisp, green tops and unblemished white
bottoms. Avoid yellow or wilted tops. Look for cylindrical, rather
than bulbous, leeks, as the latter may be tough. Refrigerate in the
vegetable crisper and use within one week. To clean, discard the
green tops and cut the white parts in half lengthwise. Wash well
under running water, removing sand or soil that often lodges between the leaves. To cook: sauté, stir-fry, braise, steam, add to
soups and stews.

Lettuce There are crisphead varieties of lettuce such as *iceberg*, softer
varieties such as *Boston* and *Bibb*, long, loose-headed lettuce such
as *romaine*, and leaf lettuces such as *red* or *green leaf*. In crisphead
lettuce, look for clean, solid heads with medium-green outer leaves
and lighter inner leaves. Romaine should be crisp and dark. The
others are softer but should be bright-colored and fresh. Avoid
discoloration and signs of decay in all varieties. Wrap lettuce in a
damp towel and store in the refrigerator in the vegetable crisper.

Loose-headed lettuce and leaf lettuce should be used within a few days. Head lettuce keeps longer. Wash and drain before using.

Mushrooms (domestic button mushrooms) Select plump mushrooms that are smooth, with light-colored caps that are closed tightly around the stem. The gills should not be showing. Wrap unwashed mushrooms in paper towels and refrigerate. They are very perishable and should be used within one to two days. To cook: grill, broil, sauté, stir-fry, add to soups and stews.

Onions Choose ones that are well shaped and hard with crisp, papery skins and no green sprouts. Onions will keep for several weeks in a cool, dry place. In warm weather, they should be refrigerated. To cook: steam, grill, broil, sauté, stir-fry, add to soups and stews.

Parsnips Resembling white carrots, parsnips should be firm and smooth. Look for smallish parsnips, avoiding the sometimes tough larger ones. They should also be firm, rather than limp. Place in a plastic bag and store in the refrigerator for up to two weeks. Unlike carrots, parsnips need to be cooked before eating. To cook: steam, braise, add to soups and stews.

Peas There are several varieties available, including *shell peas, flat snow peas,* and *plump sugar snap peas.* The latter two have edible pods. Look for smooth, bright, well-filled pods and refrigerate peas, in their pods, in loose plastic bags. Use with a few days. Wash pods and remove the strings before using. To cook: steam, stir-fry, sauté. Shell peas should be shelled just before using. To cook: steam, add to soups and stews.

Potatoes There are several groups of potatoes, among them the tender, small, thin-skinned *new potatoes,* which are ideal for potato salads, the *all-purpose potatoes,* and those that are ideal *baking potatoes,* such as the Idaho and russet. All potatoes should be firm and fairly smooth with no sprouts or decay. Avoid any with green discolorations, numerous eyes, cuts, or bruises. Store potatoes in a cool, dark, well-ventilated bin, not in the refrigerator, for two to three weeks. Before using, scrub the skin well and, if possible, do not peel. To cook: bake, boil, roast, grill, sauté, add to soups and stews.

Pumpkins Choose firm pumpkins that are heavy for their size, with few scars or bruises and no signs of decay. Store in a cool, dry place for up to a month. (*See also* Squash.) To cook: bake, boil, steam, add to soups and stews.

Radishes Look for firm, bright radishes with few scars or bruises. To store, remove the leafy tops and refrigerate for up to two weeks.

Shallots   Choose shallot bulbs with a paper-thin skin. Store in a cool, dry, well-ventilated place for up to a month.

Spaghetti squash   Look for squash with firm, hard, unblemished skin and no signs of decay. The colors can range from pale yellow to orange. Store in a cool, dry place for up to a month. Whole squash can be microwaved at full power for six minutes per pound or baked in a 375° oven in a pan with an inch of water for 45 to 60 minutes. Be sure to pierce squash with a sharp knife in several places before baking, or it might explode. (*See also* Squash.)

Spinach   Choose fresh, crisp, dark green leaves. Avoid those that are crushed, bruised, or wilted. Store, unwashed, in a plastic bag in the vegetable crisper and use within a few days. To cook: steam, stir-fry, add to soups and stews.

Squash   There are two types of squash, the tender-skinned *summer squash* such as zucchini, pattypan, and yellow crookneck, and the hard-skinned *winter squash* such as butternut, acorn, pumpkin, and Hubbard. Both types should have firm, smooth skins. Summer squash do not need to be peeled; winter squash do. Refrigerate summer squash and use within a few days. Store winter squash in a cool, dry place for up to a month. To cook summer squash: steam, grill, stir-fry. To cook winter squash: steam, bake, add to soups and stews.

Sweet potato   Look for firm potatoes with smooth, evenly-colored, yellow-brown skins. Avoid any with shriveled ends or signs of decay. Store in a cool, dry place for up to two weeks. To cook: bake, add to soups and stews.

Tomato   Look for firm, plump fruits with a bright red color and a strong tomato smell. Vine-ripened tomatoes are the best choice, however, they are only available in most areas from May to September. Tomatoes available in the winter months are often treated with gas to ripen and they are odorless (and often tasteless). Avoid tomatoes that are soft or have splits in the skin. Under-ripe tomatoes can be stored in a light spot for a few days to ripen. Ripe tomatoes can be kept at room temperature for a day or two, but for longer storage they should be refrigerated. Use ripe tomatoes as soon as possible. To cook: broil, grill, bake, add to sauces, soups, and stews.

Turnips   Choose firm, smooth turnips with fresh green tops. Avoid soft, wrinkled turnips. Remove the tops and store in the vegetable crisper for up to two weeks. To cook: steam, stir-fry, braise, add to soups and stews.

Fruits

Apples   Choose firm apples with good color. Avoid apples with
  bruises, punctures, or soft spots. Always store apples in a refrigerator or very cool place. To keep cut apples from turning brown, always cut them just before using, or dip the cut pieces in orange or
  lemon juice.

Apricots   Choose apricots that have a deep golden color and yield
  slightly to pressure. Avoid ones that are greenish and either very
  hard, bruised, or mushy. Refrigerate apricots immediately and use
  within a few days.

Avocados   Avocados may have a smooth, dark green skin or a
  greenish-black pebbly skin, depending on the variety. When
  ripe the flesh should yield slightly to pressure. Avoid those with
  dark, sunken spots or cracks. Use ripe avocados immediately. Cut
  just before using and rub any unused portions with lemon juice to
  keep flesh from turning brown. To prepare, cut avocado in half
  lengthwise and twist the halves apart. Remove the seed with a
  spoon. Hold each half cut-side up and the flesh can be scooped out
  in one piece with a spoon.

Bananas   Choose plump, firm bananas without dark bruises. Speckles
  indicate ripeness and these bananas are best in breads, cakes,
  and pies. Store bananas at room temperature until ripe, then
  they may be refrigerated for a few days. The peel will darken
  when refrigerated, but this will not hurt the banana. Peel just
  before using or dip in orange or lemon juice to prevent the flesh
  from browning.

Blueberries   Choose plump, firm, dark blue berries of uniform size.
  Avoid stained containers, which may indicate mushy fruit. Discard
  any moldy berries and store remaining ones in the refrigerator for
  up to a few days. Wash them just before using. Frozen blueberries
  can be used in place of fresh ones.

Cherries   Look for plump, glossy cherries with fresh stems and good
  color. The color will depend on the variety and may vary from pale
  yellow to very dark red. Discard any moldy or damaged cherries
  and store remaining ones in the refrigerator for up to a week. Wash
  them just before using.

Cranberries   Look for firm, plump, glossy cranberries. Avoid shriveled or light-colored ones. Refrigerate for up to a week, or freeze in
  the original container. Wash just before using.

Grapefruit   Choose firm, heavy fruit. Avoid fruit with soft spots or
  bruises; however, a brownish discoloration of the surface of the

rind will usually not affect the quality of the fruit. Refrigerate grapefruit and use within two weeks.

Grapes There are many varieties of grapes, with a broad range of colors and flavors. Each variety should be plump, well-colored, and firmly attached to the stems. Avoid shriveled or split grapes. Discard any moldy or shriveled grapes and store remaining ones in the refrigerator for up to two weeks.

Kiwi fruit Choose kiwis that are slightly firm with no signs of shriveling. When ripe, they will yield to gentle pressure. They can be ripened at room temperature and then refrigerated for up to a week.

Lemons Choose smooth-skinned lemons with a rich yellow color. Always scrub well before using the peel in any dish and only use the yellow part of the peel, called the *zest*. Lemons may be refrigerated for several weeks. To get the most juice out of a lemon, warm it in a microwave for one minute at 50 percent power or roll in on a counter top for a minute or so, pressing down on it with your palm as you roll.

Limes Look for limes with green, glossy skin. Avoid ones with a yellowish color. Limes may be refrigerated for several weeks. (*See* Lemons for preparation and juicing.)

Mangoes Choose firm mangoes with no dark spots or shriveling. Fully ripe mangoes have a lot of red and orange color and yield to gentle pressure. Green ones can be ripened at room temperature and then refrigerated for up to three days.

Melons There are many varieties of melons, with the skin ranging from smooth and glossy to furrowed and netted. Generally a ripe melon will yield to gentle pressure at the blossom end and have a light fragrance. Avoid any with soft spots, punctures, or moldy ends. Melons can be ripened at room temperature and then refrigerated for a few days.

Papaya Choose fruit that is mostly yellow, with smooth skin. Avoid any with dark spots or soft ends. A ripe papaya will yield to gentle pressure. Papayas can be ripened at room temperature and then refrigerated for several days.

Peaches Choose peaches that are fairly firm, yet yield to gentle pressure. The color should be cream or yellow with a red blush. Avoid hard, greenish fruit, very soft fruit, or fruit with bruises. Peaches can be ripened at room temperature and then refrigerated for up to a week.

Pears   There are many varieties and colors of pears. Choose ones that are free of blemishes and have good color for their variety. Pears can be ripened at room temperature and then stored in the refrigerator.

Pineapples   Choose plump, heavy fruit with fresh green leaves, a rich yellow color, and a fragrant aroma. Avoid ones that are soft, too green, or have withered brown leaves. Refrigerate ripe pineapple and use as soon as possible.

Plantains   Choose plump, firm, green to greenish-yellow fruit. The peel of the plantain is often marked with blemishes, but they generally do not affect the quality of the fruit.

Plums   There are many varieties of plums, ranging in color from yellowish-green to purple-black. Choose slightly firm fruit with a good color for the variety. Ripe plums will yield to gentle pressure. Avoid very hard plums or ones with bruises. Plums can be ripened at room temperature and then refrigerated for up to five days.

Raspberries   Choose plump berries in unstained containers. Discard any moldy berries and store remaining ones in the refrigerator. Wash berries just before using. They should be used within one day.

Strawberries   Look for bright, firm berries with a good aroma and with the green stems attached. For best flavor, choose smaller berries over larger ones. Discard any moldy berries and store remaining ones in the refrigerator. Wash berries just before using. Use within two days.

Suggested Menus

Breakfast Menus

Carrot-Pineapple Juice (page 458)
Breakfast Grains with
Apples and Grapes (page 303)
Whole wheat toast with jam

Crock Pot Applesauce (page 360)
Oatmeal
Apricot Brown Bread (page 270)
with
Fat-free cream cheese

Multigrain Raisin Muffin (page 275)
with
Jam and fat-free cream cheese
Three-Fruit Smoothie (page 448)

Lunch Menus

Refried Bean Dip (page 37)
on
Whole wheat pita
with
Lettuce and tomato
Mushroom Gazpacho
Salad (page 88)
Mangoade (page 457)

Tossed salad
with
"House" Vinaigrette (page 100)
Sweet Caribbean
Tofu Salad (page 96)
on
Whole wheat toast
Minted Pineapple Lemonade
(page 450)
Cream of Fresh
Vegetable Soup (page 66)

Italian Cunnellini Salad (page 87)
on
Bed of lettuce
Layered Lemon Cup (page 420)
Juicy Tea Combo (page 455)

Dinner Menus

Endive Salad with
Orange Curry Dressing (page 79)
Stove-Top Bean and
Noodle Casserole (page 138)
Steamed green beans
Peach-Berry Angel
Shortcake (page 421)

Fresh vegetables
with
Roasted Red Pepper
Spread (page 52)
Moroccan Pasta and
Vegetable Soup (page 57)
Grilled Portobello
Sandwich (page 207)
Sweet Potato "Fries" (page 337)
Very Peachy Tapioca (page 427)

Tossed salad
with
Maple-Dijon Vinaigrette (page 102)
Eggplant and Rice Parmesan (page 130)
Steamed broccoli
Winter Fruit Crisp (page 404)

Vegetable Broth

Many recipes, both in this book and others, call for vegetable broth. It is available in cans (in the soup section of most large grocery stores), in dry form (see Vegetable Broth Mix on page 34), or by simmering vegetables and herbs in water. Following is just one suggestion for a homemade broth. You can easily create your own by using any combination of vegetables or vegetable trimmings. There are a few vegetables that I consider a "must" in a good broth: onions (or leeks), carrots, potatoes, garlic, and celery. Other tasty possibilities include: winter squash, Swiss chard, shiitake mushrooms, eggplant, corn cobs, and tomatoes. Some vegetables have a rather strong flavor and may overpower a stock, so I avoid using them unless I want their particular flavor to be dominant: green peppers, broccoli, turnips, fennel bulbs, cauliflower, asparagus, and Brussels sprouts. Strain the finished broth for use in other recipes, or the vegetables can be puréed and served as a thick soup. Broths will keep well in the refrigerator for several days and can be frozen.

Makes 10 to 12 cups

1	large onion, chopped
1	large potato, unpeeled, cut into 1-inch pieces
2	leeks, cut into 1-inch pieces (white and green parts)
2	large carrots, cut into 1-inch pieces
2	stalks celery, with leaves, cut into 1-inch pieces
2	tomatoes, chopped
4	cloves garlic, coarsely chopped
1/4	cup chopped parsley
1	teaspoon dried basil
2	bay leaves
8	whole peppercorns
1/2	teaspoon dried thyme
1/2	teaspoon salt
1/4	teaspoon ground sage
12	cups (3 quarts) cold water

Combine all ingredients in a large soup pot. Bring to a boil over medium heat. Reduce heat to medium-low, cover, and simmer 1 hour. Strain and use as needed.

Each cup provides:

18	Calories	4 g	Carbohydrate
0 g	Protein	109 mg	Sodium
0 g	Total fat (0 g Sat. fat)	0 mg	Cholesterol

Vegetable Broth Mix

When soup recipes call for vegetable broth mix, you can either buy the ready-made mix in jars or packets or you can make your own. This is a basic mix, but don't be afraid to alter it by adding your own favorite spices. If you wish to reduce the amount of sodium, you can replace the celery salt with celery seed. This recipe can easily be doubled or tripled and, stored in a jar with a tightly fitting lid, will keep for several months. If you buy a commercial mix, be sure to read the ingredients carefully, as some of the mixes contain MSG or extremely high amounts of salt.

Important: When using commercially prepared mixes, follow the directions on the label, as some mixes recommend 1 tablespoon of mix per cup of water and others recommend 1 teaspoon.

Makes 12 servings
(1 teaspoon each serving)

1	tablespoon onion powder
1	tablespoon dried parsley flakes
1 1/2	teaspoons garlic powder
1 1/2	teaspoons celery salt
1/2	teaspoon ground sage
1/2	teaspoon dried marjoram
1/2	teaspoon dried thyme
1/2	teaspoon dried basil
1/2	teaspoon dried oregano
1/4	teaspoon pepper
1/4	teaspoon dill weed

Combine all ingredients and mix well. Store in a jar with a tightly fitting lid. Stir before each use.

Use 1 rounded teaspoonful to each cup of water.

Each serving provides:

4	Calories	1 g	Carbohydrate
0 g	Protein	81 mg	Sodium
0 g	Total fat (0 g Sat. fat)	0 mg	Cholesterol

Dips and Spreads

Dips and spreads can suit so many purposes. They're ideal for appetizers, make great snacks, can often be used as salad dressings, and can also be spread between slices of bread for an easy sandwich. They're also usually the quickest and easiest appetizers to make. Most dips require only a whirl in the blender or a mix or two, and they're ready to enjoy.

For dip accompaniments, choose cut-up fresh fruit or vegetables or whole grain breads and crackers and be sure, when buying crackers, to read the labels carefully. Crackers are often a source of unexpected, hidden fat, and some crackers can turn a healthy dip into a high-fat nightmare. Fortunately, many varieties of baked tortilla chips and potato chips are also available in grocery stores; they also make tasty dippers.

In order to keep the fat content low, the recipes in this chapter use only lowfat or nonfat dairy products. You get lots of fiber from the addition of fruits, vegetables, and even beans. They're easy and delicious and make great snacks, so don't wait for a party to try these tasty dips and spreads.

Refried Bean Dip

Canned refried beans form the basis for many quick dishes. This easy dip can be put together almost as fast as you can open the can. Be sure to read the labels carefully when buying the beans and choose the ones without any added fat.

Makes 2 1/2 cups

1	1-pound can fat-free vegetarian refried beans
1	4-ounce can chopped green chilies (hot or mild), drained
1	teaspoon dried oregano
1/4	teaspoon garlic powder
1/2	cup plain nonfat yogurt
	Salt and pepper

In a medium bowl, combine beans, chilies, oregano, and garlic powder. Mix well. Stir in yogurt, mixing until thoroughly blended.
Add salt and pepper to taste.
Chill.
Serve with (baked) tortilla chips or toasted pita triangles.
❖*Serve-again hint:* Cut off one short end of a submarine roll, scoop out part of the inside, and fill the roll with dip, shredded lettuce, and chopped tomato. What a great lunch!
You can also make a quick snack by spreading the dip on mini rice cakes and topping each one with finely chopped jalapeño peppers.

Each tablespoon provides:			
11	Calories	2 g	Carbohydrate
1 g	Protein	55 mg	Sodium
0 g	Total fat (0 g Sat. fat)	0 mg	Cholesterol

Sesame-Dill Tofu Dip

Tofu makes a perfect base for dips. Its mild, bland flavor (or lack of flavor) enables it to take on the flavor of whatever it is added to. This dip is wonderful for veggies, especially cucumbers and carrots. It's also a great salad dressing.

Makes 1 cup

1	10-ounce package reduced-fat silken tofu (Look for Mori-Nu brand available in aseptic packages in the produce section of many large grocery stores.)
1	large clove garlic, crushed
2	teaspoons dill weed
1	teaspoon onion powder
1/2	teaspoon sesame oil
1/4	teaspoon salt
1/4	teaspoon pepper

Place tofu in a blender container and blend until smooth. Spoon into a small bowl. Add remaining ingredients, mixing well.

Chill several hours to blend flavors.

❖*Serve-again hint*: If you have any leftover cooked lentils or chickpeas, you can create a Middle Eastern-style sandwich by spooning the leftover legumes into a pita and topping them with the dip and some sliced green onions.

Each tablespoon provides:			
10	Calories	1 g	Carbohydrate
1 g	Protein	50 mg	Sodium
0 g	Total fat (0 g Sat. fat)	0 mg	Cholesterol

Curried Tomato Bean Dip

Blend, chill, and serve. This tangy dip has a flavor that goes well with taco chips (baked, of course) or veggie dippers.

Makes 2¹/₂ cups

1	1-pound can pinto beans, rinsed and drained (or 2 cups of cooked beans)
1	8-ounce can salt-free (or regular) tomato sauce
2	heaping tablespoons chopped onion
³/₄	teaspoon ground cumin
³/₄	teaspoon curry powder
³/₄	teaspoon garlic powder
¹/₂	cup plain nonfat yogurt

In a blender container, combine all ingredients, *except* yogurt. Blend until smooth. Spoon mixture into a bowl and stir in yogurt, mixing well.

Chill.

✧*Serve-again hint:* The leftovers are delicious heated (in a saucepan or in a microwave) and spooned over rice or onto a baked potato.

Each tablespoon provides:

10	Calories	2 g	Carbohydrate
1 g	Protein	22 mg	Sodium
0 g	Total fat (0 g Sat. fat)	0 mg	Cholesterol

Chili and Black Olive Salsa

This chunky salsa is a perfect dip for (baked) tortilla chips and is also delicious spread on toasted French bread slices. It's great as a party food and also as a football game snack.

Makes 1 1/2 cups

1	4-ounce can chopped green chilies (hot or mild), drained
1	large, ripe tomato, chopped
12	extra-large, pitted black olives, chopped
2	green onions, thinly sliced (green and white parts)
1	large clove garlic, crushed
1 1/2	teaspoons olive oil
1	teaspoon red wine vinegar
1/2	teaspoon dried oregano
1/4	to 1/2 teaspoon pepper

Combine all ingredients in a medium bowl, mixing well. Chill.

✦*Quick tip:* A mini food processor will chop the olives in a second or two.

✧*Serve-again hint:* For a delicious sandwich, fill a sub roll with left-over salsa and add a slice of reduced-fat Cheddar cheese.

Each tablespoon provides:

9	Calories		1 g	Carbohydrate
0 g	Protein		55 mg	Sodium
1 g	Total fat (0 g Sat. fat)		0 mg	Cholesterol

Pumpkin and Black Bean Dip

Dips today can be both healthful and delicious—quite different from the dips of the past that were made with sour cream and other high-fat products. This tasty dip can be served with veggies or (baked) tortilla chips, and it can even be used to fill hollowed-out cherry tomatoes for a really festive party treat.

Makes 3 cups

1	1-pound can black beans, rinsed and drained (or 2 cups of cooked beans)
1/4	cup chopped onion
1/4	cup chopped green bell pepper
2	tablespoons plain nonfat yogurt
2	teaspoons Dijon mustard
1	1-pound can pumpkin
1	teaspoon ground coriander
1	teaspoon ground cumin
1/2	teaspoon garlic powder
1/2	teaspoon salt
1/4	teaspoon pepper

In a blender container, combine beans, onion, green pepper, yogurt, and mustard. Blend until almost smooth. (Small pieces of the beans will remain.) Spoon mixture into a medium bowl and add remaining ingredients. Mix well.

Chill.

◇*Serve-again hint:* Leftovers make a delicious sandwich filling, especially on rye bread with sliced tomato and onion. They can also be heated and rolled in tortillas to make a quick burrito dinner.

Each tablespoon provides:

10	Calories	2 g	Carbohydrate
1 g	Protein	44 mg	Sodium
0 g	Total fat (0 g Sat. fat)	0 mg	Cholesterol

Sweet 'n' Sour Red Onion Dip

This unusual recipe was shared with me by Letha Comegys, a fellow food lover. She uses it in her catering business and always gets rave reviews. Thanks, Letha.

Makes 2 cups

1	teaspoon vegetable oil
1	cup finely chopped red onions
1	tablespoon sugar
2	tablespoons water
1	tablespoon red wine vinegar
1	12-ounce container lowfat (1%) cottage cheese
3	tablespoons reduced-calorie mayonnaise
1	teaspoon bottled hot sauce
$1/4$	teaspoon salt
$1/2$	teaspoon chili powder
$1/8$	teaspoon garlic powder

Heat oil in a small nonstick skillet over medium heat. Add onions. Cook, stirring frequently, until onions are tender, about 3 minutes. Stir the sugar, water, and vinegar into the pan. Cover and cook for 1 minute. Remove from heat and let cool 10 minutes.

Place cottage cheese and mayonnaise in a blender container or food processor. Blend until smooth. (If using a blender, blend the cottage cheese in 2 or 3 batches.) Spoon into a bowl. Stir in onions and remaining ingredients. Mix well.

Chill thoroughly.

Serve with vegetable dippers or crackers.

Each tablespoon provides:

16	Calories	1 g	Carbohydrate
1 g	Protein	72 mg	Sodium
1 g	Total fat (0 g Sat. fat)	1 mg	Cholesterol

Quick-a-mole Dip

Similar to guacamole but quicker and easier, this dip makes fresh vegetables come alive. Avocado lovers will be in heaven!

Makes 1 cup

1	medium, ripe avocado, peeled and center seed discarded
1	teaspoon lime juice
1/4	teaspoon garlic powder
1/8	teaspoon chili powder

Place avocado in a small bowl and mash with a fork until smooth. Add remaining ingredients and mix well.

Enjoy right away or refrigerate for later serving.

Note: Avocados darken after being cut. The lime juice will help somewhat, and it also helps to cover the dip tightly with foil and stir just before serving. This darkening does not affect the flavor or quality of the dip.

✤*Serve-again hint:* This dip also makes a great sandwich spread. Serve it on toasted whole grain bread with lettuce, tomato, sliced cucumber, and alfalfa sprouts.

Each tablespoon provides:

27	Calories	1 g	Carbohydrate
0 g	Protein	2 mg	Sodium
2 g	Total fat (0 g Sat. fat)	0 mg	Cholesterol

Creamy Sweet Cheese

This topping is so thick, rich, and creamy, you'll swear it's high in fat. You'll be amazed that a lowfat topping can taste so good. Use it as a dip for fresh berries or any type of fruit or as a topping for reduced-fat ice cream, angel food cake, and other desserts. Let your imagination be your guide.

Makes 3 cups

1	12-ounce container lowfat (1%) cottage cheese
2¹/₂	tablespoons sugar
1	teaspoon vanilla extract
¹/₂	teaspoon ground cardamom
2	cups vanilla nonfat yogurt

In a blender container, combine all ingredients, *except* yogurt. Blend until smooth. Spoon mixture into a bowl and add yogurt. Mix well.

Chill thoroughly.

Stir again just before serving.

✧*Serve-again hint:* Make a thick spread by straining the mixture. Place a cone-shaped coffee filter (natural, unbleached) in a strainer and suspend it over a bowl to catch the drippings. (Or, you can line the strainer with several layers of cheesecloth.) Spoon topping into filter. Place in the refrigerator and let drain for 24 hours. Then, spoon mixture into a small bowl. (Discard the liquid that has drained from the yogurt.) Use it as a spread for toast, graham crackers, or sliced fresh fruit.

Each tablespoon provides:

16	Calories	2 g	Carbohydrate
1 g	Protein	35 mg	Sodium
0 g	Total fat (0 g Sat. fat)	1 mg	Cholesterol

Maple-Tahini Fruit Dip

If you love the sweet, mellow flavor of tahini, you'll flip over this easy dip. It's heavenly for dipping fresh fruit, especially apples, pears, and bananas. Tahini is made from ground sesame seeds in the same way that peanut butter is made from peanuts, and it is available in health food stores and many large grocery stores. Like peanut butter, it is relatively high in fat, making this a dip that should be used sparingly.

Makes about 1/2 cup

1/4   cup plus 2 tablespoons pure maple syrup
1/4   cup plus 1/2 tablespoon tahini

Combine maple syrup and tahini in a small bowl or custard cup. Mix well, stirring until mixture is well blended.

Serve right away or chill for later servings.

❖*Variation:* For a sinfully sweet, decadent-tasting treat, add 1 tablespoon of unsweetened cocoa and 1/4 teaspoon almond extract. Yum!

Each tablespoon provides:			
106	Calories	12 g	Carbohydrate
2 g	Protein	14 mg	Sodium
5 g	Total fat (1 g Sat. fat)	0 mg	Cholesterol

Sweet Cinnamon Tofu Dip

*For dipping fresh fruit or for topping pancakes or waffles, this versatile dip
adds all the nutrients of soy and tastes delicious. It can also be used to wake
up an otherwise boring English muffin or slice of whole wheat toast.*

Makes 1 cup

1	10-ounce package reduced-fat silken tofu (Look for Mori-Nu brand available in aseptic packages in the produce section of many large grocery stores.)
1	tablespoon maple syrup
1	tablespoon firmly packed brown sugar
1/8	teaspoon ground cinnamon
1/4	teaspoon vanilla extract
2	drops lemon extract

Place tofu in a blender container and blend until smooth. Spoon
into a small bowl. Add remaining ingredients, mixing well.

Chill several hours to blend flavors.

✦*Quick tip:* Keep a few packages of tofu in the refrigerator so it will
always be handy for dips or puddings. (Be sure to see the "No-Bake
Desserts" chapter on page 412.)

Each tablespoon provides:

15	Calories	2 g	Carbohydrate
1 g	Protein	16 mg	Sodium
0 g	Total fat (0 g Sat. fat)	0 mg	Cholesterol

Tangy Herbed Eggplant Spread

This has become one of my favorite weekend recipes. When watching a game on TV or a movie with friends or family, I like to slice a loaf of crusty French bread, put out a bowl of this tangy dip, and enjoy. It can be made ahead and served cold; however, I've also served it warm to hungry friends who loved it.

Makes 1 1/2 cups

1	medium eggplant (1 pound)
1/3	cup coarsely chopped onion
1	large clove garlic
1	tablespoon lemon juice
1	tablespoon vegetable oil
1	teaspoon Dijon mustard
1/2	teaspoon red wine vinegar
1	tablespoon dried parsley flakes
1/2	teaspoon dried oregano
1/2	teaspoon dried basil
1/2	teaspoon dill weed
1/4	teaspoon salt
1/16	teaspoon pepper

Preheat oven to 400°.

Cut off the stem end of the eggplant, place the eggplant on a sheet of aluminum foil, and bake 25 minutes, or until eggplant is very tender. Remove from oven and cut eggplant in half to cool.

In a blender container, combine onion, garlic, lemon juice, oil, mustard, and vinegar. Blend until smooth. Add eggplant, along with remaining ingredients. Blend just until smooth, turning the blender on and off several times. (Do not let mixture get soupy.)

Spoon into a bowl and chill.

◆*Quick tip:* An eggplant that is long and thin will cook faster than one that is short and fat. Also, two small eggplants will cook even faster.

Each tablespoon provides:

12	Calories		1 g	Carbohydrate
1 g	Protein		29 mg	Sodium
1 g	Total fat (0 g Sat. fat)		0 mg	Cholesterol

White Bean and Toasted Onion Spread

Browning the onions until they are crisp gives this spread a delectable flavor. It's great on crackers, sliced French bread, or toasted pita triangles, and it can also be spread on carrot or celery sticks.

Makes 1 cup

1¹/₂	teaspoons vegetable oil
1	cup finely chopped onion
1	teaspoon reduced-sodium (or regular) soy sauce
¹/₈	teaspoon pepper
1	1-pound can white kidney beans (cannellini), rinsed and drained (or 2 cups of cooked beans)

Heat oil in a medium nonstick skillet over medium heat. Add onion. Cook, stirring frequently, until onion is brown, about 10 minutes. (The secret to the flavor of the spread is to let the onions get nicely browned, but do not let them burn.)

In a food processor or blender container, combine onions with remaining ingredients. Process until smooth.

Chill.

❖*Serve-again hint:* Make a delicious quesadilla by spreading the leftovers on a flour tortilla and placing on a griddle. Fold tortilla in half and press down gently. Heat tortilla, flipping it back and forth, until hot and crispy on both sides.

Each tablespoon provides:

28	Calories	4 g	Carbohydrate
2 g	Protein	48 mg	Sodium
1 g	Total fat (0 g Sat. fat)	0 mg	Cholesterol

Hummus with Sun-Dried Tomatoes

Sun-dried tomatoes enhance this popular spread by adding a lively color and a delicious flavor that's slightly tart, yet slightly sweet. Spread on crackers or vegetable dippers, this is sure to be a favorite.

Makes 1¹/2 cups

4	sun-dried tomato halves (not packed in oil), cut into ¹/4-inch pieces
	Boiling water
1	1-pound can chickpeas (garbanzo beans), rinsed and drained (or 2 cups of cooked beans)
¹/4	cup water
2	tablespoons lemon juice
2	tablespoons tahini (sesame paste)
2	to 3 cloves garlic, chopped
1	teaspoon dried parsley flakes
	Dash pepper

Place tomatoes in a small bowl and cover with boiling water. Set aside for 10 minutes.

In a blender container, combine remaining ingredients. Blend until smooth. Add tomatoes and blend for a few seconds, until tomatoes are in tiny pieces but not completely puréed. Stir a little more water into the spread if a thinner consistency is desired.

Chill several hours to blend flavors.

❖*Serve-again hint:* Hummus piled into a pita with chopped tomato and shredded lettuce makes a terrific sandwich.

Each tablespoon provides:			
22	Calories	3 g	Carbohydrate
1 g	Protein	23 mg	Sodium
1 g	Total fat (0 g Sat. fat)	0 mg	Cholesterol

Tomato Cream Cheese Spread

This easy spread makes a perfect topping for toasted bagels. It's also a great appetizer and can be spread on melba toast or crackers or served with vegetable dippers. I've also used it to stuff celery, creating a very pretty party platter.

Makes 1¹/₂ cups

1	8-ounce container fat-free cream cheese
1	1-pound can stewed tomatoes, drained well (squeeze out as much liquid as possible)
3	tablespoons thinly sliced green onions (green and white parts)
1	teaspoon ground cumin
	Few drops bottled hot sauce, or to taste

Combine all ingredients in a bowl and mix well. (If smaller pieces of tomato are desired, chop them before adding to the cream cheese.) Chill.

✧*Serve-again hint:* Have some leftover black beans or pinto beans? Add them to the spread and stuff into a pita with lettuce and sliced onion for a great sandwich.

Each tablespoon provides:

14	Calories	2 g	Carbohydrate
2 g	Protein	94 mg	Sodium
0 g	Total fat (0 g Sat. fat)	1 mg	Cholesterol

Dilled Vegetable Spread

This has always been one of my mother's favorite ways to serve cream cheese. It's different each time she makes it, depending on the vegetables she has on hand. Use my combination as a suggestion and add whatever vegetables you like.

Makes 1¹/2 cups

1   8-ounce container fat-free cream cheese
¹/4   cup very finely chopped radish
3   tablespoons very finely chopped carrots
3   tablespoons very finely chopped green onions (green and
        white parts)
1   tablespoon very finely chopped red or green bell pepper
¹/4   teaspoon dill weed
¹/8   teaspoon pepper

Combine all ingredients in a bowl and mix until well blended.
Chill.

✦*Quick tip:* If you have a mini food processor, it can be used to chop the vegetables in a flash.

Each tablespoon provides:

9	Calories	1 g	Carbohydrate
1 g	Protein	46 mg	Sodium
0 g	Total fat (0 g Sat. fat)	1 mg	Cholesterol

Roasted Red Pepper Spread

If you keep a jar of roasted peppers in the pantry, you can always whip up this easy spread. It's delicious on crackers or toast, it can be used as a dip for fresh veggies, or it can be used as a tasty sandwich spread.

Makes ³/₄ cup

1	7-ounce jar roasted red bell peppers, rinsed and drained
1¹/₂	teaspoons lemon juice
1	teaspoon olive oil
1	teaspoon dried parsley flakes
1	teaspoon onion powder
1	clove garlic, chopped
¹/₈	teaspoon salt
¹/₈	teaspoon pepper

Combine all ingredients in a blender container. Blend until smooth. Chill.

Each tablespoon provides:

10	Calories	1 g	Carbohydrate
0 g	Protein	58 mg	Sodium
0 g	Total fat (0 g Sat. fat)	0 mg	Cholesterol

Apple-Walnut-Date Spread

If you like a sweet spread on your bagel or crackers, this one's for you. It's filled with chopped apples and dates and is enhanced with the added crunch of walnuts. I've even eaten it as a dessert, spread on graham crackers and served with fresh apple slices.

Makes 2 cups

1	cup very finely chopped Golden Delicious apple, peeled
1	teaspoon lemon juice
1	8-ounce container fat-free cream cheese
1/2	cup very finely chopped pitted dates
2	tablespoons finely chopped walnuts
1	teaspoon vanilla extract

Place apple in a medium bowl. Sprinkle with lemon juice and mix well. Add remaining ingredients. Mix until blended.

Chill.

◆*Quick tip:* A food processor will chop the apples, dates, and walnuts in no time.

Each tablespoon provides:

19	Calories	3 g	Carbohydrate
1 g	Protein	34 mg	Sodium
0 g	Total fat (0 g Sat. fat)	0 mg	Cholesterol

Honey-Pumpkin Spread

This quick, jam-like spread is delicious on graham crackers or any type of bread or muffin, and it is perfect to serve at a holiday brunch. Low-sugar fruit pectin is available in most grocery stores, often labeled as "no sugar needed fruit pectin."

Makes 3 1/2 cups

1	1-pound can pumpkin
1	cup orange juice
1/2	cup honey
1/2	teaspoon pumpkin pie spice
1/4	teaspoon ground cinnamon
1	1 3/4-ounce package low-sugar fruit pectin

In a medium saucepan, combine all ingredients, *except* pectin. Mix well.

Gradually add pectin, stirring briskly with a fork or wire whisk. Bring mixture to a boil over medium heat, stirring frequently. Continue to cook, stirring constantly, 1 minute.

Spread can be stored in a jar in the refrigerator for up to 3 weeks.

Each tablespoon provides:

20	Calories		5 g	Carbohydrate
0 g	Protein		13 mg	Sodium
0 g	Total fat (0 g Sat. fat)		0 mg	Cholesterol

Soups

Nothing says "home" like a bowl of steamy, hot soup. As a first course or as the entree itself, soups can be a valuable source of protein, vitamins, and fiber. One of the secrets to creating wholesome soups is to use healthful ingredients, such as fresh fruits, vegetables, grains, and beans. Another is to use a minimal amount of fat. This means sautéing the vegetables in just a few teaspoons of oil and making "cream" soups with evaporated skim milk instead of cream. The sodium content of soups can be kept low by using salt-free tomato products and only adding salt, if necessary, at the end of cooking, *after* you have tasted the soup.

If you don't have a lot of time to cook during the week, make a large pot of soup (maybe even two) on the weekend. Freeze some for busy nights and enjoy the rest for several days. Sometimes a hearty bowl of soup, along with a salad and some whole grain bread, is all you need for a very satisfying meal.

Moroccan Pasta and Vegetable Soup

*This thick Moroccan stew-like soup was originally made with fava beans,
however I've adapted it to use the more readily available pinto beans. What
a lively blend of flavors!*

*Makes 6 servings
(1¹/₃ cups each serving)*

2	teaspoons olive oil
1	cup chopped onion
¹/₂	cup chopped celery
3	cloves garlic, finely chopped
1	10-ounce package frozen mixed vegetables
1	28-ounce can crushed tomatoes
1	1-pound can pinto beans, rinsed and drained (or 2 cups of cooked beans)
3	cups vegetable broth, or 3 cups of water and 3 teaspoons Vegetable Broth Mix (page 34)
2	teaspoons dried basil
1	teaspoon ground coriander
1	teaspoon ground cumin
¹/₄	teaspoon ground cinnamon
¹/₄	teaspoon pepper
¹/₂	cup elbow macaroni, uncooked
	Salt

Heat oil in a large saucepan over medium heat. Add onion, celery,
and garlic. Cook, stirring frequently, until vegetables are tender,
about 5 minutes.

Add remaining ingredients, *except* macaroni and salt. Bring mixture to a boil, stirring occasionally. Then reduce heat to medium-low,
cover, and simmer 20 minutes, or until vegetables are tender.

Stir macaroni into soup. Continue to cook, covered, 10 to 12 minutes more, until pasta is tender.

Add salt and additional pepper to taste.

Each serving provides:

182	Calories	33 g	Carbohydrate
9 g	Protein	398 mg	Sodium
3 g	Total fat (0 g Sat. fat)	0 mg	Cholesterol

Spiced Red Lentil Soup

Red lentils, smaller than the brown ones, turn light in color when cooked and make a very thick soup similar to split pea soup. This one is rich and hearty and flavored with an unusual combination of aromatic spices. Red lentils are available at most health food stores.

Makes 6 servings
(1 cup each serving)

2	teaspoons vegetable oil
1	cup chopped onion
	Water
1	1-pound can salt-free (or regular) tomatoes, drained and chopped (reserve liquid)
1	cup red lentils, uncooked
1/4	cup dry red wine
3	teaspoons Vegetable Broth Mix (page 34)
1	bay leaf
1	teaspoon chili powder
1/4	teaspoon dried thyme
1/4	teaspoon dried marjoram
1/4	teaspoon ground cumin
1/4	teaspoon *each* salt and pepper
1/2	teaspoon ground allspice

Heat oil in a large saucepan over medium heat. Add onion. Cook, stirring frequently, 3 to 5 minutes, until onion is tender.

Add water to tomato liquid to equal 4$\frac{1}{2}$ cups. Add to saucepan, along with remaining ingredients. Bring to a boil, stirring occasionally. Then reduce heat to medium-low, cover, and simmer 25 to 30 minutes.

Remove and discard bay leaf.

Add additional salt and pepper to taste.

✦*Quick tip:* Red lentils cook quickly, and if you have frozen, chopped onions in the freezer and a can of tomatoes, you can throw this soup together in no time.

Each serving provides:			
152	Calories	25 g	Carbohydrate
10 g	Protein	149 mg	Sodium
2 g	Total fat (0 g Sat. fat)	0 mg	Cholesterol

Succotash Soup

This delicious chowder of corn and lima beans needs only a salad and a toasted cheese sandwich to make a quick and easy lunch or light dinner.

Makes 5 servings
(1 cup each serving)

2	teaspoons vegetable oil
1	cup chopped onion
2	cloves garlic, crushed
1	1-pound can salt-free (or regular) cream-style corn
1	8-ounce can salt-free (or regular) whole kernel corn, drained
1	cup skim milk
1	cup vegetable broth, or 1 cup of water and 1 teaspoon Vegetable Broth Mix (page 34)
1	10-ounce package frozen baby lima beans
1	tablespoon prepared yellow mustard
1/4	teaspoon dried thyme
1/4	teaspoon pepper

Heat oil in a large saucepan over medium heat. Add onion and garlic. Cook 5 minutes, stirring frequently. Add small amounts of water as necessary, about a tablespoon at a time, to prevent sticking.

Add remaining ingredients. Bring to a boil, stirring occasionally. Then cover, reduce heat to medium-low, and simmer 15 to 20 minutes, until lima beans are tender.

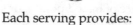

	Each serving provides:		
221	Calories	44 g	Carbohydrate
9 g	Protein	121 mg	Sodium
3 g	Total fat (0 g Sat. fat)	1 mg	Cholesterol

No-Cook Tomato Vegetable Soup

Soup can't get any fresher than this! Rather than reach for a can, reach for some fresh veggies instead. Your soup can be ready in minutes.

Makes 4 servings
(1 cup each serving)

2	large, very ripe tomatoes, cut in half (if the tomatoes are not very red and ripe, use one 1-pound can of tomatoes, undrained)
1	carrot, cut into large chunks
1	cabbage wedge (about 1/8 of a medium cabbage), cut into large chunks
1	green onion (green and white parts), cut into thirds
1	teaspoon Vegetable Broth Mix (page 34)
1/4	teaspoon garlic powder
1	cup boiling water
	Salt and pepper

In a blender container, combine tomatoes, carrot, cabbage, onion, broth mix, and garlic powder. Blend on medium speed until blended. Blend on high speed 2 minutes.

Add boiling water to blender. Blend until combined.

Pour soup into a saucepan and heat through. If you prefer, you can pour the soup into a bowl and heat in the microwave.

Add salt and pepper to taste.

Serve with crushed crackers, or add cooked rice or noodles.

❖*Variations:* Experiment by adding other vegetables, such as a few broccoli flowerets, a piece of baked potato, or some leftover corn. You can also add your favorite herbs.

Each serving provides:

36	Calories	8 g	Carbohydrate
1 g	Protein	40 mg	Sodium
0 g	Total fat (0 g Sat. fat)	0 mg	Cholesterol

Cream of Wheat Soup

What? Cream of Wheat? Yep, that's right! This is about as soothing and "down home" as a soup can get. Filled with tiny, pearl-like bits of wheat, it's a perfect cold weather pick-me-up.

Makes 8 servings
(1 cup each serving)

2	teaspoons vegetable oil
1/2	cup Quick Cream of Wheat, uncooked
1/2	cup finely chopped onion
4	cups vegetable broth, or 4 cups of water and 4 teaspoons Vegetable Broth Mix (page 34)
4	cups skim milk
1/4	teaspoon pepper
1/16	teaspoon ground nutmeg
	Salt
4	teaspoons chopped chives, fresh or dried

Heat oil in a medium saucepan over medium heat. Add Cream of Wheat. Cook, stirring constantly, 2 minutes. Add onion. Continue to cook and stir 2 more minutes. Be careful not to let it burn. (Don't take your eyes off the pot.)

Add broth and milk. Bring to a boil, stirring frequently. Reduce heat to medium-low and simmer, uncovered, 15 minutes, stirring occasionally.

Stir in pepper, nutmeg, and salt to taste.

Spoon into serving bowls and top each serving with 1/2 teaspoon chopped chives.

Each serving provides:

106	Calories	17 g	Carbohydrate
6 g	Protein	147 mg	Sodium
1 g	Total fat (0 g Sat. fat)	2 mg	Cholesterol

Orange-Carrot Soup

Like golden coins, thin slices of carrots dot the delicate, orange-flavored broth. It's a soothing, feel-good soup that is also good with thin noodles added in place of the rice.

Makes 6 servings
(1 cup each serving)

1	cup carrots, sliced crosswise into 1/8-inch slices
1/4	cup finely chopped onion
3	cups vegetable broth, or 3 cups of water and 3 teaspoons Vegetable Broth Mix (page 34)
2	cups orange juice
1/2	teaspoon ground ginger
2	whole cloves
1	small bay leaf
1	cup cooked brown rice
	Salt and pepper

In a medium saucepan, combine carrots, onion, and 1 cup of the broth. Bring to a boil over medium heat. Reduce heat to medium-low, cover, and simmer 10 minutes.

Add remaining 2 cups broth, orange juice, ginger, cloves, and bay leaf. Increase heat to medium, and when soup boils, reduce heat to medium-low once more, cover, and simmer 20 minutes.

Remove and discard bay leaf and cloves.

Stir in rice and heat through.

Add salt and pepper to taste.

◆*Quick tip:* Use leftover rice or make quick cooking brown rice, which can be cooked while the soup is simmering.

Each serving provides:

94	Calories	21 g	Carbohydrate
2 g	Protein	64 mg	Sodium
0 g	Total fat (0 g Sat. fat)	0 mg	Cholesterol

Fresh Broccoli Soup with Basil

Fresh broccoli, available in most large grocery stores throughout the year, makes a quick, nutritious soup that adds calcium, vitamins, and fiber to your diet. If you like, you can turn it into a cream soup by stirring in about a half cup of evaporated skim milk just before serving.

Makes 6 servings
(1 cup each serving)

2	teaspoons vegetable oil
1½	cups chopped onion
3	cloves garlic, finely chopped
1½	pounds broccoli, chopped (6½ cups) (peel the tough parts of the stalks, chop the stalks into ¼-inch pieces, and chop the tops into small flowerets)
5	cups vegetable broth, or 5 cups of water and 5 teaspoons Vegetable Broth Mix (page 34)
1	tablespoon dried basil
	Salt and pepper

Heat oil in a medium saucepan over medium heat. Add onion and garlic. Cook, stirring frequently, until onion is tender, about 5 minutes. Add small amounts of water as necessary, about a tablespoon or two at a time, to prevent sticking.

Add broccoli, broth, and basil. When mixture boils, reduce heat to medium-low, cover, and simmer 15 to 20 minutes, until broccoli is tender.

Place soup in a blender, a few cups at a time, and blend until smooth. If you like, you can leave 1 cup of the broccoli in pieces to add texture to the soup. Return soup to saucepan and add salt and pepper to taste. Heat through.

✦*Quick tip:* A food processor will chop the broccoli in a few seconds.

Each serving provides:			
74	Calories	13 g	Carbohydrate
4 g	Protein	118 mg	Sodium
2 g	Total fat (0 g Sat. fat)	0 mg	Cholesterol

Sweet Spiced Cream of Pumpkin Soup

Sweet and spicy, this unusual soup is perfect with a sandwich on a Sunday afternoon. It also makes a great beginning for a holiday meal and is reminiscent of warm pumpkin pie.

Makes 6 servings
(1 cup each serving)

2	teaspoons vegetable oil
1	cup finely chopped onion
1/2	cup finely chopped celery
2	cloves garlic, crushed
1 1/2	teaspoons grated fresh ginger root
4	cups vegetable broth, or 4 cups of water and 4 teaspoons Vegetable Broth Mix (page 34)
1	1-pound can pumpkin
1/4	cup firmly packed brown sugar
2	bay leaves
1/4	teaspoon *each* dried thyme, pepper, and ground cinnamon
1/8	teaspoon ground cloves
1	cup evaporated skim milk

Heat oil in a large saucepan over medium heat. Add onion, celery, garlic, and ginger root. Cook, stirring frequently, until vegetables are tender, about 5 minutes. Add small amounts of water as necessary, a tablespoon or two at a time, to prevent sticking.

Add remaining ingredients, *except* milk. Bring mixture to a boil, stirring occasionally. Reduce heat to medium-low, cover, and simmer 25 minutes. Remove soup from heat and stir in milk. Remove and discard bay leaves.

Each serving provides:			
134	Calories	26 g	Carbohydrate
5 g	Protein	139 mg	Sodium
2 g	Total fat (0 g Sat. fat)	2 mg	Cholesterol

Barley-Lentil Soup with Caraway

My good friend, Judy Katz, came up with the idea for this delicious and un-usual soup. The barley and lentils cook right in the broth, making a wonder-ful, thick soup with a sweet and zesty flavor.

Makes 8 servings
(1 1/4 cups each serving)

2	teaspoons vegetable oil
1	cup chopped onion
1	cup chopped carrots
3	cloves garlic, crushed
2	1-pound cans salt-free (or regular) tomatoes, chopped, undrained
4	cups vegetable broth, or 4 cups of water and 4 teaspoons Vegetable Broth Mix (page 34)
2	cups apple juice (I prefer the "natural" apple juice that's sold in health food stores)
2	cups cabbage, thinly shredded
2	tablespoons apple cider vinegar
2	tablespoons ketchup
1 1/2	tablespoons caraway seeds
3	bay leaves
1/2	teaspoon salt
1/2	cup barley, uncooked
1/2	cup lentils, uncooked
	Pepper

Heat oil in a large saucepan over medium heat. Add onion, carrots, and garlic. Cook 5 minutes, stirring frequently. Add small amounts of water as necessary, about a tablespoon at a time, to prevent sticking.

Add remaining ingredients, *except* barley, lentils, and pepper. Bring to a boil, stirring occasionally. Stir in barley and lentils. Cover, reduce heat to medium-low, and simmer 45 minutes, until barley and vegetables are tender.

Remove and discard bay leaves. Add pepper to taste.

Each serving provides:			
181	Calories	36 g	Carbohydrate
7 g	Protein	264 mg	Sodium
2 g	Total fat (0 g Sat. fat)	0 mg	Cholesterol

Cream of Fresh Vegetable Soup

The flavors of the different vegetables blend perfectly to create a thick, rich, cream-style soup that is a perfect beginning to any meal. You can chop the vegetables into any size pieces, however if they're fairly uniform, they will all cook in the same amount of time.

Makes 6 servings
(1¹/2 cups each serving)

2	teaspoons vegetable oil
2	cups chopped potatoes, unpeeled
1	cup chopped onion
1	cup chopped mushrooms
1	cup chopped zucchini, unpeeled
1	cup chopped green beans, ends trimmed and strings removed
1	cup chopped carrots
1	cup chopped tomato
1	cup chopped broccoli
1	cup chopped leek, white part only
3	cloves garlic, coarsely chopped
2	bay leaves
5	cups vegetable broth, or 5 cups of water and 5 teaspoons Vegetable Broth Mix (page 34)
1/2	cup evaporated skim milk
	Salt and pepper

Heat oil in a large saucepan over medium heat. Add the vegetables and garlic. Cook 15 minutes, stirring frequently. Add small amounts of water as necessary, a few tablespoons at a time, to prevent sticking.

Add bay leaves and broth. Bring to a boil, then cover, reduce heat to medium-low, and simmer 15 to 20 minutes, until vegetables are tender.

Remove and discard bay leaves.

Place soup in blender, a few cupfuls at a time, and blend until smooth. Return to saucepan and stir in milk. Add salt and pepper to taste. Heat through, but do not boil.

Each serving provides:			
136	Calories	26 g	Carbohydrate
5 g	Protein	139 mg	Sodium
2 g	Total fat (0 g Sat. fat)	1 mg	Cholesterol

Tomato and Butter Bean Soup

Butter beans make a thick, rich soup, creating a perfect background for the lively flavors of garlic, oregano, and cumin. A delicious accompaniment to this soup is the Multigrain Cheese Bread on page 259. Add a salad, and that's all you need for a filling and nutritious lunch or dinner.

Makes 5 servings
(1 cup each serving)

2	teaspoons vegetable oil
1	cup chopped onion
1	cup chopped green bell pepper
2	1-pound cans butter beans, rinsed and drained
1	1-pound can salt-free (or regular) tomatoes
1	cup vegetable broth, or 1 cup of water and 1 teaspoon Vegetable Broth Mix (page 34)
4	to 5 large cloves garlic
1	tablespoon red wine vinegar
1¹/2	teaspoons ground cumin
1¹/2	teaspoons dried oregano
	Salt and pepper

Heat oil in a large saucepan over medium heat. Add onion and green pepper. Cook 6 to 8 minutes, until tender, stirring frequently and adding small amounts of water as necessary, about a tablespoon at a time, to prevent sticking.

In a blender container, combine one can of the beans, tomatoes, broth, and garlic. Blend until smooth. Add to saucepan along with remaining ingredients, *except* salt and pepper.

Bring to a boil, stirring occasionally. Cover, reduce heat to medium-low, and simmer 15 minutes.

Add salt and pepper to taste.

❖*Serve-again hint:* Leftovers are delicious heated and spooned over a baked potato.

Each serving provides:			
183	Calories	33 g	Carbohydrate
9 g	Protein	328 mg	Sodium
3 g	Total fat (0 g Sat. fat)	0 mg	Cholesterol

Zucchini Soup with Garlic and Rosemary

Fresh rosemary gives this creamy soup a delectable flavor. Although it's great year-round, it's a perfect summer soup, providing a delicious way to use those ever-abundant zucchini.

Makes 8 servings
(1 cup each serving)

2	teaspoons vegetable oil
1	cup chopped onion
4	cloves garlic, coarsely chopped
1	large potato (about 9 ounces), unpeeled, chopped into 1/4- to 1/2-inch pieces
5	cups vegetable broth, or 5 cups of water and 5 teaspoons Vegetable Broth Mix (page 34)
4	cups zucchini, unpeeled, cut into 1/2-inch pieces
2	teaspoons finely chopped fresh rosemary (dried rosemary doesn't work well here)
	Salt and pepper

Heat oil in a large saucepan over medium heat. Add onion, garlic, and potato. Cook 5 minutes, stirring frequently. Add small amounts of water as necessary, about a tablespoon at a time, to prevent sticking.

Add broth, zucchini, and rosemary. When mixture boils, reduce heat to medium-low, cover, and simmer 15 to 20 minutes, until zucchini is tender.

Purée soup in a blender in 2 or 3 batches, then return soup to saucepan. Add salt and pepper to taste.

Each serving provides:

64	Calories	12 g	Carbohydrate
2 g	Protein	73 mg	Sodium
1 g	Total fat (0 g Sat. fat)	0 mg	Cholesterol

Potato, Apple, and White Bean Soup

I knew when I made this soup for the first time that it was either a crazy combination or a delicious new taste treat. We loved it!

Makes 8 servings
(1 cup each serving)

2	teaspoons vegetable oil
2	medium leeks, thinly sliced (white parts only)
1/2	cup chopped onion
3	large cloves garlic, finely chopped
1	pound baking potatoes (2 medium potatoes), unpeeled, cut into 1/2-inch pieces
4	cups vegetable broth, or 4 cups of water and 4 teaspoons Vegetable Broth Mix (page 34)
1	19-ounce can white kidney beans (cannellini), rinsed and drained (or 2 1/4 cups of cooked beans)
2	medium Granny Smith apples, peeled, chopped into 1/2-inch pieces
1	cup evaporated skim milk
	Salt and pepper

Heat oil in a large saucepan over medium heat. Add leeks, onion, and garlic. Cook 3 to 5 minutes, stirring frequently, until onion starts to brown. Add small amounts of water as necessary, about a tablespoon at a time, to prevent sticking.

Add potatoes. Continue to cook, stirring frequently, 3 to 5 minutes, continuing to add water, a little at a time, to prevent sticking.

Add broth, beans, and apples. Bring mixture to a boil, stirring occasionally. Reduce heat to medium-low, cover, and simmer 25 to 30 minutes, until potatoes are tender.

Using a strainer, remove about *half* of the potatoes, beans, and apples from the soup. Place in a blender container and blend until smooth, adding a little of the broth if necessary for blending. Return mixture to the soup, along with the milk, and salt and pepper to taste.

Heat through but do not boil.

	Each serving provides:		
175	Calories	33 g	Carbohydrate
8 g	Protein	185 mg	Sodium
2 g	Total fat (0 g Sat. fat)	1 mg	Cholesterol

Curried Lentil Soup with Root Vegetables

Spicy and delicious, this soup combines the "zippy" flavor of turnips, parsnips, and rutabagas with the "heat" of the curry powder. It's a thick and chunky delight.

Makes 9 servings
(1¹/4 cups each serving)

2	teaspoons vegetable oil
1	cup *each* chopped carrots, turnip, parsnips, and rutabaga, in ¹/4- to ¹/2-inch pieces
¹/2	cup chopped onion
¹/4	cup chopped celery
3	cloves garlic, crushed
8	cups vegetable broth, or 8 cups of water and 8 teaspoons Vegetable Broth Mix (page 34)
1¹/2	cups lentils, uncooked
1	6-ounce can tomato paste
1	to 2 tablespoons curry powder
¹/2	teaspoon ground cumin
2	bay leaves
	Salt

Heat oil in a large saucepan over medium heat. Add carrots, turnip, parsnips, rutabaga, onion, celery, and garlic. Cook, stirring frequently, 5 minutes.

Add remaining ingredients, *except* salt. Bring mixture to a boil, stirring occasionally. Reduce heat to medium-low, cover, and simmer 45 minutes, or until lentils and vegetables are tender.

Add salt to taste.

Remove and discard bay leaves before serving.

Each serving provides:

185	Calories	34 g	Carbohydrate
11 g	Protein	275 mg	Sodium
2 g	Total fat (0 g Sat. fat)	0 mg	Cholesterol

Lentil and Split Pea Soup

After enjoying lentils and split peas separately, I thought I'd put them to-gether. The result is a soup that's as thick and rich as a soup can be. Any thicker and you'd have to eat it with a fork!

Makes 8 servings
(1¹/₄ cups each serving)

2	teaspoons vegetable oil
1	cup chopped onion
1	28-ounce can salt-free (or regular) tomatoes, chopped, undrained
6	cups water
1	cup split peas, uncooked
1	cup lentils, uncooked
1	large potato (about 12 ounces), peeled, chopped into ¹/₄- to ¹/₂-inch pieces
2	large cloves garlic, crushed
3	teaspoons Vegetable Broth Mix (page 34)
2	bay leaves
¹/₂	teaspoon dried thyme
	Salt and pepper

Heat oil in a large saucepan over medium heat. Add onion. Cook, stirring frequently, until onion is tender, about 5 minutes. Add small amounts of water as necessary, about a tablespoon at a time, to prevent sticking.

Add remaining ingredients, *except* salt and pepper. Bring to a boil, stirring occasionally. Then, reduce heat to medium-low, cover, and simmer 1 hour.

Remove and discard bay leaves before serving.

Add salt and pepper to taste.

Each serving provides:

232	Calories	41 g	Carbohydrate
15 g	Protein	52 mg	Sodium
2 g	Total fat (0 g Sat. fat)	0 mg	Cholesterol

Corn and Red Pepper Chowder

The red bell pepper adds a wonderful, delicate sweetness to this rich, thick soup. It looks so pretty, too, with the chunks of red and yellow.

Makes 4 servings
(1 cup each serving)

2	teaspoons vegetable oil
1¹/₂	cups chopped red bell pepper
1	cup chopped onion
¹/₂	cup chopped celery
2¹/₂	cups vegetable broth, or 2¹/₂ cups of water and 2¹/₂ teaspoons Vegetable Broth Mix (page 34)
1	10-ounce package frozen corn
³/₄	teaspoon dried basil
³/₄	teaspoon ground cumin
	Salt and pepper

Heat oil in a medium saucepan over medium heat. Add red pepper, onion, and celery. Cook, stirring frequently, until vegetables are tender, about 8 minutes. Add small amounts of water as necessary, about a tablespoon at a time, to prevent sticking.

Add broth, corn, basil, and cumin. When mixture boils, reduce heat to medium-low, cover, and simmer 30 minutes.

Reserve ³/₄ cup of the vegetables and puree remaining soup in a blender. Return soup to saucepan and add reserved vegetables.

Add salt and pepper to taste.

	Each serving provides:		
123	Calories	24 g	Carbohydrate
3 g	Protein	86 mg	Sodium
3 g	Total fat (0 g Sat. fat)	0 mg	Cholesterol

Creamy Carrot Bisque

This creamy soup is thick and rich and makes a wonderful, soothing begin-
ning to any meal. It also makes a filling lunch when served with a salad and
a chunk of crusty bread.

Makes 6 servings
(1 cup each serving)

2	teaspoons vegetable oil
1	pound carrots, coarsely chopped (3 cups)
1	cup coarsely chopped mushrooms
1	cup coarsely chopped celery, including leaves
1/2	cup thinly sliced green onion (green and white parts)
5	cups vegetable broth, or 5 cups of water and 5 teaspoons Vegetable Broth Mix (page 34)
1/4	teaspoon dried thyme
1	bay leaf
1	cup evaporated skim milk
	Pepper

Heat oil in a large saucepan over medium heat. Add carrots, mushrooms, celery, and green onion. Cook, stirring frequently, 10 minutes.

Add broth, thyme, and bay leaf. When mixture boils, cover, reduce
heat to medium-low, and simmer 35 minutes, or until vegetables are
tender.

Remove and discard bay leaf.

Reserve 1/2 cup of the vegetables and puree remaining soup in two
batches in a blender or food processor. Return soup to saucepan. Add
reserved vegetables, along with milk. Heat through, but do not boil.

Add pepper to taste.

Each serving provides:			
103	Calories	18 g	Carbohydrate
5 g	Protein	185 mg	Sodium
2 g	Total fat (0 g Sat. fat)	2 mg	Cholesterol

Cold Banana Bisque
with Cinnamon Croutons

This unusual and exotic Caribbean recipe makes a fabulous beginning to any summer meal. It's very rich and can be served in small dessert bowls or champagne glasses. For the sweetest soup, make sure the bananas are very ripe.

Makes 4 servings
(1/2 cup each serving)

Soup

2	medium, very ripe bananas, sliced
1	12-ounce can evaporated skim milk (1 1/2 cups)
2	tablespoons sugar
1	teaspoon vanilla extract

Croutons

2	slices whole wheat bread (1-ounce slices)
	Nonstick cooking spray
1	teaspoon sugar
1/2	teaspoon ground cinnamon

In a blender container, combine bananas, milk, sugar, and vanilla. Blend until smooth.

Chill thoroughly, for several hours or overnight.

To prepare the croutons, preheat oven to 300°. Place bread on a nonstick baking sheet. Spray both sides lightly and evenly with nonstick cooking spray. Combine sugar and cinnamon and sprinkle evenly on bread, covering both sides.

Cut bread into small cubes.

Place in oven for 10 minutes, then turn oven off and leave bread cubes in oven until cool. Store in a loosely covered container until serving time.

To serve, beat soup with a fork or wire whisk until smooth. Pour into serving bowls and top with croutons.

Serve right away.

Each serving provides:

198	Calories	39 g	Carbohydrate
9 g	Protein	185 mg	Sodium
2 g	Total fat (0 g Sat. fat)	4 mg	Cholesterol

Tropical Fruit Soup

The chunks of tropical fruits sparkle like gemstones in this luscious cold soup. As a meal starter or a light dessert, this one truly looks as good as it tastes. And, with most tropical fruits available in large grocery stores all year, you can enjoy this treat any time.

Makes 4 servings
(³/₄ cup each serving)

1	ripe papaya, peeled, cut into ¹/₂-inch pieces, seeds discarded
1	ripe mango, peeled, cut into ¹/₂-inch pieces, center seed discarded
1	ripe kiwi, peeled, cut into ¹/₂-inch pieces
1¹/₂	cups apricot nectar
2	teaspoons sugar
¹/₂	teaspoon vanilla extract
¹/₂	teaspoon grated fresh lime peel
¹/₈	teaspoon ground cardamom
¹/₈	teaspoon ground cinnamon
1¹/₂	tablespoons lime juice
¹/₂	cup vanilla nonfat yogurt

In a medium bowl, combine chopped fruit. Add apricot nectar, followed by remaining ingredients, *except* yogurt. Mix well.

Chill thoroughly.

Just before serving, spoon yogurt into a small bowl. Add a few tablespoons of the juice from the soup. Stir until smooth. Add a few more tablespoons and stir again. Add yogurt mixture to soup and mix well.

Serve right away.

❖*Serve-again hint:* Leftovers in the blender make a delicious, thick fruit shake.

Each serving provides:

164	Calories	40 g	Carbohydrate
3 g	Protein	28 mg	Sodium
0 g	Total fat (0 g Sat. fat)	1 mg	Cholesterol

Salads and Salad Dressings

Salads provide a delicious way to "dose up" on vitamins, minerals, and necessary fiber. Different fruits and vegetables provide different nutrients, so the more varieties you include in your salads, the more wholesome the salads will be. Remember that the darker the greens, the more vitamins they contain, so romaine and red leaf or green leaf lettuce are better nutritional choices than iceberg lettuce.

Assembling a salad can be a bit time consuming, but don't forgo the great health benefits because of this. For the most part, salads can be made ahead of time. This means that you can prepare them when you have the time and serve them with very little last-minute fuss. If salads contain lettuce or other very perishable ingredients, you can prepare the salad and the dressing ahead, refrigerate them separately, and add the dressing just before serving.

To keep the fat content down, the amount of oil in salad dressings can be reduced and some of it replaced with fruit juice, broth, or water. Fat-free yogurt and reduced-fat tofu make tasty replacements for sour cream. The oils that many health professionals recommend are canola oil and olive oil. They contain high amounts of mono-unsaturated fat and very low amounts of saturated fat.

Be creative. Add cooked beans, grains, or pasta to a salad, and it can easily become a whole meal. "Borrow" the dressing from one salad and create a new one. There are endless varieties of fruits and vegetables to explore.

Spinach Salad with Orange Vinaigrette

For a "wilted" salad, you can heat the dressing before spooning it over the spinach. Served either way, this colorful salad will definitely be a favorite. If you like, you can double the vinaigrette recipe so there will be some left over.

Makes 4 servings

Orange Vinaigrette
1/4	cup orange juice
2	tablespoons vegetable oil
1 1/2	tablespoons red wine vinegar
1/2	teaspoon dried basil
1/8	teaspoon salt
1/8	teaspoon pepper
1/16	teaspoon garlic powder

Salad
6	cups fresh spinach, torn into bite-size pieces, stems removed
1	medium, ripe tomato, cut into thin wedges
1/4	cup red onion, sliced vertically into thin slivers
1	large orange, peeled and sectioned (discard white membranes)
4	large mushrooms, thinly sliced

In a small bowl or jar, combine all vinaigrette ingredients. Mix well. Chill several hours or overnight to blend flavors.

At serving time, divide spinach evenly onto 4 individual serving plates. Arrange tomato, onion, orange sections, and mushrooms over spinach. Spoon dressing (either hot or cold) over salads. (There will be a little less than 2 tablespoons of dressing for each salad.)

◆*Quick tip:* Make the dressing ahead and have all of the vegetables washed and refrigerated. At serving time, it can all be assembled quickly.

Each serving provides:			
127	Calories	14 g	Carbohydrate
4 g	Protein	141 mg	Sodium
7 g	Total fat (1 g Sat. fat)	0 mg	Cholesterol

Endive Salad with Orange Curry Dressing

The often-forgotten Belgian endive is right at home in this tangy salad. It's an elegant way to start a meal.

Makes 6 servings

Dressing

2	tablespoons cider vinegar
2	tablespoons olive oil
2	tablespoons water
2	tablespoons orange juice
1	small clove garlic, crushed
1¹/₂	teaspoons Dijon mustard
¹/₄	teaspoon curry powder
1¹/₄	teaspoons sugar
¹/₁₆	teaspoon salt
¹/₁₆	teaspoon pepper

Salad

4	Belgian endives, cut in half lengthwise, then cut crosswise into ¹/₂-inch slices (remove and discard cores)
2	oranges, peeled and sectioned (discard white membranes)
¹/₄	cup raisins
6	cups torn romaine lettuce

Combine all dressing ingredients in a small bowl or jar. Mix well. Chill several hours or overnight.

When ready to assemble, combine endives, orange sections, and raisins in a bowl. Shake dressing and add to bowl. Toss gently until mixed well.

Divide lettuce onto 6 individual salad plates. Divide endive mixture evenly and pile onto lettuce.

Serve right away.

❖*Variation:* The raisins can be soaked overnight in Grand Marnier, adding a wonderful flavor to the salad.

Each serving provides:

104	Calories	15 g	Carbohydrate
2 g	Protein	60 mg	Sodium
5 g	Total fat (1 g Sat. fat)	0 mg	Cholesterol

Chinese Vegetable Salad
with Tangy Soy Dressing

What a lovely way to start any meal! This recipe makes a lot of salad, but you can eat some, save the rest for later, and add dressing as needed.

Makes 8 servings
(with dressing left over)

Dressing

1/3	cup vegetable broth, or 1/3 cup water and 1/2 teaspoon Vegetable Broth Mix (page 34)
1/4	cup vegetable oil
3	tablespoons reduced-sodium (or regular) soy sauce
1	tablespoon firmly packed brown sugar
2	teaspoons lime juice
2	teaspoons cider vinegar
1 1/2	teaspoons sesame oil
2	teaspoons grated fresh ginger root
4	cloves garlic, crushed

Salad

2	cups (packed) romaine lettuce, cut into thin strips
1 1/2	cups Chinese cabbage (packed), cut into thin strips
1	cup fresh bean sprouts
1	cup mushrooms, thinly sliced
1	cup snow peas, cut diagonally into 1/2-inch slices, strings removed
1/2	cup cucumber, cut in half lengthwise, then very thinly sliced
1/2	cup carrot, cut into matchstick-size pieces
1/2	cup red bell pepper, cut into thin strips, about 1-inch long
1/2	cup chopped green onions (green and white parts)
1/2	cup red onion, sliced vertically into thin slivers
1/4	cup radishes, very thinly sliced

Combine all dressing ingredients in a small bowl or jar. Mix well. Chill several hours or (preferably) overnight.

Combine vegetables in a large bowl. Toss.

To serve, for each serving (a heaping cup) of salad, add 1 tablespoon of dressing. Toss until vegetables are coated with dressing.

Serve right away.

◆*Quick tip:* Prepare dressing up to 2 days ahead and salad up to 1 day ahead. Add dressing and toss before serving.

Each serving provides:			
114	Calories	10 g	Carbohydrate
3 g	Protein	241 mg	Sodium
8 g	Total fat (1 g Sat. fat)	0 mg	Cholesterol

Southwest Jicama Salad

Jicama (pronounced HEE-kah-mah) is a crisp, sweet root vegetable shaped like a large turnip with a light brown skin. It has a texture similar to water chestnuts and makes a wonderful, crunchy addition to salads. This salad, with the combination of red and green leaf lettuce, red peppers and orange slices, is a perfect backdrop for introducing a new and distinctive vegetable.

Makes 8 servings

Dressing

1/4	cup red wine vinegar
3	tablespoons honey
2	tablespoons water
1 1/4	teaspoons chili powder
1/2	teaspoon anise seed, crushed
1/8	teaspoon salt
1/8	teaspoon pepper
3	tablespoons vegetable oil

Salad

8	cups (packed) red and green leaf lettuce, torn into bite-size pieces
1	8-ounce can mandarin orange slices (packed in juice), drained
1 1/2	cups jicama, peeled and coarsely shredded
1	cup red bell pepper, coarsely chopped
3	green onions, thinly sliced (green and white parts)

Combine all dressing ingredients, *except* oil, in a small bowl. Gradually whisk in oil. (This can be made up to a day ahead and refrigerated until needed.)

Place lettuce in a large salad bowl. Top with orange slices, jicama, red pepper, and green onions. Spoon dressing over salad. Toss and serve.

Note: If you wish, you can make individual salads and spoon 1½ tablespoons of the dressing over each salad.

♦*Quick tip:* To make last-minute preparation easy, you can cut and wash the vegetables (except the jicama) and make the dressing up to a day ahead. At serving time, just toss it all together. The jicama is best when shredded just before using.

Each serving provides:			
112	Calories	16 g	Carbohydrate
2 g	Protein	50 mg	Sodium
5 g	Total fat (1 g Sat. fat)	0 mg	Cholesterol

Sweet 'n' Sour Mixed Vegetable Salad

My good friend Anne Atkins suggested this easy salad, and we loved it from the start. It tastes best on the second (or even third) day, so you can put it together whenever you have the time and refrigerate it until needed. Because it uses frozen vegetables, it can be enjoyed any time of the year.

Makes 4 servings

1	10-ounce package frozen mixed vegetables (or you can use half of a 1-pound bag)
1	small tomato, chopped (about 1/3 cup)
1/4	cup chopped celery
3	tablespoons sliced green onion (green and white parts)
1/4	cup water
31/2	tablespoons vinegar
2	tablespoons sugar
1/4	teaspoon celery seed
1/4	teaspoon salt
1/8	teaspoon pepper

Cook frozen vegetables for *half* the recommended cooking time. Drain.

Place vegetables in a shallow bowl and toss with tomato, celery, and green onion.

Combine remaining ingredients in a small bowl and stir to dissolve sugar. Pour over vegetables. Mix well.

Cover and chill at least several hours or preferably overnight. Stir several times while chilling.

✦*Quick tip:* If you're in a super hurry, while you're picking up the veggies, you might want to pick up the celery, tomato, and green onion at the grocery store salad bar. It's a real luxury to have a vegetable salad that requires no chopping.

✧*Serve-again hint:* This makes a great addition to a tossed salad. Also, for a nutritious sandwich, try tossing the leftovers with cooked beans and spooning it all into a pita.

Each serving provides:

77	Calories	18 g	Carbohydrate
3 g	Protein	177 mg	Sodium
0 g	Total fat (0 g Sat. fat)	0 mg	Cholesterol

Lentil Salad with Feta

This tasty, herbed salad can be mounded on a bed of lettuce, used to fill a hollowed-out tomato, or piled into a pita for a delicious sandwich. If you can, plan to make it ahead; it tastes even better the next day.

Makes 8 servings

2¹/₂	cups water
1	cup lentils, uncooked
1	bay leaf
¹/₂	teaspoon garlic powder
¹/₂	cup coarsely shredded carrots
¹/₂	cup finely chopped tomato
¹/₂	cup finely chopped red onion
¹/₂	cup finely chopped red bell pepper
3	tablespoons red wine vinegar
2	tablespoons water
1	tablespoon vegetable oil
1	teaspoon dried oregano
1	teaspoon ground cumin
¹/₈	teaspoon *each* salt and pepper
¹/₂	cup feta cheese, crumbled (3 ounces)

Bring water to a boil in a medium saucepan over medium heat. Add lentils, bay leaf, and garlic powder. Cover, reduce heat to medium-low, and simmer 30 minutes, or until lentils are just tender. (Do not let them get mushy.) Drain, place lentils in a bowl, and discard bay leaf. Let lentils cool 5 to 10 minutes.

Add remaining ingredients, *except* feta cheese, and mix well. Add feta and mix again.

Chill.

Note: If you plan to serve this the next day, reserve the chopped tomato and add it just before serving.

❖*Serve-again hint:* For a delicious spread or sandwich filling, put leftovers in a food processor, add a few drops of oil, and process until smooth.

Each serving provides:

139	Calories	17 g	Carbohydrate
9 g	Protein	161 mg	Sodium
4 g	Total fat (2 g Sat. fat)	9 mg	Cholesterol

Lemon-Tangy Potato Salad

Lemon juice and Dijon mustard add a delicious tang to this mayonnaise-free potato salad. It can be made a day or two ahead; the flavor will just improve. Save time (and add fiber) by choosing thin-skinned potatoes and leaving the skin on. Like other do-ahead salads, the real ease is at serving time.

Makes 8 servings

1 1/2	pounds all-purpose potatoes, unpeeled, cut into 1-inch cubes (4 cups)
1/2	cup finely chopped celery
1/4	cup thinly sliced green onions (green and white parts)
1/4	cup lemon juice
3	tablespoons water
2	tablespoons vegetable oil
2	teaspoons Dijon mustard
1 1/2	teaspoons sugar
1	teaspoon Vegetable Broth Mix (page 34)
1/4	teaspoon garlic powder
1/8	teaspoon pepper

Place potatoes in 2 inches of boiling water in a medium saucepan. Cover and cook over medium heat 15 minutes, or until potatoes are tender. Do not let them get mushy. (Length of cooking time will depend on the variety of potatoes used.)

Drain potatoes and set them aside to cool (hot potatoes absorb liquid quickly, which could possibly make the salad too dry). Place in a large bowl. Add celery and green onions and mix well.

In a small bowl, combine remaining ingredients. Mix well and add to potatoes. Toss until potatoes are evenly coated.

Chill several hours to blend flavors.

Each serving provides:

102	Calories	16 g	Carbohydrate
2 g	Protein	55 mg	Sodium
4 g	Total fat (0 g Sat. fat)	0 mg	Cholesterol

Italian Cannellini Salad

Choose your favorite brand of dressing for this super-quick salad that blends the smooth texture of white kidney beans (cannellini) with the crunch of onion and the tang of olives. Mound it on a bed of greens, add a tossed salad and a chunk of crusty bread, and you have an easy, nutritious, light meal.

Makes 6 servings

1	1-pound can white kidney beans (cannellini), rinsed and drained (or 2 cups of cooked beans)
1/2	cup finely chopped red onion
2	tablespoons finely chopped, stuffed green olives (about 8 medium olives)
1/4	cup fat-free Italian dressing

In a medium bowl, combine all ingredients, mixing well. Chill.

❖*Serve-again hint:* Add a chopped tomato to the leftovers, scoop out the inside of a crusty roll, and fill the roll with the salad. It makes a great lunch.

Each serving provides:

65	Calories	10 g	Carbohydrate
4 g	Protein	260 mg	Sodium
1 g	Total fat (1 g Sat. fat)	0 mg	Cholesterol

Mushroom Gazpacho Salad

Borrowing the exquisite flavors of the popular cold soup, this salad is always a hit. Pile it on a bed of lettuce and serve it as a first course or side dish. It has a festive color and flavor that adds life to a buffet table.

Makes 8 servings

2	cups sliced mushrooms
2	cups chopped tomatoes
1	cup chopped cucumber, peeled and seeded
1/2	cup chopped green bell pepper
1/2	cup red onion, sliced vertically into thin slivers
3	tablespoons vegetable oil
3	tablespoons apple cider vinegar
2	tablespoons water
1	teaspoon onion powder
1/2	teaspoon dried oregano
1/2	teaspoon dried basil
1/4	teaspoon garlic powder
1/4	teaspoon salt
1/8	teaspoon pepper

Combine all of the vegetables in a large bowl.

In a small bowl, combine remaining ingredients, mixing well. Spoon over vegetables. Mix well.

Chill.

❖*Serve-again hint:* Make a delicious sandwich by piling the left-overs into a pita bread and adding a slice of reduced-fat cheese.

Each serving provides:

70	Calories		6 g	Carbohydrate
1 g	Protein		75 mg	Sodium
5 g	Total fat (1 g Sat. fat)		0 mg	Cholesterol

Broccoli in Dilled Vinaigrette

If you love dill pickles, you'll really love this unusual broccoli salad. It makes a great picnic dish and is perfect to serve alongside a veggie burger.

Makes 6 servings

5	cups broccoli, cut into flowerets
2	tablespoons red wine vinegar
2	tablespoons water
1¹/₂	teaspoons Dijon mustard
1	teaspoon dried chives
¹/₂	teaspoon dill weed
¹/₈	teaspoon garlic powder
	Salt and pepper
2	tablespoons vegetable oil

Place a steamer rack in the bottom of a medium saucepan. Add enough water to come almost up to the bottom of the rack. Place saucepan over medium heat. When water boils, add broccoli, cover saucepan, and cook 5 to 8 minutes, or until broccoli is just tender-crisp. Remove from heat and rinse the broccoli under cold water. Drain.

In a small bowl, combine remaining ingredients, *except* oil. Mix well. Add oil gradually, stirring constantly.

Place broccoli in a shallow bowl. Top with vinaigrette.

Chill thoroughly, stirring several times.

Stir again before serving.

Serve cold.

◆*Quick tip:* It *is* more expensive, but if you're in a major rush, you can pick up the broccoli, already cut, at your local grocery store salad bar.

Each serving provides:			
75	Calories	6 g	Carbohydrate
4 g	Protein	56 mg	Sodium
5 g	Total fat (1 g Sat. fat)	0 mg	Cholesterol

Basil, Corn, and Bean Salad

This delicious salad, served on a bed of greens, makes a colorful appetizer or side dish. You can also use it to serve four as a main dish, adding a tossed green salad and a slice of whole grain bread.

Makes 8 servings

1	1-pound can corn, rinsed and drained
1	1-pound can pinto beans, rinsed and drained (or 2 cups of cooked beans)
3	medium, plum tomatoes, chopped (1¹/₂ cups)
¹/₃	cup finely chopped onion
2	tablespoons vegetable oil
2	tablespoons lemon juice
1	tablespoon plus 1 teaspoon dried basil
¹/₂	teaspoon garlic powder
	Salt and pepper

In a large bowl, combine all ingredients. Mix well. Chill.

❖*Serve-again hint:* Pile the leftovers into a pita bread, add some romaine or green leaf lettuce, and you have a delicious, hearty sandwich.

Each serving provides:

119	Calories	19 g	Carbohydrate
4 g	Protein	250 mg	Sodium
4 g	Total fat (1 g Sat. fat)	0 mg	Cholesterol

Sweet 'n' Tangy Zucchini Salad

My family loves this sweet and sour salad. It can be served as is, but we like to pile it on a tossed salad and use the liquid in place of salad dressing.

Makes 10 servings

2	medium zucchini (about 8 ounces each), unpeeled, sliced cross-wise into paper-thin slices
2	medium onions, sliced crosswise into paper-thin slices
$^1/_2$	cup vinegar
$^1/_2$	cup water
$^1/_2$	cup sugar
$^1/_2$	teaspoon salt
$^1/_8$	teaspoon pepper

Layer zucchini and onions in a jar or bowl. Combine remaining ingredients, mixing well. Pour over vegetables. Press vegetables down into juice.

Chill overnight.

Stir before serving.

❖*Serve-again hint:* This salad makes a delicious addition to a cheese sandwich or veggie burger.

Each serving provides:

59	Calories	15 g	Carbohydrate
1 g	Protein	112 mg	Sodium
0 g	Total fat (0 g Sat. fat)	0 mg	Cholesterol

French Green Bean Salad

French-style green beans flavored with oregano and lemon juice make this salad tasty and colorful. It can be served alone or piled atop a fresh, tossed salad.

Makes 6 servings

1	10-ounce package frozen French-style green beans
1/4	cup finely chopped onion
1	2-ounce jar sliced pimientos, drained
2	tablespoons lemon juice, preferably fresh
2	teaspoons olive oil
1 1/4	teaspoons dried oregano
1/4	teaspoon dry mustard
1/8	teaspoon salt

Cook green beans according to package directions. Drain.

In a large bowl, combine green beans (while still hot), onion, and pimientos. Toss to combine.

In a small bowl or custard cup, combine remaining ingredients, mixing well. Add to beans. Toss until beans are evenly coated with herb mixture.

Chill several hours or overnight.

Stir before serving.

❖*Serve-again hint:* Pile leftovers into a pita bread, add a slice of reduced-fat cheese and a slice of tomato, and enjoy a quick, delicious lunch.

Each serving provides:

36	Calories	5 g	Carbohydrate
1 g	Protein	49 mg	Sodium
2 g	Total fat (0 g Sat. fat)	0 mg	Cholesterol

Greek Artichoke Salad

This tangy salad can be served as a side dish, an appetizer, or a delicious, perky topper for a leafy green salad. It tastes best on the second or third day, so try to make it ahead.

Makes 6 servings

1	9-ounce package frozen artichoke hearts
1/4	cup onion, cut vertically into thin slivers
2	tablespoons finely chopped green bell pepper
2	tablespoons chopped pimiento, drained
1/4	cup vinegar
2	tablespoons water
2	teaspoons vegetable oil
1	clove garlic, crushed
1	teaspoon sugar
1/4	teaspoon salt
1/8	teaspoon pepper

Cook artichoke hearts according to package directions. Drain. Place in a shallow bowl and toss with onion, green pepper, and pimiento.

In a small bowl, combine remaining ingredients, mixing well. Spoon over artichoke mixture.

Chill several hours or overnight, mixing several times.

✧*Serve-again hint:* Fill a pita bread with this salad, along with lettuce and tomato, for a quick, light lunch. A sprinkling of crumbled feta cheese also adds a delicious touch.

Each serving provides:			
38	Calories	6 g	Carbohydrate
1 g	Protein	111 mg	Sodium
2 g	Total fat (0 g Sat. fat)	0 mg	Cholesterol

Oriental Pasta Salad

Sesame oil and hoisin sauce give this salad a distinct, rich flavor. You'll find hoisin sauce in specialty stores and in the imported foods section of most large grocery stores.

Makes 4 servings

4	ounces elbow macaroni, uncooked (about 3/4 cup)
1	cup cauliflower, cut into tiny flowerets
1	cup broccoli, cut into tiny flowerets
1/4	cup red bell pepper, cut into matchstick-size pieces
2	tablespoons reduced-sodium (or regular) soy sauce
1	tablespoon hoisin sauce
2	teaspoons sesame oil
2	teaspoons red wine vinegar
1	teaspoon honey
1/8	teaspoon garlic powder
1/8	teaspoon ground ginger

Cook macaroni according to package directions.

While macaroni is cooking, place cauliflower, broccoli, and red pepper in a colander. When macaroni is done, pour into the colander over the vegetables. (The hot water will lightly steam the vegetables.) Drain and place pasta and vegetables in a large bowl.

Combine remaining ingredients in a small bowl. Mix well. Add to pasta and toss until pasta is evenly coated.

Chill.

Serve cold.

Each serving provides:

165	Calories	29 g	Carbohydrate
6 g	Protein	392 mg	Sodium
3 g	Total fat (0 g Sat. fat)	0 mg	Cholesterol

Sweet 'n' Tangy Couscous Salad

If the taste is familiar, you have probably eaten a type of mayonnaise-free cabbage slaw that is especially popular in the Pennsylvania Dutch communities. It was my Mom's idea to adapt the flavor to this quick-cooking grain (couscous is available in most grocery stores, usually with the imported foods). The result is a delicious salad.

Makes 6 servings

1¹/₂	cups water
1	cup couscous, uncooked
¹/₃	cup finely chopped onion
¹/₃	cup finely chopped green pepper
1	medium carrot, finely shredded
2	tablespoons finely chopped radish
¹/₂	cup water
¹/₄	cup sugar
¹/₄	cup plus 2 tablespoons vinegar
¹/₂	teaspoon celery seed
¹/₂	teaspoon salt
¹/₄	teaspoon pepper

Bring water to a boil in a small saucepan. Remove from heat, stir in couscous, cover, and let stand 5 minutes.

Fluff cooked couscous with a fork and stir in vegetables.

In a small bowl, combine remaining ingredients, stirring to dissolve sugar. Add to couscous and mix well.

Chill. .

Mix well before serving. Serve by itself or mounded on a bed of lettuce, garnished with sliced tomatoes and cucumbers.

Each serving provides:			
161	Calories	35 g	Carbohydrate
4 g	Protein	191 mg	Sodium
0 g	Total fat (0 g Sat. fat)	0 mg	Cholesterol

Sweet Caribbean Tofu Salad

A perfect light lunch, this tasty, sweet salad can be mounded on a bed of let-tuce and garnished with any type of fresh fruit. It can also be piled into a pita bread or used as a spread for graham crackers or rice cakes.

Makes 6 servings

1	pound medium tofu, sliced and drained between layers of towels
1	8-ounce can crushed pineapple (packed in juice), drained (reserve 2 tablespoons of the juice)
$1/3$	cup golden raisins
$1/4$	cup coarsely shredded carrot
$2^1/2$	tablespoons chopped almonds or walnuts
$1/2$	cup vanilla nonfat yogurt
1	tablespoon honey
1	teaspoon lemon juice
1	teaspoon grated fresh lemon peel
$1/2$	teaspoon coconut extract
$1/2$	teaspoon vanilla extract
$1/2$	teaspoon ground cinnamon
$1/4$	teaspoon ground cardamom

Place tofu in a large bowl and mash with a fork or potato masher. Stir in pineapple, raisins, carrot, and nuts.

In a small bowl, combine remaining ingredients, including re-served pineapple juice. Mix well. Add to tofu and mix until well blended.

Chill thoroughly.

◇*Serve-again hint:* For a take-along lunch, pack a container of this delicious salad, along with some graham crackers or rice cakes for spreading.

Each serving provides:

160	Calories	20 g	Carbohydrate
10 g	Protein	26 mg	Sodium
5 g	Total fat (1 g Sat. fat)	0 mg	Cholesterol

Fruit Salad with Cinnamon-Curry Dressing

Any combination of fresh fruits will work with this exotic dressing. You can mix it in a minute and keep it in the refrigerator until serving time. It has a tongue-tingling bite and makes a wonderful dip for fresh fruit.

Makes 6 servings

1	cup vanilla nonfat yogurt
1	tablespoon orange juice
$1/2$	teaspoon sugar
$1/2$	teaspoon ground cinnamon
$1/2$	teaspoon curry powder
	Pinch salt
$41/2$	cups cut-up fresh fruit (any combination of chopped apples, pears, oranges, grapes, peaches, nectarines, or other fruit)

In a small bowl, combine all ingredients, *except* fruit. Mix well. Chill.

Combine fruit in a large bowl. Cover and chill. (If there are no oranges among the fruits, add a tablespoon of orange or lemon juice to the fruit to keep it from discoloring.)

To serve, spoon $3/4$ cup of the fruit into each individual serving bowl. Top each serving with $21/2$ tablespoons of the dressing.

✦*Quick tip:* Make the dressing ahead, then stop by the local supermarket salad bar and pick up a container of fresh fruit salad.

✧*Serve-again hint:* The fruit and dressing make a wonderful topping for your morning oatmeal.

Each serving provides:

100	Calories	23 g	Carbohydrate
3 g	Protein	49 mg	Sodium
0 g	Total fat (0 g Sat. fat)	1 mg	Cholesterol

Waldorf Rice Salad

Brown rice adds a nutty flavor and chewy texture to this old familiar salad that's so pretty served on a bed of lettuce. Here's a great use for that leftover cup of rice.

Makes 4 servings

1	medium Golden Delicious apple, unpeeled, finely chopped
1	tablespoon orange juice
1	cup cooked brown rice (rice should be either cold or at room temperature)
1/2	cup vanilla nonfat yogurt
1/4	cup finely chopped celery
1/4	cup raisins
2	tablespoons chopped walnuts
1/8	teaspoon ground cinnamon

Combine apple with orange juice in a medium bowl. Toss to coat apples. Add remaining ingredients, mixing well.

Chill.

❖*Serve-again hint:* What a delicious and nutritious, high-fiber breakfast!

Each serving provides:

154	Calories	30 g	Carbohydrate
4 g	Protein	30 mg	Sodium
3 g	Total fat (0 g Sat. fat)	1 mg	Cholesterol

Cranberry Fruit Salad

Not only a perfect accompaniment to a holiday meal, this refreshing fruit combo also makes a delicious year-round dessert. For extra flair, serve it in tall-stemmed sherbet glasses and top each serving with a dollop of any fruit-flavored nonfat yogurt.

Makes 6 servings

1	1-pound can whole-berry cranberry sauce
1	8-ounce can crushed pineapple (packed in juice), drained (reserve 1 tablespoon of the juice)
1	medium Golden Delicious apple, unpeeled, finely chopped
1	large orange, peeled, sectioned, cut into small pieces (discard white membrane)
2	tablespoons coarsely chopped almonds
1	tablespoon honey
$1/2$	teaspoon almond extract
$1/4$	teaspoon orange extract

In a large bowl, combine cranberry sauce, pineapple, apple, orange, and almonds. Mix well.

In a small bowl or custard cup, combine reserved pineapple juice with remaining ingredients. Mix well, stirring until thoroughly blended. Add to fruit, mixing well.

Chill several hours or overnight, to blend flavors.

◆*Quick tip:* You can make entertaining easier by preparing this dish up to 3 days ahead and refrigerating until serving time.

Each serving provides:

194	Calories	46 g	Carbohydrate
1 g	Protein	23 mg	Sodium
2 g	Total fat (0 g Sat. fat)	0 mg	Cholesterol

Salad of Greens with Apple Vinaigrette

This attractive yet very simple salad is made by tossing lettuce and sliced apples with a deliciously different apple vinaigrette. The dressing can be made up to 2 days ahead and chilled until needed and, if you prefer, the recipe can easily be doubled or tripled. Regular apple juice will work, but it's definitely worth a trip to the health food store to purchase a good, all natural apple juice.

Makes 8 servings

Dressing

1/4	cup apple juice
2	tablespoons vegetable oil
2	tablespoons cider vinegar
1/2	teaspoon Dijon mustard
1/4	teaspoon salt
1/8	teaspoon pepper
1/4	cup very finely chopped Granny Smith apple, unpeeled

Salad

8	cups (packed) romaine or green leaf lettuce, torn into bite-size pieces
1	medium, Red or Golden Delicious apple, unpeeled, sliced into 1/8-inch slices (do not slice until just before serving)

Combine dressing ingredients in a small bowl or jar. Mix well. Chill several hours, or overnight, to blend flavors.

To serve, place the lettuce and sliced apple in a large bowl. Top with the dressing and toss until evenly mixed.

Serve right away.

Note: To make fewer than 8 servings, toss the desired amount of lettuce and apples with 1 1/2 tablespoons of dressing per serving.

Each serving provides:

60	Calories	6 g	Carbohydrate
1 g	Protein	82 mg	Sodium
4 g	Total fat (0 g Sat. fat)	0 mg	Cholesterol

"House" Vinaigrette

For years I've been making this easy dressing that my family has affection-
ately named the "house" dressing. (I've never measured the ingredients until
now!) Spoon it over a mixed salad or drizzle it on a veggie or cheese sand-
wich. It doubles or triples easily and keeps in the refrigerator for several
weeks.

Makes 1 cup

1/4	cup plus 2 tablespoons vegetable oil
1/4	cup plus 2 tablespoons water
1/4	cup red wine vinegar
1 1/2	teaspoons grated Parmesan cheese
1/2	teaspoon *each* dried oregano and basil
1/2	teaspoon sugar
1/4	teaspoon dill weed
1/8	teaspoon *each* garlic powder and onion powder
1/8	teaspoon *each* salt and pepper

Combine all ingredients in a jar and mix well.
Chill several hours to blend flavors.

Each tablespoon provides:

47	Calories	0 g	Carbohydrate
0 g	Protein	20 mg	Sodium
5 g	Total fat (1 g Sat. fat)	0 mg	Cholesterol

Maple-Dijon Vinaigrette

This tasty dressing is sweetened with maple syrup and accented with the tang of Dijon mustard. It tastes great over any type of mixed vegetable salad.

Makes 3/4 cup

1/4	cup red wine vinegar
3	tablespoons vegetable oil
2	tablespoons pure maple syrup
2	tablespoons water
1	tablespoon Dijon mustard
1/8	teaspoon salt
1/8	teaspoon pepper

In a small bowl, combine all ingredients. Mix with a fork or wire whisk until blended.

Chill several hours to blend flavors.

Each tablespoon provides:

41	Calories	2 g	Carbohydrate
0 g	Protein	53 mg	Sodium
3 g	Total fat (1 g Sat. fat)	0 mg	Cholesterol

French Dressing à l'Orange

In this popular dressing, I've replaced some of the oil with orange juice, adding a delicate, sweet flavor that enhances any mixed vegetable salad.

Makes 1 cup

1/4	cup vegetable oil
1/4	cup orange juice
2	tablespoons water
2	tablespoons red wine vinegar
2	tablespoons lemon juice
2	tablespoons sugar
1	teaspoon paprika
1/2	teaspoon dry mustard
1/4	teaspoon salt
1/8	teaspoon garlic powder
	Dash cayenne pepper

Combine all ingredients in a bowl or jar. Mix well with a fork or wire whisk.

Chill several hours to blend flavors.

Each tablespoon provides:

39	Calories	2 g	Carbohydrate
0 g	Protein	34 mg	Sodium
3 g	Total fat (1 g Sat. fat)	0 mg	Cholesterol

Tofu-Tahini Dressing

If you like your dressing thick and rich, this one's for you. Soft tofu blends well with tahini, adding a creamy texture to the sweet, nutty flavor of the tahini.

Makes 1 cup

1/2	10-ounce package reduced-fat silken tofu*
1/4	cup tahini (sesame paste)
1	tablespoon reduced-sodium (or regular) soy sauce
1 1/2	teaspoons lemon juice
1/8	teaspoon garlic powder
1/3	cup skim milk

Place tofu in a blender container and blend until smooth. Spoon into a small bowl. Add tahini, soy sauce, lemon juice, and garlic powder, mixing until smooth. Gradually add milk, stirring until well blended.

Chill.

Note: After chilling, dressing may thicken slightly. If a thinner consistency is desired, stir in a little more skim milk.

❖*Serve-again hint:* This dressing doubles as a delicious dip for fresh veggies or as a creamy addition to a simple sandwich of sliced lettuce, tomato, and cucumber.

*You can double the recipe and use the whole package or use the rest of the tofu to make one of the easy blender puddings in the "No-Bake Desserts" chapter.

Each tablespoon provides:

29	Calories	1 g	Carbohydrate
1 g	Protein	52 mg	Sodium
2 g	Total fat (0 g Sat. fat)	0 mg	Cholesterol

Casseroles and Oven-Baked Dishes

For generations, casseroles have ranked high among favorite American dinners. Traditionally, though, quite a few of these favorites have been loaded with high-fat ingredients. However, with some tasty alterations and substitutions, you'll see how delicious—and nutritious—a casserole can be.

In most cases there is only one pot to wash, which is a definite plus. I've always maintained that if the ingredients are tasty and the right combination of spices is used, everything can be put together in one pot, baked, and voilà—a delicious casserole.

Be sure to read "The Well-Stocked Lowfat Pantry" on page 10. If you keep a healthful variety of foods on hand along with your favorite spices, there's no end to the combinations of tasty dishes you can create.

Mexican Beans 'n' Beer

This is a shortened and lightened version of a Mexican bean dish that is usually made with dark beer and pork and simmered for several hours. There's lots of delicious, rich "gravy," making this a perfect dish to spoon over rice.

Makes 6 servings

2	teaspoons vegetable oil
1¹/₂	cups chopped onion
5	large cloves garlic, sliced lengthwise into paper-thin slices
¹/₄	cup all-purpose flour
2	teaspoons ground cumin
2	teaspoons chili powder
2	teaspoons sugar
1	teaspoon ground coriander
1	1-pound salt-free (or regular) tomatoes, chopped and drained (reserve liquid)
2	1-pound cans pinto beans, rinsed and drained (or 4 cups of cooked beans)
1	12-ounce can light beer

Heat oil in a medium nonstick skillet over medium heat. Add onion and garlic. Cook, stirring frequently, until onion begins to brown, about 5 minutes.

Preheat oven to 375°.

Lightly oil a 2¹/₂-quart casserole or spray with a nonstick cooking spray.

In a small bowl, combine flour, cumin, chili powder, sugar, and coriander. Gradually add reserved tomato liquid, stirring constantly to prevent lumps.

In prepared casserole, combine onion, flour mixture, tomatoes, beans, and beer. Mix well.

Bake, uncovered, 1 hour.

Each serving provides:			
185	Calories	29 g	Carbohydrate
8 g	Protein	267 mg	Sodium
4 g	Total fat (0 g Sat. fat)	0 mg	Cholesterol

Cheddar Bean Loaf Supreme

My favorite pasta sauce for topping this delicious loaf is one with lots of vegetable chunks in it. Read the labels carefully and choose a reduced-fat pasta sauce, as some commercial sauces are quite high in fat.

Makes 6 servings

1	1-pound can pinto beans, rinsed and drained (or 2 cups of cooked beans)
1	15-ounce jar reduced-fat, meatless spaghetti sauce
1/2	cup vegetable broth, or 1/2 cup of water and 1/2 teaspoon Vegetable Broth Mix (page 34)
1/2	cup dry bread crumbs
1/2	cup wheat germ
1/3	cup very finely chopped onion
1/3	cup very finely chopped green bell pepper
2	tablespoons very finely chopped celery
4	ounces shredded reduced-fat Cheddar cheese (1 cup)
2	egg whites
1/2	teaspoon garlic powder
1/4	teaspoon pepper

Preheat oven to 350°.

Lightly oil a 4 × 8-inch loaf pan or spray with a nonstick cooking spray.

Place beans in a large bowl. Mash *half* of the beans, using a fork or potato masher. Add 2 tablespoons of the spaghetti sauce. Set remaining sauce aside.

Add remaining ingredients, *except* spaghetti sauce, to beans. Mix well. Spoon mixture into prepared pan and press down firmly with the back of a spoon.

Bake, uncovered, 45 minutes.

Let stand 5 minutes, then run a knife around the edges of the loaf and invert onto a serving plate.

While loaf is standing, heat remaining spaghetti sauce in a saucepan or by using a microwave. Spoon about ¼ cup of sauce over each serving.

✧*Serve-again hint:* Slice any leftover loaf and make hot or cold sandwiches, topped with leftover pasta sauce or ketchup.

Each serving provides:

215	Calories	26 g	Carbohydrate
15 g	Protein	596 mg	Sodium
6 g	Total fat (3 g Sat. fat)	13 mg	Cholesterol

Tofu Tamale Casserole

There's a surprise layer of cheese under the corn bread crust, adding flavor and interest to this unique casserole. Just mash the tofu, open a few cans, and you're almost there.

Makes 6 servings

Tofu Filling
1   pound firm or medium tofu, thickly sliced and drained well between towels
2   tablespoons skim milk
3   egg whites
2¹/₂   teaspoons chili powder
1   teaspoon dried oregano
¹/₂   teaspoon garlic powder
1   1-pound can stewed tomatoes, drained
1   8-ounce can corn, drained
³/₄   cup shredded reduced-fat Cheddar cheese (3 ounces)

Corn Bread Crust
²/₃   cup yellow cornmeal
¹/₄   cup whole wheat flour
1   teaspoon baking powder
¹/₈   teaspoon salt
³/₄   cup water
2   teaspoons vegetable oil

Preheat oven to 350°.

Lightly oil a 9-inch square baking pan or spray with a nonstick cooking spray.

Place tofu in a large bowl. Mash well, using a fork or potato masher. Add milk, egg whites, and spices. Mash again, mixing well. Stir in tomatoes and corn.

Spoon mixture into prepared pan. Press down gently with the back of a spoon.

Sprinkle cheese evenly over the mixture.

To make the crust, in a small bowl, combine cornmeal, flour, baking powder, and salt. Mix well. Stir in water and oil, mixing until all ingredients are moistened. Drop mixture by tablespoonfuls onto cheese. Spread evenly with the back of a spoon.

Bake, uncovered, 35 to 40 minutes, until crust is set and begins to brown.

Each serving provides:

266	Calories	31 g	Carbohydrate
18 g	Protein	582 mg	Sodium
9 g	Total fat (3 g Sat. fat)	10 mg	Cholesterol

Chili-Bean and Corn Bread Casserole

Bottled chili sauce and canned beans form the basis for this scrumptious casserole. Imagine having your bowl of chili and your corn bread all in one pan!

Makes 6 servings

Bean Filling
1	teaspoon vegetable oil
$1/2$	cup finely chopped onion
$1/2$	cup finely chopped green bell pepper
1	1-pound can vegetarian baked beans
1	1-pound can kidney beans, rinsed and drained (or 2 cups of cooked beans)
$1/3$	cup bottled chili sauce
2	tablespoons firmly packed brown sugar
$3/4$	teaspoon dry mustard
$1/4$	teaspoon garlic powder

Corn Bread Crust
$2/3$	cup yellow cornmeal
$1/4$	cup whole wheat flour
1	teaspoon baking powder
$1/8$	teaspoon salt
$3/4$	cup water
1	tablespoon vegetable oil

Heat oil in a small nonstick skillet over medium heat.

Add onion and green pepper. Cook 5 minutes, stirring frequently. Preheat oven to 350°.

Lightly oil a 7 × 11-inch baking pan.

In a large bowl, combine onions and peppers with remaining filling ingredients. Mix well. Spoon into prepared pan.

To make the crust, in a small bowl, combine cornmeal, flour, baking powder, and salt. Mix well. Stir in water and oil, mixing until all ingredients are moistened. Drop mixture by tablespoonfuls onto bean mixture. Spread evenly with the back of a spoon.

Bake, uncovered, 30 minutes, until crust is firm.

Let stand 5 minutes before serving.

Each serving provides:

273	Calories	50 g	Carbohydrate
10 g	Protein	726 mg	Sodium
5 g	Total fat (1 g Sat. fat)	0 mg	Cholesterol

Timeless Tofu Casserole

The name comes from the fact that this easy dish tastes great any time of day. From brunch to dinner, you'll love the fact that you can change it by using a different sauce as a topping. (It's delicious topped with hoisin sauce and served with a side dish of the Stir-Fried Asparagus with Garlic and Ginger on page 306.)

Makes 4 servings

Casserole
2	teaspoons vegetable oil
1	cup chopped onion
1/2	cup chopped green bell pepper
1	pound firm or medium tofu, thickly sliced and drained well between towels
2	egg whites
2	tablespoons skim milk
3/4	teaspoon garlic powder
1/2	teaspoon turmeric
1/2	teaspoon salt
1/4	to 1/2 teaspoon pepper
2	teaspoons wheat germ or dry bread crumbs
1	teaspoon grated Parmesan cheese

Topping
1	cup reduced-fat meatless pasta sauce or pizza sauce *or* 1 one-pound can stewed tomatoes

Heat oil in a medium nonstick skillet over medium heat. Add onion and green pepper. Cook, stirring frequently, 5 minutes, until onion begins to brown.

Preheat oven to 350°.

Lightly oil a 1-quart baking dish or spray with a nonstick cooking spray.

Place tofu in a large bowl and mash with a fork or potato masher. Add egg whites, milk, garlic powder, turmeric, salt, and pepper. Mash again, mixing well. Stir in onion and green pepper. Spoon mixture into prepared baking dish. Press down gently with the back of a spoon.

Combine wheat germ and Parmesan cheese and sprinkle evenly over top of casserole.

Bake, uncovered, 30 to 35 minutes, until set and lightly browned.

Heat topping, divide evenly, and spoon over each serving.

Each serving provides:			
195	Calories	14 g	Carbohydrate
16 g	Protein	522 mg	Sodium
9 g	Total fat (1 g Sat. fat)	0 mg	Cholesterol

Swiss Spinach, Rice, and Tofu Casserole

Swiss cheese adds a slightly smoky flavor to this hearty casserole. I usually serve it for dinner, but it also makes a terrific egg-free brunch dish.

Makes 6 servings

2	teaspoons vegetable oil
1	cup chopped onion
4	cloves garlic, finely chopped
1	1-pound can stewed tomatoes, undrained
1	teaspoon *each* dried basil and oregano
1/2	teaspoon salt
1/4	teaspoon pepper
1	10-ounce package reduced-fat silken tofu
2	cups cooked brown rice
1	10-ounce package frozen chopped spinach, thawed and drained well
3	ounces reduced-fat Swiss cheese, shredded or torn into small pieces (3/4 cup)

Preheat oven to 350°.

Lightly oil an 8-inch square baking pan or spray with a nonstick cooking spray.

Heat oil in a medium nonstick skillet over medium heat. Add onion and garlic. Cook, stirring frequently, 5 minutes, until onion begins to brown. Remove from heat. Stir in stewed tomatoes, basil, oregano, salt, and pepper. Mix well.

Place tofu in a blender container and blend until smooth. Add to skillet, along with rice, spinach, and 2 ounces (1/2 cup) of the cheese. Mix well. Spoon into prepared pan. Pat mixture down gently into pan.

Cover tightly and bake 40 minutes. Remove cover and sprinkle remaining cheese over casserole. Return to oven for 10 more minutes.

◆*Quick tip:* If you don't have any leftover rice, prepare quick-cooking brown rice while you sauté the onion.

Each serving provides:			
203	Calories	27 g	Carbohydrate
10 g	Protein	467 mg	Sodium
7 g	Total fat (2 g Sat. fat)	7 mg	Cholesterol

Peachy Salsa Beans

Peach jam adds a delectable sweetness to this quick bean casserole. While the beans bake, the rice can be cooking, making an easy dinner with a Mexican flair. This is a great dish to make ahead—the flavor is even better when it's reheated.

Makes 4 servings

1	8-ounce jar salsa (mild or hot)
1/4	cup fruit-only peach (or apricot) spread
1/2	teaspoon chili powder
1/2	teaspoon dried oregano
1/4	teaspoon ground cumin
1	1-pound can kidney beans, rinsed and drained (or 2 cups of cooked beans)

Preheat oven to 375°.

Lightly oil a 1-quart casserole or spray with a nonstick cooking spray.

In a large bowl, combine all ingredients, *except* beans. Mix well. Stir in beans. Pour mixture into prepared casserole.

Bake, covered, 30 minutes.

Serve over brown rice or any other cooked grain.

❖*Serve-again hint:* The leftovers can be reheated and rolled in flour tortillas for quick burritos.

Each serving provides:

152	Calories	27 g	Carbohydrate
6 g	Protein	730 mg	Sodium
2 g	Total fat (0 g Sat. fat)	0 mg	Cholesterol

Mozzarella Veggie Casserole

This easy casserole consists of steamed veggies that are topped with tomatoes, herbs, and cheese and then baked. What could be more delicious? Serve it alongside rice or mashed potatoes, and that's all you need for a tasty, nutritious meal. A special thanks to a special friend—Rowena Wilson—for sharing this delightful idea.

Makes 6 servings

3	heaping cups cauliflower flowerets (about 1¹/₄ pounds)
3	heaping cups zucchini (about 12 ounces), unpeeled, sliced crosswise into ¹/₄-inch slices (if the zucchini is large, cut it lengthwise into quarters, then slice crosswise)
3	cups eggplant (about 1 pound), unpeeled, cut lengthwise into quarters, then sliced crosswise into ¹/₄-inch slices (choose small eggplants—large ones tend to be full of seeds)
4	1-ounce slices whole wheat bread, cut into cubes
1	1-pound can salt-free (or regular) tomatoes, chopped, undrained
1	8-ounce can salt-free (or regular) tomato sauce
2	tablespoons grated Parmesan cheese
1	teaspoon each dried basil, oregano, sage, savory, and garlic powder
¹/₄	teaspoon pepper
1¹/₂	cups shredded reduced-fat mozzarella cheese (6 ounces)

Place a steamer rack in the bottom of a large saucepan. Add enough water to come almost up to the bottom of the rack. Place saucepan over medium heat. When water boils, add vegetables, cover saucepan, and cook 10 minutes, or until vegetables are tender. Drain. (Save the liquid for use in a future vegetable broth.)

Preheat oven to 350°.

Lightly oil a 9 × 13-inch baking pan or spray with a nonstick cooking spray.

Arrange vegetables in baking pan. Top with bread cubes, mixing them among the vegetables.

In a small bowl, combine tomatoes, tomato sauce, Parmesan cheese, and spices. Mix well. Spoon evenly over vegetables. Top with mozzarella cheese.

Cover with foil and bake 40 minutes. (Spray the foil lightly with cooking spray to keep it from sticking to the cheese.)

◆*Quick tip:* The veggies can be steamed a day ahead, making the casserole easy to assemble at the last minute. You can heat the veggies briefly in a microwave before assembling the casserole.

◇*Serve-again hint:* This makes a delectable filling for a pita sandwich. Heat and enjoy.

Each serving provides:			
202	Calories	27 g	Carbohydrate
14 g	Protein	316 mg	Sodium
6 g	Total fat (3 g Sat. fat)	11 mg	Cholesterol

Pinto Burrito Pie

A spicy bean mixture is layered between flour tortillas and served in pie-shaped wedges for a change-of-pace Mexican meal. It's delicious topped with lots of salsa and perhaps a dollop of yogurt.

Makes 6 servings

2	teaspoons vegetable oil
1	cup chopped onion
1	cup chopped green bell pepper
4	cloves garlic, finely chopped
1	teaspoon ground cumin
1	teaspoon chili powder
1	teaspoon dried oregano
1	tablespoon lime juice
2	1-pound cans pinto beans, rinsed and drained (or 4 cups of cooked beans)
3	8-inch or 9-inch flour tortillas
1¹/₂	cups shredded reduced-fat Cheddar cheese (6 ounces)
	Salsa (hot or mild)
	Plain nonfat yogurt (optional)

Heat oil in a large nonstick skillet over medium heat. Add onion, green pepper, and garlic. Cook, stirring frequently, 7 minutes, or until vegetables are tender. Add small amounts of water while cooking, about a tablespoon at a time, to prevent sticking. Remove from heat and stir in spices and lime juice. Stir in beans, mixing well.

Preheat oven to 350°.

Lightly oil a 9-inch pie pan or spray with a nonstick cooking spray.

Place 1 tortilla in the prepared pan. Spoon *half* of the bean mixture evenly over the tortilla, staying ¹/₂ inch away from the edges. Sprinkle one-third of the cheese over the beans.

Top with a second tortilla, followed by the remaining beans and another one-third of the cheese. Top with remaining tortilla.

Cover tightly with aluminum foil and bake 35 minutes. Uncover, sprinkle with remaining cheese, and bake 10 minutes more.

Cut into pie-shaped wedges.

Top each serving liberally with salsa (and yogurt, if desired).

✦*Quick tip:* The bean mixture can be made ahead, whenever you have time, and refrigerated for up to several days before you make the pie.

Each serving provides:

262	Calories	28 g	Carbohydrate
17 g	Protein	555 mg	Sodium
9 g	Total fat (4 g Sat. fat)	20 mg	Cholesterol

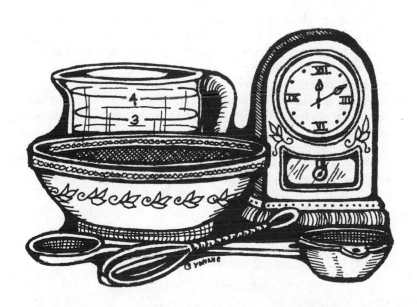

Tofu Picadillo

This spicy casserole can be made as hot or as mild as you like. Along with the sweet burst of raisins in every bite, the combination of flavors will surprise and delight you.

Makes 4 servings

2	4-ounce cans whole green chilies (hot or mild), drained
1	16-ounce jar salsa (hot or mild)
2	tablespoons all-purpose flour
1/4	teaspoon ground cinnamon
1/8	teaspoon ground cloves
1/4	cup raisins
3	tablespoons slivered almonds
1	pound firm or medium tofu, cut into 1/4- to 1/2-inch cubes, drained well between layers of towels
1/2	cup shredded reduced-fat Cheddar or Monterey Jack cheese
1	cup plain nonfat yogurt
2	egg whites

Preheat oven to 375°.

Lightly oil an 8-inch square baking pan or spray with nonstick cooking spray.

Cut chilies in half lengthwise and arrange in a single layer in prepared pan.

In a medium bowl, combine salsa, flour, cinnamon, and cloves. Mix well. Stir in raisins and almonds. Gently stir in tofu. Spoon mixture evenly over chilies. Press down gently with the back of a spoon.

Sprinkle cheese evenly over tofu.

In a small bowl, combine yogurt and egg whites. Beat with a fork or wire whisk until smooth. Spread over casserole.

Bake, uncovered, 40 to 45 minutes, until center is set.

❖*Serve-again hint:* As a delicious filling, the leftovers can be piled into scooped-out tomatoes or zucchini halves and baked in a 350° oven until hot.

Each serving provides:			
321	Calories	29 g	Carbohydrate
23 g	Protein	1711 mg	Sodium
12 g	Total fat (3 g Sat. fat)	11 mg	Cholesterol

Butter Bean and Cheddar Casserole

A thick, creamy, cheese sauce, laced with sherry, surrounds the tender butter beans, making a sumptuous casserole that both family and guests will love.

Makes 4 servings

2	tablespoons all-purpose flour
1	cup skim milk
1	teaspoon Vegetable Broth Mix (page 34)
1/8	teaspoon pepper
1	tablespoon ketchup
1	tablespoon dry sherry
1	4-ounce jar chopped pimientos, drained
1/2	cup shredded reduced-fat Cheddar cheese (2 ounces)
2	1-pound cans butter beans, rinsed and drained (or 4 cups of cooked beans)
2	tablespoons wheat germ or dry bread crumbs

Preheat oven to 350°.

Lightly oil a 1-quart baking dish or spray with a nonstick cooking spray.

Place flour in a small saucepan. Gradually add milk, stirring until mixture is smooth. Add broth mix and pepper. Cook over medium-low heat, stirring constantly, until mixture comes to a boil. Continue to cook, stirring, 1 to 2 minutes, until mixture has thickened. Remove from heat and stir in ketchup, sherry, pimientos, and cheese.

Place beans in prepared baking dish. Spoon sauce over beans. Mix gently.

Sprinkle evenly with wheat germ.

Bake, uncovered, 30 minutes.

Each serving provides:

264	Calories	39 g	Carbohydrate
17 g	Protein	575 mg	Sodium
5 g	Total fat (2 g Sat. fat)	11 mg	Cholesterol

Tangy Baked Beans

Three types of mustard are used in these beans, making them tangy and delicious. Serve over brown rice or add this tasty dish to your next cookout menu.

Makes 4 servings

2	teaspoons vegetable oil
1/2	cup chopped onion
1	1-pound can pinto beans, rinsed and drained (or 2 cups of cooked beans)
1/4	cup molasses
1/4	cup apple juice
2	teaspoons firmly packed brown sugar
2	teaspoons prepared yellow mustard
2	teaspoons Dijon mustard
1/2	teaspoon dry mustard
1/4	teaspoon ground ginger
1/8	teaspoon ground allspice
1/8	teaspoon garlic powder

Heat oil in a small nonstick skillet over medium heat. Add onion. Cook, stirring frequently, until tender, about 3 to 5 minutes. Remove from heat and stir in beans.

Preheat oven to 375°.

Lightly oil a 1-quart baking dish or spray with nonstick cooking spray.

Combine remaining ingredients in a medium bowl and mix well. Stir in onion and beans. Spoon mixture into prepared baking dish.

Cover and bake 45 minutes.

Note: If a thicker sauce is desired, uncover beans and continue to cook another 5 to 10 minutes.

❖*Serve-again hint:* Heated leftovers make a delicious topping for baked potatoes, or serve the cold leftovers as a tasty topping for a tossed salad.

Each serving provides:			
177	Calories	31 g	Carbohydrate
5 g	Protein	286 mg	Sodium
4 g	Total fat (0 g Sat. fat)	0 mg	Cholesterol

Easy Layered Beans and Rice

There's nothing to chop in this easy dish. Just open a few cans, layer everything in a casserole, and pop it in the oven. If you have some extra time, you can sauté chopped onions and green peppers and add them to any one of the layers. Or, add whatever spices you wish, such as basil, oregano, chili powder, or garlic.

Makes 4 servings

1   cup long-grain white rice, uncooked
4   sun-dried tomato halves (not packed in oil), cut into small
        pieces
1   8-ounce can corn, drained
1¹/4   cups boiling vegetable broth, or 1¹/4 cups boiling water and
        1¹/4 teaspoons Vegetable Broth Mix (page 34)
2   cups reduced-fat, meatless spaghetti sauce
1   1-pound can pinto beans, rinsed and drained (or 2 cups of
        cooked beans)
1   cup shredded reduced-fat mozzarella cheese (4 ounces)
1   tablespoon grated Parmesan cheese

Preheat oven to 375°.

Lightly oil a deep 2-quart casserole or spray with a nonstick cooking spray.

Spread rice in the casserole. Sprinkle with sun-dried tomatoes. Spread corn evenly over the rice. Gently pour broth over the corn.

Spoon *half* of the spaghetti sauce evenly over the corn. Spoon beans over the sauce, followed by remaining sauce.

Cover tightly and bake 45 minutes.

Uncover, sprinkle with both cheeses, and return to oven until cheese is melted and begins to brown, 5 to 10 minutes.

✧*Serve-again hint:* Here's everything you need for a bean and rice burrito, including the cheese. Just roll the leftovers in flour tortillas, heat in an oven or microwave, then top with salsa.

Each serving provides:			
413	Calories	71 g	Carbohydrate
19 g	Protein	938 mg	Sodium
6 g	Total fat (3 g Sat. fat)	11 mg	Cholesterol

Pinto Popover

This easy casserole, filled with beans and corn, is topped with a delicious, cheesy crust. It serves six as a filling entrée or it can serve twelve as a side dish. Its delicious herbed flavor makes it at home anywhere from a dinner buffet to a backyard picnic.

Makes 6 servings

Bean Filling
2	1-pound cans pinto beans, rinsed and drained (or 4 cups of cooked beans)
1	12-ounce can corn, drained
1	8-ounce can salt-free (or regular) tomato sauce
2	green onions, thinly sliced
2	tablespoons ketchup
1	tablespoon firmly packed brown sugar
1	teaspoon onion powder
1	teaspoon dried oregano
1/4	teaspoon dry mustard
1/8	teaspoon *each* salt and pepper

Topping
1	cup shredded reduced-fat Cheddar cheese (4 ounces)
2	egg whites
1/2	cup skim milk
1 1/2	teaspoons vegetable oil
1/2	cup all-purpose flour
1/2	teaspoon baking powder
2	green onions, thinly sliced

Preheat oven to 425°.

Lightly oil a 7 × 11-inch baking pan or spray with a nonstick cooking spray.

In a large bowl, combine all filling ingredients, mixing well. Place in prepared pan.

Sprinkle evenly with cheese.

In a small bowl, combine remaining topping ingredients. Beat with a wire whisk until blended. Spoon evenly over casserole.

Bake, uncovered, 25 to 30 minutes, until topping is lightly browned.

Each serving provides:

282	Calories	42 g	Carbohydrate
17 g	Protein	731 mg	Sodium
7 g	Total fat (3 g Sat. fat)	14 mg	Cholesterol

Tex-Mex Tofu Cutlets

This unusual blend of ingredients turns tofu into a spicy delight. I like to arrange the cutlets over a bed of brown rice and pass the extra picante sauce.

Makes 4 servings

1	pound firm tofu, sliced 1/2-inch thick
1	cup picante sauce (hot or mild), preferably the thick-and-chunky variety
2	tablespoons firmly packed brown sugar
2¹/₂	teaspoons Dijon mustard
¹/₈	teaspoon garlic powder

Heat oven to 375°.

Lightly oil a 7 × 11-inch baking pan or spray with a nonstick cooking spray.

Place tofu slices between two clean kitchen towels and press out as much water as possible.

In a small bowl, combine remaining ingredients, mixing well. Spread about 3 tablespoons of the sauce in the bottom of the prepared pan. Arrange tofu cutlets over sauce. Spoon remaining sauce over tofu.

Bake, uncovered, 30 minutes, until sauce is hot and bubbly and edges of tofu begin to brown.

❖*Serve-again hint:* Hot or cold, the leftovers make delicious sandwiches.

Each serving provides:

160	Calories	13 g	Carbohydrate
11 g	Protein	475 mg	Sodium
6 g	Total fat (1 g Sat. fat)	0 mg	Cholesterol

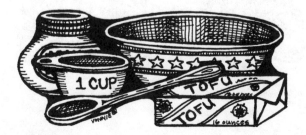

Chili Hominy Casserole

Thanks to my dear friend, Anne Atkins, for this delicious casserole. If you've never tried hominy, you're in for a new and exciting taste adventure. This plump white corn has the same toasted corn flavor as tortillas.

Makes 6 servings

2	teaspoons vegetable oil
1	cup chopped onions
3	cloves garlic, finely minced
2	1-pound cans hominy, rinsed and drained
1	1-pound can salt-free (or regular) tomatoes, chopped, undrained
1	tablespoon cornstarch
1	teaspoon chili powder (or more, if desired)
1	cup shredded reduced-fat Cheddar cheese (4 ounces)

Preheat oven to 350°.

Lightly oil 1³/₄-quart casserole or spray with a nonstick cooking spray.

Heat oil in a large nonstick skillet over medium heat. Add onions and garlic. Cook, stirring, 1 minute. Add hominy. Cook, stirring frequently, 3 minutes. Remove from heat.

Add tomatoes to skillet, reserving ¹/₄ cup of the liquid. Dissolve cornstarch in the reserved liquid and add to skillet. Add chili powder. Mix well.

Reserve ¹/₄ cup of the cheese and stir remaining cheese into skillet.

Bake, covered, 45 minutes. Then uncover, sprinkle with reserved cheese and bake 5 minutes more.

✧*Serve-again hint:* Leftovers make a tasty topper for baked potatoes.

Each serving provides:

216	Calories	29 g	Carbohydrate
9 g	Protein	480 mg	Sodium
7 g	Total fat (3 g Sat. fat)	13 mg	Cholesterol

Eggplant and Rice Parmesan

I've added a layer of rice to this popular dish, creating a filling casserole that only needs a steamed green vegetable to make the meal complete. If you're in a hurry, use quick-cooking brown rice and let it cook while you prepare the eggplant.

Makes 6 servings

1	medium eggplant (1¹/₂ pounds), peeled, sliced crosswise into ¹/₂-inch slices
	Nonstick cooking spray
	Salt, pepper, and garlic powder
¹/₃	cup Italian-seasoned bread crumbs
3	cups cooked brown rice
1	28-ounce jar reduced-fat, meatless spaghetti sauce
3	tablespoons grated Parmesan cheese
1	cup shredded reduced-fat mozzarella cheese (4 ounces)

Preheat the broiler. Place eggplant slices in a single layer on a nonstick baking sheet. Spray each side lightly with nonstick spray and sprinkle each side lightly with salt, pepper, and garlic powder. Broil 3 to 4 minutes on each side, until lightly browned.

Reduce oven temperature to 375°.

Lightly oil a 9 × 13-inch baking pan or spray with nonstick cooking spray.

Arrange eggplant in slightly overlapping layers in prepared pan. Sprinkle evenly with bread crumbs.

In a large bowl, combine rice, spaghetti sauce, and Parmesan cheese. Spoon evenly over eggplant.

Cover tightly and bake 25 minutes. Uncover, sprinkle with mozzarella cheese and return to oven for 5 minutes.

❖*Serve-again hint:* Hot or cold, leftovers make a delicious sandwich.

Each serving provides:			
270	Calories	43 g	Carbohydrate
12 g	Protein	738 mg	Sodium
6 g	Total fat (2 g Sat. fat)	8 mg	Cholesterol

All-in-One Rice and Beans

Rice and beans are perfect together, both health-wise and taste-wise. Mixed with corn and tomato sauce and flavored with onions and basil, this is really a winning combination.

Makes 4 servings

1	cup brown rice, uncooked
2¹/2	cups water
1	1-pound can cream-style corn
1	1-pound can kidney beans, rinsed and drained (or 2 cups of cooked beans)
1	8-ounce can salt-free (or regular) tomato sauce
¹/3	cup thinly sliced green onions (green and white parts)
1¹/2	teaspoons dried basil
¹/8	to ¹/4 teaspoon pepper

Cook rice according to the directions on page 20.

Preheat oven to 375°.

Lightly oil a 2-quart casserole or spray with a nonstick cooking spray.

In a large bowl, combine cooked rice with remaining ingredients. Mix well. Spoon into prepared casserole.

Bake, covered, 30 minutes, until hot and bubbly.

◆*Quick tip:* If you have leftover rice in the refrigerator or freezer, run it under hot water, drain, and it's ready to use. Quick-cooking brown rice is also a time-saver.

Each serving provides:

367	Calories	74 g	Carbohydrate
12 g	Protein	482 mg	Sodium
4 g	Total fat (1 g Sat. fat)	0 mg	Cholesterol

Skillet and Stove-Top Dinners

What could be easier than chopping some vegetables, opening a few cans, and preparing your dinner in one skillet or saucepan with no oven to heat or broiler to wash? Most of the dishes in this section cook in 30 minutes or less and some of them can be prepared in as little as 10 minutes. Many of the recipes are for bean dishes that are served over grains. So, if you keep cooked rice in your freezer or use quick-cooking grains such as couscous, bulgur, or quick-cooking brown rice, the grain can be ready as quickly as the entrée. For a change of pace, many of the dishes in this section can also be spooned over baked potatoes, which can be cooked quickly in a microwave.

A large nonstick skillet is the only cooking necessity for these dishes. It not only makes cleanup easier but also enables you to prepare foods using a minimal amount of oil.

So, if you're in a hurry, try these easy entrées. They're easy to prepare and economical, too. They'll make your life easier and will save you lots of time and money. And the bonus? They taste great!

Bombay Kidney Beans

Beans and rice make an easy, nutritious dinner. A perfect meal when you're in a hurry, it can be made with many different spice combinations. This Indian blend is one of my favorites. It's also delicious over couscous.

Makes 4 servings

1	1-pound can kidney beans, rinsed and drained (or 2 cups of cooked beans)
1	1-pound can salt-free (or regular) tomatoes, chopped, undrained
2	teaspoons honey
1	teaspoon curry powder
1/4	teaspoon ground cumin
1/4	teaspoon ground ginger
1/8	teaspoon ground allspice
1/8	teaspoon salt
1/8	teaspoon pepper (optional)
1	tablespoon cornstarch
1 1/2	tablespoons water

In a medium saucepan, combine all ingredients, *except* cornstarch and water. Bring to a boil over medium heat, stirring occasionally. Reduce heat to medium-low, cover, and simmer 10 minutes.

Combine cornstarch and water in a small bowl or custard cup. Stir to dissolve cornstarch. Add to saucepan. Cook, stirring constantly, 2 to 3 minutes, until mixture has thickened slightly.

Serve with rice.

◆*Quick tip:* Always keep canned beans and tomatoes in the pantry!

Each serving provides:			
124	Calories	23 g	Carbohydrate
7 g	Protein	226 mg	Sodium
1 g	Total fat (0 g Sat. fat)	0 mg	Cholesterol

Pumpkin and White Bean Stew

Served over brown rice, this mellow stew is a perfect fall entree. It also makes a great meatless alternative for Thanksgiving dinner.

Makes 6 servings

2	teaspoons vegetable oil
1	cup chopped onion
1	cup sliced mushrooms
3	cloves garlic, finely chopped
1	teaspoon ground cumin
1/4	teaspoon ground cinnamon
31/2	cups pumpkin, peeled, cut into 1/2-inch to 3/4-inch cubes (about 11/2 pounds)
1	cup vegetable broth, or 1 cup of water and 1 teaspoon Vegetable Broth Mix (page 34.)
1	19-ounce can white kidney beans (cannellini), rinsed and drained (or 21/4 cups of cooked beans)
1	1-pound can salt-free (or regular) tomatoes, chopped, undrained
1/4	teaspoon salt
1/8	teaspoon pepper

Heat oil in a large saucepan over medium heat. Add onion, mushrooms, and garlic. Sprinkle with cumin and cinnamon. Cook, stirring frequently, 5 minutes, or until vegetables are tender.

Add remaining ingredients, mixing well. When mixture boils, reduce heat to medium-low, cover, and cook 35 to 40 minutes, until pumpkin is tender.

If desired, add additional salt and pepper to taste.

◆*Quick tip:* Peel and chop the pumpkin up to a day ahead and store it, covered, in the refrigerator.

Each serving provides:

141	Calories	25 g	Carbohydrate
7 g	Protein	233 mg	Sodium
2 g	Total fat (0 g Sat. fat)	0 mg	Cholesterol

Korean Spiced Beans

Fresh garlic and ginger give this Korean dish an intense flavor and a zip you'll love. Serve it over brown rice, add a green vegetable—and dinner is complete.

Makes 6 servings

3	tablespoons reduced-sodium (or regular) soy sauce
3	tablespoons firmly packed brown sugar
1/3	cup water
1	tablespoon ketchup
3	cloves garlic, crushed
1/2	teaspoon grated fresh ginger root
2	1-pound cans kidney beans, rinsed and drained (or 4 cups of cooked beans)
2	teaspoons cornstarch dissolved in 1/4 cup water

In a medium saucepan, combine soy sauce, brown sugar, water, ketchup, garlic, and ginger root. Mix well. Stir in beans. Bring to a boil over medium heat, stirring occasionally.

Stir cornstarch mixture and add to beans. Continue to cook, stirring constantly, 1 to 2 minutes.

✧*Serve-again hint:* Leftovers are a perfect topping for a baked potato.

Each serving provides:

146	Calories	26 g	Carbohydrate
8 g	Protein	521 mg	Sodium
1 g	Total fat (0 g Sat. fat)	0 mg	Cholesterol

Savory Spiced Split Peas

If you love split peas but thought they were just for soup, you'll love this thick stew-like mix that can be served over any cooked grain. I especially like it over a mildly spiced dish, such as the Spiced Raisin Rice on page 290. .

Makes 4 servings

1	cup split peas, uncooked
2¹/₂	cups vegetable broth, or 2¹/₂ cups water plus 2¹/₂ teaspoons Vegetable Broth Mix (page 34)
³/₄	teaspoon ground cumin
¹/₂	teaspoon ground ginger
¹/₂	teaspoon ground coriander
¹/₄	teaspoon ground cinnamon
¹/₁₆	teaspoon ground cloves
¹/₁₆	teaspoon cayenne pepper
¹/₂	cup hot water
	Salt to taste

In a medium saucepan, combine all ingredients, *except* hot water and salt. Bring to a boil over medium heat, then cover, reduce heat to medium-low, and simmer 30 minutes.

Stir in hot water, cover, and continue to cook 10 minutes more. Add salt to taste.

Spoon over rice or any other cooked grain.

❖*Serve-again hint:* For a tasty soup, stir vegetable broth into the leftovers until a desired consistency is reached, then heat and serve.

Each serving provides:

182	Calories	33 g	Carbohydrate
12 g	Protein	76 mg	Sodium
1 g	Total fat (0 g Sat. fat)	0 mg	Cholesterol

Stove-Top Bean and Noodle Casserole

My dear friend, Lynda Bell, gave me the idea for this "old standby" dish. It's like everyone's favorite beef and noodle casserole but without the beef. One of the things you'll love about it is that it can be varied in so many ways. For an Italian flair, add basil and oregano; for a Mexican dish, add chili powder and cumin. You can also add chopped green pepper, corn, or green chilies, or enjoy its homestyle flavor just the way it is.

Makes 4 servings

2	teaspoons vegetable oil
1	cup chopped onion
2	cups thinly sliced mushrooms
1	1-pound can salt-free (or regular) tomatoes, undrained
1	1-pound can kidney beans, rinsed and drained (or 2 cups of cooked beans)
1/2	cup water
1	teaspoon Vegetable Broth Mix (page 34)
3/4	teaspoon garlic powder
1/2	teaspoon onion powder
1 1/2	cups medium (yolk-free) noodles, uncooked (about 3 ounces)
	Salt and pepper to taste

Heat oil in a medium saucepan over medium heat. Add onion. Cook until tender, 5 to 7 minutes. Stir occasionally and add water as necessary, about a tablespoon at a time, to prevent sticking.

Add remaining ingredients, *except* noodles, salt, and pepper. Bring mixture to a boil, stirring occasionally and breaking up the tomatoes with the spoon. Add noodles, then stir gently and press noodles down into liquid.

Cover, reduce heat to medium-low, and simmer 20 minutes, stirring once halfway through cooking time.

Add salt and pepper to taste.

✧*Serve-again hint:* Pile the leftovers into hollowed-out tomatoes and serve them cold as a nutritious bean and pasta salad.

	Each serving provides:		
225	Calories	38 g	Carbohydrate
11 g	Protein	184 mg	Sodium
4 g	Total fat (0 g Sat. fat)	0 mg	Cholesterol

Baked Beans Dressed for Dinner

This recipe proves that "Necessity is the mother of invention." I came up with it one night when I was in a hurry and there was truly nothing in the house to eat. To our surprise, we loved it!

Makes 6 servings

2	teaspoons vegetable oil
1	cup chopped onion
1/2	cup chopped green bell pepper
2	1-pound cans vegetarian baked beans
1	8-ounce can crushed pineapple (packed in juice), drained (reserve juice)
1	tablespoon cornstarch
1	teaspoon chili powder
1/2	teaspoon garlic powder
1/16	teaspoon ground cloves
1/16	teaspoon ground allspice

Heat oil in a medium saucepan over medium heat. Add onion and green pepper. Cook, stirring frequently, until tender. Add small amounts of water as necessary, about a tablespoon at a time, to prevent sticking.

Stir in beans and pineapple.

Add cornstarch to reserved pineapple juice and stir to dissolve cornstarch. Add to saucepan, along with spices. Cook, stirring, until mixture comes to a boil. Continue to cook and stir 1 minute.

Serve over brown rice or any cooked grain.

♦*Quick tip:* That extra brown rice in the freezer will really come in handy here!

Each serving provides:

196	Calories	41 g	Carbohydrate
8 g	Protein	607 mg	Sodium
2 g	Total fat (0 g Sat. fat)	0 mg	Cholesterol

Hominy and White Bean Chili

Hominy adds a delightful corn flavor to this unusual version of a popular dish. It's really a delicious blend of tastes and textures. If you like, you can garnish each bowlful with a dollop of plain nonfat yogurt and a sprinkling of fresh cilantro or a bit of shredded reduced-fat Cheddar cheese.

Makes 6 servings

2	teaspoons vegetable oil
1	cup *each* chopped onion and chopped celery
4	cloves garlic, crushed
2	cups chopped mushrooms
1	cup *each* chopped green bell pepper and red bell pepper
1	cup chopped zucchini, unpeeled
1	28-ounce can crushed tomatoes
1	6-ounce can tomato paste
1	cup water
1	1-pound can Great Northern beans, rinsed and drained (or 2 cups of cooked beans)
1	1-pound can hominy, drained
1	tablespoon chili powder (or to taste)
2	teaspoons dried oregano
1 1/2	teaspoons ground cumin

Heat oil in a large saucepan over medium heat. Add onion, celery, and garlic. Cook, stirring frequently, 5 minutes.

Add mushrooms, green and red peppers, and zucchini. Continue to cook, stirring frequently, 10 more minutes.

Add remaining ingredients, mixing well. When mixture boils, reduce heat to medium-low, cover, and simmer 20 minutes, stirring several times.

Each serving provides:

202	Calories	37 g	Carbohydrate
8 g	Protein	755 mg	Sodium
4 g	Total fat (0 g Sat. fat)	0 mg	Cholesterol

Curried Chickpeas and Spinach

You can serve this Indian specialty over any cooked grain, but it just begs to be served with the Spiced Bulgur on page 286. Try it and you'll see why.

Makes 4 servings

2	teaspoons olive oil
1/2	cup chopped onion
1/2	cup chopped green bell pepper
3	cloves garlic, finely chopped
1	1-pound can salt-free (or regular) tomatoes, chopped, undrained
1	1-pound can chickpeas (garbanzo beans), rinsed and drained (or 2 cups of cooked beans)
1	10-ounce package frozen chopped spinach, thawed and drained well
1/4	cup water
1 1/2	to 2 teaspoons chili powder
1	teaspoon Vegetable Broth Mix (page 34)
	Salt to taste

Heat oil in a medium saucepan over medium heat. Add onion, green pepper, and garlic. Cook 5 minutes, stirring frequently. Add small amounts of water as necessary, about a tablespoon at a time, to prevent sticking.

Add remaining ingredients, *except* salt. Bring mixture to a boil, stirring occasionally. Cover and cook 10 minutes. Add salt to taste.

✦*Quick tip:* Place the frozen spinach in the refrigerator the day before so it will be thawed and ready to use when you need it.

✧*Serve-again hint:* Leftovers reheat nicely in a saucepan or a microwave, and they can be spooned into a pita bread for a delicious hot sandwich.

Each serving provides:			
156	Calories	23 g	Carbohydrate
8 g	Protein	225 mg	Sodium
5 g	Total fat (0 g Sat. fat)	0 mg	Cholesterol

Beans with Tomatoes and Feta

When I asked Harry what I should call this recipe, his answer was "I'd call it good!" It's one of his favorites and it can be served over any cooked grain or even over pasta. Be sure to choose a good brand of tomatoes—they're vital to this dish.

Makes 4 servings

2	teaspoons vegetable oil
1¹/₂	cups chopped onion
1	28-ounce can Italian plum tomatoes, drained, chopped
¹/₄	cup dry white wine
2	teaspoons dried oregano
1	1-pound can kidney beans, rinsed and drained (or 2 cups of cooked beans)
¹/₂	cup crumbled feta cheese (3 ounces)
	Freshly ground black pepper

Heat oil in a large nonstick skillet over medium heat. Add onion. Cook, stirring frequently, 5 to 8 minutes, or until onion is tender and begins to brown.

Add tomatoes, wine, and oregano, mixing well. Stir in beans. When mixture boils, reduce heat to medium-low, cover, and simmer 15 minutes.

Spoon over rice or any cooked grain.

Divide feta cheese evenly and sprinkle on top of each serving. Top with freshly ground black pepper.

Each serving provides:

237	Calories	29 g	Carbohydrate
12 g	Protein	751 mg	Sodium
8 g	Total fat (4 g Sat. fat)	19 mg	Cholesterol

Barbecue Beans and Rice

Barbecue sauce adds just the right spark to this hearty skillet dinner. Feel free to add any other veggies you like along with the onion and green pepper. Tasty additions are broccoli, mushrooms, zucchini, carrots, or celery.

Makes 4 servings

2	teaspoons vegetable oil
1	cup chopped onion
1	cup chopped green bell pepper
3	cloves garlic, crushed
2^1/$_2$	cups cooked brown rice
1	1-pound can pinto beans, rinsed and drained (or 2 cups of cooked beans)
1	8-ounce can salt-free (or regular) tomato sauce
^{1}/$_4$	cup barbecue sauce

Heat oil in a large nonstick skillet over medium heat. Add onion, green pepper, and garlic. Cook, stirring frequently, until vegetables are tender, about 5 minutes.

Add remaining ingredients to skillet. Reduce heat slightly. Cook, stirring frequently, until mixture is heated through.

✦*Quick tip:* Have some quick-cooking brown rice, which cooks in 10 to 12 minutes, on hand. Or, keep plenty of cooked rice in the freezer for dishes like this.

✧*Serve-again hint:* Heat the leftovers and roll them in a tortilla with lettuce and tomato for an unusual barbecue burrito.

Each serving provides:

275	Calories	50 g	Carbohydrate
9 g	Protein	331 mg	Sodium
4 g	Total fat (1 g Sat. fat)	0 mg	Cholesterol

Spicy Red Lentils and Cauliflower

The delectable flavors of India abound in this fragrant dish. You'll love the way the house smells while the dish is cooking, but, better than that, you'll love the exotic flavor. Look for red lentils in any health food store. They're smaller than green lentils, cook quickly, and have a delicious, thick consistency.

Makes 6 servings

2	teaspoons vegetable oil
1¹/₂	cups chopped onion
1¹/₂	teaspoons ground cumin
1¹/₂	teaspoons ground coriander
1	teaspoon chili powder
1	teaspoon turmeric
¹/₄	to ¹/₂ teaspoon pepper
¹/₄	teaspoon *each* salt and garlic powder
1	cup red lentils, uncooked
3	cups vegetable broth, or 3 cups of water and 3 teaspoons Vegetable Broth Mix (page 34)
1	tablespoon lemon juice
4	cups cauliflower, cut into small flowerets

Heat oil in a large nonstick skillet over medium heat. Add onion. Cook, stirring frequently, until onion is tender, about 5 minutes.

While onion is cooking, combine spices in a small bowl. Sprinkle spices evenly over onion and continue to cook, stirring, 30 seconds.

Stir in lentils.

Add broth, lemon juice, and cauliflower, mixing well. Bring mixture to a boil, stirring frequently. Then cover, reduce heat to medium-low, and simmer 20 minutes, or until cauliflower is tender. Remove from heat and stir.

Serve over rice.

❖*Serve-again hint:* Leftovers make a delicious topping for a baked potato, turning it into a whole meal.

Each serving provides:			
168	Calories	28 g	Carbohydrate
11 g	Protein	165 mg	Sodium
2 g	Total fat (0 g Sat. fat)	0 mg	Cholesterol

Tofu Barbecue

This quick dish is delicious spooned over cooked couscous or bulgur. Since both grains cook quickly, this tasty dinner can be ready in about 20 minutes.

Makes 4 servings

2	teaspoons vegetable oil
1/2	cup finely chopped onion
1/2	cup finely chopped green bell pepper
3	cloves garlic, finely minced
1	pound firm or medium tofu, drained slightly, cut into 1/4-inch to 1/2-inch cubes
2	8-ounce cans salt-free (or regular) tomato sauce
2	tablespoons firmly packed brown sugar
2	tablespoons sweet pickle relish
2	teaspoons reduced-sodium (or regular) soy sauce
1 1/2	teaspoons dry mustard
	Few drops bottled hot sauce

Heat oil in a large nonstick skillet over medium heat. Add onion, green pepper, and garlic. Cook, stirring frequently, until tender, about 5 minutes. Stir in remaining ingredients, *except* hot sauce. When mixture boils, reduce heat to medium-low, cover, and simmer 10 minutes. Add hot sauce to taste.

◆*Quick tip:* Keep chopped onions and green peppers in the freezer where they will be handy for easy dishes such as this.

Each serving provides:

217	Calories	24 g	Carbohydrate
14 g	Protein	198 mg	Sodium
8 g	Total fat (1 g Sat. fat)	0 mg	Cholesterol

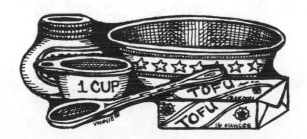

Tofu Cacciatore

Pile some noodles on your plate, then top them with this Italian-favorite-turned-veggie. All you need is a salad and a slice of Italian bread, and you've created a gourmet feast.

Makes 4 servings

2	teaspoons vegetable oil
1	cup onion, sliced vertically into thin slices
1	cup green bell pepper, cut into thin 2-inch strips
1	cup sliced mushrooms
4	cloves garlic, crushed
1	1-pound can salt-free (or regular) tomatoes, chopped, undrained
1	8-ounce can salt-free (or regular) tomato sauce
1/2	cup water
1	bay leaf
1	teaspoon dried oregano
1/2	teaspoon dried rosemary, crumbled
1/8	teaspoon pepper
1	pound firm or medium tofu, cut into 1 × 2-inch rectangles, 1/4-inch thick, drained well between layers of towels
	Salt to taste

Heat oil in a large nonstick skillet over medium heat. Add onion, green pepper, mushrooms, and garlic. Cook, stirring frequently, until vegetables are tender, about 8 minutes.

Add tomatoes, tomato sauce, water, and spices. Bring to a boil, stirring occasionally. Add tofu, stirring very gently to keep tofu from breaking apart. Reduce heat to medium-low, cover, and simmer 20 minutes, stirring occasionally.

Remove and discard bay leaf.

Add salt to taste.

Serve over medium (yolk-free) noodles.

❖*Serve-again hint:* Hollow out a submarine roll and fill it with the tofu mixture. Hot or cold, it's a delicious sandwich.

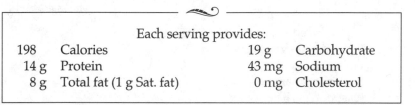

Each serving provides:			
198	Calories	19 g	Carbohydrate
14 g	Protein	43 mg	Sodium
8 g	Total fat (1 g Sat. fat)	0 mg	Cholesterol

Fried Rice with Tofu and Scallions

A favorite in Chinese restaurants, fried rice is often served as an entree. I've added tofu and lots of green onions (scallions), adding protein and flavor to this easy dinner-in-a-skillet. Start with soup, add a side dish of steamed green beans, and that's all you need.

Makes 4 servings

1/4	cup reduced-sodium (or regular) soy sauce
1 1/2	tablespoons dry sherry
1	tablespoon water
1/2	teaspoon sesame oil
1/2	teaspoon garlic powder
1/2	teaspoon ground ginger
	Few drops of bottled hot sauce (optional)
1	large bunch green onions (about 7 medium green onions)
2 1/2	teaspoons vegetable oil
1	pound firm or medium tofu, cut into 1/2-inch cubes, drained well between layers of towels
1	cup sliced mushrooms
4	cups cooked brown rice, cooled (preferably cold)

In a small bowl or custard cup, combine soy sauce, sherry, water, sesame oil, garlic powder, ginger, and hot sauce. Mix well and set aside.

Slice the white ends of the green onions into 1/2-inch pieces. Thinly slice the green parts. (You should have about 1/2 cup of the white parts and 1 cup of the green parts.)

Heat vegetable oil in a large nonstick skillet over medium-high heat. Add the white parts of the green onions, along with the tofu and mushrooms. Sprinkle with 1 tablespoon of the soy mixture. Cook, stirring constantly, 5 minutes, or until tofu is lightly browned. Stir gently, with a tossing motion, being careful not to break up the tofu.

Add rice, green parts of the green onions, and remaining soy mixture. Continue to cook, stirring constantly, until mixture is thoroughly combined and rice is hot and sizzling.

◆*Quick tip:* You can make the rice and slice the green onions and mushrooms up to a day ahead and keep them in the refrigerator until needed.

Each serving provides:

379	Calories	52 g	Carbohydrate
18 g	Protein	628 mg	Sodium
11 g	Total fat (1 g Sat. fat)	0 mg	Cholesterol

Israeli Simmered
Vegetables over Spiced Couscous

Amy Pessah, the daughter of one of my dearest friends, brought this recipe home from Israel, where it came from her friend Andrea. It's too easy for words and makes a delicious and filling homestyle dinner.

Makes 6 servings

Vegetables

1	small cabbage, cut into 6 wedges (cut the cabbage vertically through the core and do not remove the core, as it will keep the cabbage from falling apart)
4	large carrots, cut crosswise into thirds
2	medium zucchini, unpeeled, cut in half crosswise, then in half lengthwise
2	medium onions, quartered vertically, leaving the root end intact (this will help keep the onion from falling apart)
2	medium potatoes, unpeeled, cut into eighths
1	19-ounce can chickpeas (garbanzo beans), rinsed and drained (or 2 1/4 cups of cooked beans)
5	cups vegetable broth, or 5 cups of water and 5 teaspoons Vegetable Broth Mix (page 34)
1/2	teaspoon garlic powder

Couscous

1 1/2	cups water
1	cup couscous, uncooked
1/4	teaspoon *each* ground cinnamon and ground cumin

Additional

Salt and freshly ground black pepper

Place cabbage wedges in the bottom of a large soup pot. Top with remaining vegetables and chickpeas. Pour broth over vegetables. Add garlic powder. Bring mixture to a boil over medium heat. Reduce heat to medium-low, cover, and simmer 30 minutes, or until vegetables are tender.

When vegetables are almost ready, prepare couscous: bring water to a boil in a small saucepan. Stir in couscous and spices. Cover, remove from heat, and let stand 5 minutes. Fluff with a fork before serving.

To serve, place $1/2$ cup of couscous in the center of each soup bowl. Arrange vegetables and chickpeas around couscous. Spoon $1/2$ cup of broth over the couscous. Sprinkle with salt and freshly ground black pepper to taste.

✧*Serve-again hint:* Put the leftover veggies and broth in the blender for a thick, rich soup. Stir in couscous and heat through, adding vegetable broth if soup is too thick.

Each serving provides:

332	Calories	68 g	Carbohydrate
13 g	Protein	246 mg	Sodium
2 g	Total fat (0 g Sat. fat)	0 mg	Cholesterol

Chinese Barbecue Stir-Fry

Hoisin is a slightly sweet, rich sauce that adds a definite zing to food. Look for it in specialty stores and in many large groceries. The one important thing to remember here is to have all of your ingredients sliced and ready before you begin to stir-fry.

Makes 4 servings

1	8-ounce can salt-free (or regular) tomato sauce
1/4	cup hoisin sauce
1	tablespoon red wine vinegar
2	teaspoons firmly packed brown sugar
2	teaspoons cornstarch
1/4	teaspoon garlic powder
1/8	teaspoon pepper
1	pound firm tofu, cut into $2^{1}/_{2} \times {}^{1}/_{2} \times {}^{1}/_{2}$-inch strips, drained well between layers of towels
1	teaspoon vegetable oil
1	large red bell pepper, sliced vertically into thin strips
1	large onion, sliced vertically into thin strips
2	cups thinly shredded cabbage

In a small bowl, combine tomato sauce, hoisin, vinegar, brown sugar, cornstarch, garlic powder, and pepper. Mix well, stirring to dissolve cornstarch. Set aside.

Spray a large nonstick skillet with nonstick cooking spray. Heat over medium-high heat. Add tofu strips. Cook, stirring constantly with a tossing motion, until tofu is lightly browned on all sides. Remove tofu to a bowl and cover to keep warm.

Return skillet to heat and add oil.

Add red pepper and onion. Cook, again stirring constantly with a tossing motion, 2 minutes. Add cabbage. Cook, stirring, 2 more minutes.

Return tofu to skillet and add hoisin sauce mixture. Cook, stirring constantly, 30 seconds. Remove from heat.

Serve with rice.

✧*Serve-again hint:* The heated leftovers make a perfect filling for flour tortillas.

Each serving provides:

229	Calories	28 g	Carbohydrate
13 g	Protein	349 mg	Sodium
7 g	Total fat (1 g Sat. fat)	0 mg	Cholesterol

Hungarian Paprikash

This thick, potato-based stew is a typical Hungarian dish. I replaced the traditional meat with beans, creating a delicious dish that's as healthy as it is hearty.

Makes 6 servings

Stew

2	teaspoons vegetable oil
1	cup chopped onion
1	cup chopped green bell pepper
1	cup chopped red bell pepper
1	1-pound can stewed tomatoes, undrained
1	1-pound can white kidney beans (cannellini), rinsed and drained (or 2 cups of cooked beans)
1½	cups vegetable broth, or 1½ cups of water and 1½ teaspoons Vegetable Broth Mix (page 34.)
1	tablespoon paprika
1½	teaspoons caraway seeds
1	teaspoon garlic powder
½	teaspoon *each* salt and pepper
4	medium potatoes (8 ounces each), peeled, sliced crosswise into ⅛-inch slices

Topping

1	cup plain nonfat yogurt
½	cup thinly sliced green onions (green part only)

Heat oil in a large nonstick skillet over medium heat. Add onion, green pepper, and red pepper. Cook, stirring frequently, 6 to 8 minutes, until vegetables are tender.

Add remaining ingredients, *except* potatoes and topping ingredients, to skillet. Mix well. Add potatoes, stirring to separate potato slices. When mixture boils, reduce heat to medium-low, cover, and

simmer 20 to 25 minutes, stirring several times, until potatoes are tender. (Length of cooking time will depend on the variety of potatoes used; all-purpose potatoes cook faster than baking potatoes.)

Top each serving with 2 1/2 tablespoons of yogurt and a heaping tablespoon of green onions.

Each serving provides:

231	Calories	44 g	Carbohydrate
10 g	Protein	535 mg	Sodium
3 g	Total fat (0 g Sat. fat)	1 mg	Cholesterol

Chili Dogs

Kids of all ages love frankfurters, and this delicious dish is no exception. There are many meatless franks on the market today. Some are canned, some are refrigerated, and others are frozen. You may have to try several brands before you find the one you love. Be sure to read the labels carefully and choose a brand that is either very low in fat or fat-free.

Makes 4 servings

2	teaspoons vegetable oil
1	cup finely chopped onion
1	cup finely chopped green bell pepper
3	cloves garlic, crushed
1	1-pound can salt-free (or regular) stewed tomatoes
1	8-ounce can salt-free (or regular) tomato sauce
1	4-ounce can chopped green chilies (hot or mild), drained
4	lowfat, meatless frankfurters, sliced crosswise into 1/4-inch slices
1	tablespoon molasses
1	to 2 teaspoons chili powder
1/2	cup shredded reduced-fat Cheddar cheese (2 ounces)

Heat oil in a medium saucepan over medium heat. Add onion, green pepper, and garlic. Cook, stirring frequently, 6 to 8 minutes, until vegetables are tender.

Add remaining ingredients, *except* cheese. Bring mixture to a boil, stirring frequently. Then reduce heat to medium-low, cover, and simmer 15 minutes.

Serve over rice or any other cooked grain.

Top each serving with 2 tablespoons of Cheddar cheese.

Each serving provides:

219	Calories	27 g	Carbohydrate
18 g	Protein	679 mg	Sodium
5 g	Total fat (2 g Sat. fat)	10 mg	Cholesterol

Mushroom-Bean Ragout

A simple, yet hearty meal, this stew is delicious over rice or noodles. Flavored with thyme and lightly laced with sherry, this is a perfect company dish as well as an easy family treat.

Makes 4 servings

2	teaspoons vegetable oil
1	pound small mushrooms, quartered (if the mushrooms are large, cut them into sixths or eighths)
1/2	cup finely chopped onion
3	cloves garlic, crushed
1	1-pound can salt-free (or regular) tomatoes, chopped, undrained
1	1-pound can kidney beans, rinsed and drained (or 2 cups of cooked beans)
1/2	cup dry sherry
1/2	teaspoon dried thyme
1/4	teaspoon salt
1/4	teaspoon pepper
2	teaspoons cornstarch
1	tablespoon water

Heat oil in a large saucepan over medium-high heat. Add mushrooms, onion, and garlic. Cook, stirring frequently, 3 to 4 minutes.

Add tomatoes, beans, sherry, thyme, salt, and pepper. When mixture boils, reduce heat to medium and simmer, uncovered, 3 to 4 more minutes, stirring frequently.

Dissolve cornstarch in water in a small bowl or custard cup. Add to skillet. Cook, stirring, 1 to 2 minutes, until mixture has thickened slightly.

✧*Serve-again hint:* For a delicious appetizer, heat the leftovers and serve them over toast points. Add a flavor twist by sprinkling each serving with a little grated Parmesan cheese.

Each serving provides:

206	Calories	28 g	Carbohydrate
10 g	Protein	299 mg	Sodium
3 g	Total fat (0 g Sat. fat)	0 mg	Cholesterol

Three-Bean Chili

One of the thickest, richest chilies around, this one is also quick and easy. Just chop a few veggies, open a few cans, and cook for 20 minutes. It's a great dish to throw together for a casual dinner when unexpected guests drop in.

Makes 6 servings
(1½ cups each serving)

2	teaspoons vegetable oil
1	cup chopped onion
1	cup chopped green bell pepper
4	large cloves garlic, crushed
1	28-ounce can crushed tomatoes
1	1-pound can pinto beans, rinsed and drained (or 2 cups of cooked beans)
1	1-pound can black beans, rinsed and drained (or 2 cups of cooked beans)
1	1-pound can cannellini (white kidney beans), rinsed and drained (or 2 cups of cooked beans)
1	10-ounce package frozen corn (or one 12-ounce can corn, drained)
2	tablespoons chili powder (more if you like it extra spicy)
1½	teaspoons dried oregano
1	teaspoon ground cumin
½	teaspoon salt
2	teaspoons red wine vinegar

Heat oil in a large saucepan over medium heat. Add onion, green pepper, and garlic. Cook, stirring frequently, 6 to 8 minutes, until tender. Add small amounts of water, a few tablespoons at a time, to prevent sticking.

Add remaining ingredients, mixing well. Bring to a boil, stirring occasionally. Then cover, reduce heat to medium-low, and simmer 20 minutes. Stir several times while cooking.

◆*Quick tip:* If you keep chopped onions and green peppers in the freezer, you have a head start.

Each serving provides:

247	Calories	44 g	Carbohydrate
13 g	Protein	765 mg	Sodium
4 g	Total fat (0 g Sat. fat)	0 mg	Cholesterol

Potato and Bean Curry

Thick and chunky, with the delicious flavors of India, this hearty dish can be made hot or mild. You control the heat!

Makes 4 servings

2	teaspoons vegetable oil
1	cup chopped onion
4	cloves garlic, finely chopped
1	tablespoon grated fresh ginger root
1	teaspoon ground coriander
1	teaspoon turmeric
1	teaspoon ground cinnamon
3/4	teaspoon ground cumin
1/4	teaspoon ground cloves
1/2	teaspoon salt
1/4	teaspoon pepper
1/8	to 1/4 teaspoon cayenne pepper (optional)
3	medium potatoes (1 1/2 pounds total), unpeeled, chopped into 1/2-inch pieces
1	1-pound can salt-free (or regular) tomatoes, chopped, undrained
1	1-pound can kidney beans, rinsed and drained (or 2 cups of cooked beans)
1 1/2	cups water
1	cup frozen green peas, thawed

Heat oil in a large nonstick skillet over medium heat. Add onion, garlic, and ginger root. Cook, stirring frequently, 3 to 4 minutes, until onion is tender.

While onion is cooking, combine spices in a small bowl or custard cup. Sprinkle over onion mixture and continue to cook, stirring, 2 more minutes.

Add remaining ingredients *except* peas, mixing well. When mixture boils, reduce heat slightly, cover, and simmer 25 to 30 minutes, or until potatoes are tender. Stir occasionally (about every 5 minutes) while cooking. Add a little water if mixture becomes too dry.

Uncover and add peas. Cook, stirring frequently, 2 to 3 minutes, until peas are heated through. Add a little more water if mixture becomes too dry.

✦*Serve-again hint:* For a unique, cross-cultural dish, heat the leftovers, then roll them in flour tortillas along with a dollop of plain nonfat yogurt and a sprinkling of green onions and chopped fresh cilantro.

Each serving provides:			
303	Calories	57 g	Carbohydrate
13 g	Protein	485 mg	Sodium
4 g	Total fat (0 g Sat. fat)	0 mg	Cholesterol

Burgundy Bean Stew

Burgundy wine gives a gourmet flavor to this hearty stew. Serve it with a salad, some crusty bread, and a fruit dessert for a delicious, filling, and very nutritious meal.

Makes 6 servings
(1¹/₂ cups each serving)

2	teaspoons vegetable oil
1	cup sliced leeks (white part only)
4	cloves garlic, crushed
3	cups vegetable broth, or 3 cups of water and 3 teaspoons Vegetable Broth Mix (page 34)
¹/₂	cup burgundy wine
2	1-pound cans kidney beans, rinsed and drained (or 4 cups of cooked beans)
2	cups carrots, sliced crosswise into ¹/₂-inch slices
3	medium potatoes (1¹/₂ pounds total), unpeeled, cut into 1-inch cubes
2	medium onions, each cut vertically into 6 wedges (leave the root ends intact to help keep the onions from falling apart)
1¹/₂	cups turnips, peeled, cut into 1-inch cubes
3	bay leaves
1	teaspoon paprika
1	teaspoon sugar
¹/₂	teaspoon dried oregano
¹/₄	teaspoon pepper
	Pinch dried thyme
2	tablespoons all-purpose flour
3	tablespoons water
	Salt to taste

Heat oil in a large saucepan over medium heat. Add leeks and garlic. Cook 5 minutes, stirring frequently. Add small amounts of water as necessary, a few tablespoons at a time, to prevent sticking.

Add remaining ingredients, *except* flour, 3 tablespoons of water, and salt. When mixture boils, reduce heat slightly, cover, and simmer 20 minutes, or until vegetables are tender.

Place flour in a small bowl or custard cup. Gradually stir in water, forming a smooth paste. Stir into stew. Continue to cook, stirring occasionally, 10 minutes.

Remove and discard bay leaves.

Add salt and additional pepper to taste.

Each serving provides:

289	Calories	55 g	Carbohydrate
13 g	Protein	292 mg	Sodium
3 g	Total fat (0 g Sat. fat)	0 mg	Cholesterol

Sweet 'n' Sour Chickpea Stew

An unusual and delectable combination of flavors awaits you in this delicious stew, full of potatoes, cabbage, chickpeas, and raisins. All you need is a chunk of crusty rye bread to make your meal complete.

Makes 8 servings
(1¹/₂ cups each serving)

2	teaspoons vegetable oil
2	medium onions, sliced
2	1-pound cans salt-free (or regular) tomatoes, chopped, undrained
1	19-ounce can chickpeas, rinsed and drained (or 2¹/₄ cups of cooked beans)
1	cup water
¹/₂	cup molasses
¹/₂	cup vinegar
¹/₂	cup raisins
1	cup carrots, sliced crosswise into ¹/₂-inch slices
2	large potatoes (1¹/₄ pounds total), unpeeled, cut into ¹/₂-inch chunks
¹/₂	medium cabbage, coarsely chopped (about 4 cups)
1	teaspoon celery salt
³/₄	teaspoon ground ginger
¹/₄	teaspoon pepper

Heat oil in a large soup pot over medium heat. Add onions, separating them into rings. Cook 5 minutes, stirring frequently, and adding small amounts of water, a few tablespoons at a time, to prevent sticking.

Add remaining ingredients. Bring to a boil, stirring frequently. Then reduce heat to medium-low, cover, and simmer 40 minutes, or until vegetables are tender.

Each serving provides:

246	Calories	52 g	Carbohydrate
6 g	Protein	195 mg	Sodium
3 g	Total fat (0 g Sat. fat)	0 mg	Cholesterol

Pasta and Pasta Sauces

When it comes to preparing quick meals, pasta is definitely an all-star. It can be kept on hand, cooks quickly, and can be topped with an infinite variety of sauces and toppings. Be sure to keep a few jars of reduced-fat pasta sauces in the pantry. With the simple addition of some steamed or sautéed vegetables or a can of beans, commercial sauces can be turned into gourmet meals.

You can also adapt your own favorite pasta recipes and make them healthier by reducing the amount of oil, replacing any meat with beans or tofu cubes, and adding lots of vegetables. You can also create healthful "cream" sauces by using skim milk and healthful cheese sauces by using reduced-fat cheeses. Pasta sauces can also be used to top cooked grains or an endless variety of combinations of grains and vegetables.

Pasta, once thought of as "fattening," can be enjoyed often as the delicious, high-carbohydrate base of a healthful diet.

Pasta Alfredo with Broccoli and Mushrooms

An easy way to steam the broccoli is to place it in the colander and pour the hot pasta over it. The broccoli cooks while the pasta drains. This delicious, light Alfredo sauce has all of the flavor of the original with just a fraction of the fat and calories.

Makes 4 servings

8	ounces ziti or penne pasta, uncooked
2	cups broccoli, cut into very small flowerets
2	teaspoons vegetable oil
1	cup sliced mushrooms
1/2	cup chopped onion
5	cloves garlic, finely chopped
2	tablespoons all-purpose flour
1	cup skim milk
1/2	cup vegetable broth, or 1/2 cup water and 1/2 teaspoon Vegetable Broth Mix (page 34)
1/4	teaspoon salt
1/4	teaspoon pepper
3	tablespoons grated Parmesan cheese

Cook pasta according to package directions. Place broccoli in colander and pour cooked pasta over the broccoli. Let drain for a few minutes.

While pasta is cooking, heat oil in a medium saucepan over medium heat. Add mushrooms, onion, and garlic. Cook 5 minutes, stirring frequently.

Place flour in a small bowl. Gradually add milk, stirring until mixture is smooth. Add broth, salt, and pepper. Stir into mushroom mixture. Cook, stirring constantly, until mixture comes to a boil. Continue to cook, stirring, 1 to 2 minutes, until mixture has thickened. Remove from heat and stir in Parmesan cheese.

Toss pasta and broccoli and place in a large shallow bowl. Spoon sauce over pasta.

Each serving provides:			
323	Calories	56 g	Carbohydrate
14 g	Protein	272 mg	Sodium
5 g	Total fat (1 g Sat. fat)	4 mg	Cholesterol

Baked Ziti Goes Southwest

I re-created an easy favorite and, using a different combination of flavors, came up with a new twist on an old theme.

Makes 6 servings

8	ounces ziti, uncooked
1	8-ounce can salt-free (or regular) tomato sauce
1	8-ounce jar salsa (hot or mild)
3/4	cup reduced-fat ricotta cheese
1	cup shredded reduced-fat mozzarella cheese (4 ounces)
1	11-ounce can corn, drained
1	4-ounce can chopped green chilies (hot or mild), drained
1	teaspoon dried oregano
1/8	teaspoon pepper
1	tablespoon grated Parmesan cheese

Cook pasta according to package directions, using the shorter amount of cooking time given. Drain.

Preheat oven to 375°.

Lightly oil an 8-inch square baking pan or spray with a nonstick cooking spray.

Combine tomato sauce and salsa in a small bowl.

In a large bowl, combine ricotta cheese with *half* of the mozzarella cheese. Stir in *half* of the sauce, along with the corn, chilies, oregano, and pepper. Add the cooked ziti and mix well. Spoon into prepared casserole.

Spread remaining sauce over top of casserole, then sprinkle with remaining mozzarella cheese and then the Parmesan cheese.

Cover and bake 20 minutes. Uncover and continue to bake 15 more minutes.

✦*Quick tip:* This entire casserole can be prepared a day ahead and baked when needed. You will need to remove it from the refrigerator about an hour before baking and add about 20 minutes to the (covered) baking time.

Each serving provides:

304	Calories	47 g	Carbohydrate
15 g	Protein	810 mg	Sodium
7 g	Total fat (3 g Sat. fat)	17 mg	Cholesterol

Taco Stuffed Shells

Italy meets Mexico in this cross-cultural version of a popular favorite. Just fill the shells with refried beans, top with a quick sauce, add cheese, and bake. It's pretty enough for a party and sure to please the family as well.

Makes 4 servings

16	jumbo pasta shells, uncooked
1	1-pound can fat-free vegetarian refried beans (available in most grocery stores)
1	8-ounce can salt-free (or regular) tomato sauce
1	8-ounce jar picante sauce (hot or mild)
3/4	cup shredded reduced-fat Cheddar cheese (3 ounces)
1/2	cup plain nonfat yogurt
1/4	cup thinly sliced green onions (green and white parts)

Cook shells according to package directions. Drain. Place shells on wax paper in a single layer to keep them from sticking together.

Preheat oven to 350°.

Lightly oil a 6 × 10-inch baking pan or spray with a nonstick cooking spray.

Fill shells with beans, placing 2 tablespoonfuls in each shell.

Combine tomato sauce and picante sauce in a small bowl. Mix well. Spread 1/2 cup of the sauce in the bottom of the pan. Place shells in pan. Spoon remaining sauce over shells. Cover tightly and bake 20 minutes.

Sprinkle cheese evenly over shells. Return to oven and continue to bake, uncovered, 10 minutes more, until cheese is hot and bubbly.

To serve, top each shell with about 1 1/2 teaspoons of yogurt and sprinkle with about 1/2 teaspoon of sliced green onions.

◆*Quick tip:* Always keep a can of refried beans in the pantry. It comes in handy.

Each serving provides:			
381	Calories	61 g	Carbohydrate
21 g	Protein	946 mg	Sodium
6 g	Total fat (3 g Sat. fat)	16 mg	Cholesterol

Pasta Fagioli

Pronounced "pasta fazool," this Italian favorite can be made quickly and easily in one skillet, with very little cleanup. This deliciously herbed dish of pasta and beans can be served with a salad and a chunk of crusty Italian bread for a light yet hearty meal.

Makes 4 servings

2	teaspoons olive oil
1	cup finely chopped onion
1	cup coarsely shredded carrots
1/2	cup finely chopped celery
3	cloves garlic, crushed
1	1-pound can salt-free (or regular) tomatoes, chopped, undrained
1	1-pound can white kidney beans (cannellini) or pinto beans, rinsed and drained (or 2 cups of cooked beans)
2 1/2	cups vegetable broth, or 2 1/2 cups of water and 2 1/2 teaspoons Vegetable Broth Mix (page 34)
1 1/2	teaspoons dried oregano
1 1/2	cups elbow macaroni, uncooked
	Salt and freshly ground black pepper

Heat oil in a large nonstick skillet over medium heat. Add onion, carrots, celery, and garlic. Cook, stirring frequently, 5 minutes.

Add tomatoes, beans, broth, and oregano to skillet. Mix well. When mixture boils, stir in macaroni. Reduce heat to medium-low, cover, and simmer 15 minutes.

Add salt and pepper to taste.

✧*Serve-again hint:* Add more broth, heat, and enjoy. If you wish, you can add a lot of broth and serve it as a delicious, hearty soup.

Each serving provides:			
314	Calories	57 g	Carbohydrate
13 g	Protein	251 mg	Sodium
4 g	Total fat (0 g Sat. fat)	0 mg	Cholesterol

Skillet Macaroni Barbecue

Barbecue sauce adds just the right spicy touch to this easy skillet dinner. Choose the barbecue sauce you like, either spicy, hickory smoked, or any other flavor. Just be sure to read the label carefully. Most are fat-free; however, some are very high in sodium.

Makes 4 servings

2	teaspoons vegetable oil
1	large onion, cut vertically into thin strips
1	large green bell pepper, cut vertically into thin strips
2	cloves garlic, finely chopped
1¹/₄	cups water
1	1-pound can salt-free (or regular) stewed tomatoes
¹/₃	cup barbecue sauce
1¹/₂	cups elbow macaroni, uncooked
1	8-ounce can corn, drained
³/₄	cup shredded reduced-fat Cheddar cheese (3 ounces)

Heat oil in a large nonstick skillet over medium heat. Add onion, green pepper, and garlic. Cook, stirring frequently, until vegetables are tender, about 5 minutes.

Add water, stewed tomatoes, and barbecue sauce. When mixture boils, stir in macaroni and corn. Reduce heat to medium-low, cover, and simmer 15 minutes.

Turn heat off. Sprinkle cheese evenly over macaroni. Replace lid and let stand 5 minutes to allow cheese to melt.

✦*Quick tip:* You can cut the onion and pepper up to a day ahead and refrigerate until needed. The rest can be done very quickly.

Each serving provides:

347	Calories	57 g	Carbohydrate
16 g	Protein	512 mg	Sodium
8 g	Total fat (3 g Sat. fat)	15 mg	Cholesterol

Herbed Orzo with Basil

Orzo—tiny, rice-shaped pasta—cooks quickly and makes this a perfect side dish to serve alongside a bean casserole, baked tofu, or a veggie burger. This recipe can also be used to serve three people as an entrée and only needs a salad and some steamed vegetables to make a quick, filling dinner.

Makes 6 servings

2	teaspoons vegetable oil
1	cup finely chopped onion
2	cloves garlic, crushed
2	cups vegetable broth, or 2 cups of water and 2 teaspoons Vegetable Broth Mix (page 34)
2	tablespoons reduced-sodium (or regular) soy sauce
1	teaspoon dried basil
1/16	teaspoon pepper
1	cup orzo, uncooked

Heat oil in a medium saucepan over medium heat. Add onion and garlic. Cook, stirring frequently, until onion is tender, about 4 minutes. Add small amounts of water as necessary, about a tablespoon at a time, to prevent sticking.

Add remaining ingredients, *except* orzo. Bring mixture to a boil, then stir in orzo. Cover, reduce heat to medium-low, and cook 15 minutes, until the liquid has been absorbed.

Fluff with a fork before serving.

❖*Serve-again hint:* Heat the leftovers in clear vegetable broth, and you have a delectable noodle soup.

Each serving provides:

158	Calories	30 g	Carbohydrate
5 g	Protein	240 mg	Sodium
2 g	Total fat (0 g Sat. fat)	0 mg	Cholesterol

Black Bean and Noodle Casserole with Feta

"Easy" is an understatement for this noodle casserole made with uncooked noodles. Just mix a few ingredients, layer them with the noodles, and bake. It's simple and delicious.

Makes 8 servings

3	egg whites
3/4	cup skim milk
1	8-ounce container plain nonfat yogurt
1/2	cup crumbled feta cheese, rinsed and drained (3 ounces)
1	tablespoon all-purpose flour
2	teaspoons parsley flakes
2	teaspoons dried basil
1/2	teaspoon dried oregano
6	ounces medium (yolk-free) noodles, uncooked (about 4 cups)
1	1-pound can black beans, rinsed and drained (or 2 cups of cooked beans)
1	16-ounce jar salsa (hot or mild)

Preheat oven to 350°.

Lightly oil a 7 × 11-inch baking pan or spray with a nonstick cooking spray.

In a large bowl, combine egg whites, milk, yogurt, feta cheese, and flour. Beat with a fork until blended. Add spices, mixing well.

Place *half* of the noodles in the prepared pan. Top with *half* of the beans, followed by *half* of the salsa. Spoon *half* of the cheese mixture evenly over the top.

Repeat layers, using remaining noodles, beans, and salsa. Spoon remaining cheese mixture over the top, covering all of the noodles. Press noodles down lightly into the sauce.

Cover with aluminum foil and bake 45 minutes.

Let stand 5 minutes before serving.

Each serving provides:			
192	Calories	29 g	Carbohydrate
10 g	Protein	855 mg	Sodium
4 g	Total fat (2 g Sat. fat)	10 mg	Cholesterol

Chili Peanut Noodles

Chili sauce and peanut butter combine to make a slightly sweet sauce that gets some added zip from hot pepper sauce. For a light dinner, these delicious noodles can be served with soup and a salad and fresh fruit for dessert.

Makes 4 servings

2¹/₂	tablespoons peanut butter, creamy or chunky (choose one without added sugar or fat)
2	tablespoons bottled chili sauce
1	tablespoon firmly packed brown sugar
2	teaspoons reduced sodium (or regular) soy sauce
³/₄	teaspoon garlic powder
1	cup vegetable broth, or 1 cup of water and 1 teaspoon Vegetable Broth Mix (page 34)
1	tablespoon cornstarch
8	ounces linguine, uncooked
	Bottled hot pepper sauce
2	cups very thinly shredded Chinese (napa) cabbage
¹/₂	cup thinly sliced green onions (green and white parts)

In a small saucepan, combine peanut butter, chili sauce, brown sugar, soy sauce, and garlic powder. Mix well. Gradually add broth, stirring until mixture is smooth. Add cornstarch, mixing until completely dissolved. Set aside.

Cook linguine according to package directions.

While linguine is cooking, cook peanut butter mixture over medium heat, stirring constantly, until mixture boils. Continue to cook, stirring, for 1 minute. Remove from heat and stir in hot sauce to taste.

Drain pasta and place in a large bowl. Add peanut sauce, cabbage, and green onions. Toss and serve.

❖*Serve-again hint:* Served cold, this is a ready-made pasta salad.

Each serving provides:			
320	Calories	55 g	Carbohydrate
11 g	Protein	292 mg	Sodium
6 g	Total fat (0 g Sat. fat)	0 mg	Cholesterol

Pasta with Fresh Tomatoes and Basil

This is a delicious way to enjoy pasta—without *cooking the sauce. The hot pasta is simply tossed with fresh tomatoes and basil. When red, ripe summer tomatoes are available, nothing can taste fresher. I like it with the long, thin spaghetti; Harry prefers it with the tiny shells (he says they're like little cups that hold the tomatoes). Why not try it both ways?*

Makes 4 servings

1	pound ripe tomatoes, at room temperature, chopped into 1/4-inch pieces
1/3	cup thinly sliced fresh basil leaves (dried basil doesn't work well here)
1	large clove garlic, crushed
2	teaspoons olive oil
1/2	teaspoon sugar
1/4	teaspoon salt
	Freshly ground black pepper
8	ounces thin spaghetti, uncooked
	Grated Parmesan cheese (optional)

In a medium bowl, combine all ingredients, *except* pasta and Parmesan cheese. Mix well. Set aside and let stand while pasta is cooking (or up to 1 hour).

Cook pasta according to package directions. Drain, but do not rinse.

Place pasta in a large serving bowl and top with tomato mixture. Toss gently.

Serve right away, topping each serving with a light sprinkling of cheese if desired.

✥*Serve-again hint:* Served cold, you have a ready-made pasta salad.

Each serving provides:

261	Calories	49 g	Carbohydrate
8 g	Protein	150 mg	Sodium
4 g	Total fat (0 g Sat. fat)	0 mg	Cholesterol

Pizza-style Pasta

Just like pizza, here's sauce and cheese with crisp veggies on top. Instead of a crust, there are pasta spirals, which really hold onto the sauce, making them moist and tasty. Feel free to top the casserole with your choice of vegetables, such as mushrooms, zucchini, and broccoli.

Makes 4 servings

8	ounces spiral-shaped pasta, uncooked
2^1/$_2$	cups reduced-fat, meatless spaghetti sauce
1	cup shredded reduced-fat mozzarella cheese (4 ounces)
1	teaspoon grated Parmesan cheese
^{1}/$_2$	cup onion, sliced vertically into thin slivers
^{1}/$_2$	cup green bell pepper, thinly sliced

Cook pasta according to package directions. Drain.

Lightly oil an 8-inch square baking pan or spray with a nonstick cooking spray.

Preheat oven to 375°.

Place pasta in a large bowl and add spaghetti sauce, mixing well. Pour into prepared pan. Top with both cheeses. Sprinkle onion and pepper evenly over the casserole.

Bake, uncovered, 20 minutes, or until cheese is melted and vegetables begin to brown.

Each serving provides:

353	Calories	57 g	Carbohydrate
17 g	Protein	648 mg	Sodium
6 g	Total fat (2 g Sat. fat)	10 mg	Cholesterol

Pasta with Broccoli

Little bits of broccoli "collect" in the pasta spirals, creating this colorful and unusual dish that I created one day when broccoli was on sale (I couldn't resist buying several bunches).

Makes 6 servings

1	pound pasta spirals, uncooked
2	teaspoons vegetable oil
3	cloves garlic, finely chopped
4	cups finely chopped broccoli (use the flowerets and about 1 inch of the stems—save the remaining stems for soups or salads)
1/2	cup plus 2 tablespoons of water
1	teaspoon Vegetable Broth Mix (page 34)
1/4	cup dry white wine
1	cup shredded reduced-fat mozzarella cheese
3	tablespoons grated Parmesan cheese (4 ounces)

Cook pasta according to package directions. Drain.

While pasta is cooking, heat oil in a large nonstick skillet over medium heat. Add garlic. Cook until garlic just begins to brown.

Add broccoli, mixing well. Add 2 tablespoons of the water, cover, reduce heat slightly, and cook 2 minutes. Combine remaining water, broth mix, and wine. Pour over broccoli, cover, and continue to cook 3 minutes more. Remove from heat.

Place drained pasta in a large bowl (preferably a large, shallow pasta bowl). Spoon broccoli and pan juices over pasta. Sprinkle with both cheeses.

Toss gently and serve.

✧*Serve-again hint:* Place leftovers in a lightly oiled casserole, stir in your favorite pasta sauce, and heat in an oven or microwave.

Each serving provides:			
370	Calories	60 g	Carbohydrate
17 g	Protein	181 mg	Sodium
6 g	Total fat (2 g Sat. fat)	8 mg	Cholesterol

Italian Pasta Salad

Broccoli and tomatoes add color and flavor to this ever-popular salad. You can serve it as a side dish or pile it on a bed of lettuce for a delicious light lunch.

Makes 12 servings

3	cups broccoli, cut into very small flowerets
1	pound spiral shaped pasta, uncooked
1/3	cup vegetable oil
1/3	cup water
1/3	cup red wine vinegar
6	medium plum tomatoes, chopped
1/2	cup green onions, thinly sliced (green and white parts)
1	3/4-ounce packet Italian dressing mix
1	teaspoon dried oregano
1	teaspoon dried basil
1/2	teaspoon dill weed
	Salt and pepper

Place broccoli in a colander. Cook pasta according to package directions. Pour pasta and cooking water into colander, over the broccoli (this will lightly steam the broccoli). Let drain for a few minutes.

Place pasta and broccoli in a large bowl. Add remaining ingredients and mix well.

Chill.

Mix well before serving.

◆*Quick tip:* All of the ingredients, except the broccoli and pasta, can be combined and chilled a day ahead, making the remaining preparation much easier.

Each serving provides:

215	Calories	33 g	Carbohydrate
6 g	Protein	251 mg	Sodium
7 g	Total fat (1 g Sat. fat)	0 mg	Cholesterol

Spicy Peanut-Lime Noodles

My noodles of choice for this easy dish are the somen noodles that are found in health food stores, Asian food stores, and many large groceries. They're usually made from whole wheat flour and cook in about 5 minutes. If you can't find them, linguine will also work.

Makes 4 servings

8	ounces somen noodles, uncooked
1/4	cup water
3	tablespoons reduced-sodium (or regular) soy sauce
2 1/2	tablespoons creamy peanut butter (choose one without added sugar or oil)
2	tablespoons lime juice, preferably freshly squeezed
2	tablespoons ketchup
2	teaspoons firmly packed brown sugar
1/2	teaspoon garlic powder
1/2	teaspoon ground ginger
2	cups very finely sliced Chinese (napa) cabbage
1/4	cup thinly sliced green onion (green and white parts)

Cook noodles according to package directions.

While noodles are cooking, combine remaining ingredients, *except* cabbage and green onion, in a small bowl. Whisk with a fork or wire whisk until well blended.

Drain noodles and place in a large bowl. Add cabbage and green onion and toss to combine. Add peanut butter mixture and toss until noodles are evenly coated.

Serve right away.

❖*Serve-again hint:* Serve the leftovers as a delicious cold salad.

Each serving provides:

297	Calories	52 g	Carbohydrate
11 g	Protein	1635 mg	Sodium
6 g	Total fat (1 g Sat. fat)	0 mg	Cholesterol

Pasta with Broccoli Pesto

Steamed broccoli, fresh basil, and white wine form the basis for this unusual variation of a popular dish. It's also much lighter than the original oil-laden version, calling for only two teaspoons of oil.

Makes 4 servings

2	cups broccoli, cut into small flowerets
1/3	cup dry white wine
1/4	cup fresh basil, loosely packed
2	cloves garlic, coarsely chopped
1	tablespoon grated Parmesan cheese
2	teaspoons olive oil
1/8	teaspoon pepper
8	ounces elbow macaroni, uncooked

Cook broccoli until tender (either in a steamer basket over boiling water for about 8 minutes, or microwaved with a little water for about 3 minutes). Drain.

In a blender container or food processor, combine broccoli with remaining ingredients, *except* pasta. Process until smooth.

Cook macaroni according to package directions. Drain. Place in a large bowl and add broccoli mixture. Mix well.

Serve right away.

✧*Serve-again hint:* Leftovers make a delicious cold pasta salad. You can add any chopped veggies, either cooked or raw, and a little reduced-fat Italian salad dressing if the mixture is too dry.

Each serving provides:

274	Calories	10 g	Carbohydrate
10 g	Protein	44 mg	Sodium
4 g	Total fat (1 g Sat. fat)	1 mg	Cholesterol

One-Pot Pasta

What if you were to cook the macaroni and the sauce all in one pot at the same time? It works! It's thick and delicious, and there's only one pot to wash.

Makes 4 servings

2	teaspoons olive oil
1/2	cup onion, cut vertically into thin slivers
1	cup sliced mushrooms
1	28-ounce can tomatoes, chopped, undrained
1	8-ounce can salt-free (or regular) tomato sauce
1	cup water
2	teaspoons dried basil
1	teaspoon dried oregano
1	teaspoon sugar
1/4	teaspoon garlic powder
1/4	teaspoon pepper
8	ounces elbow macaroni, uncooked

Heat oil in a large nonstick skillet over medium heat (a nonstick pan is essential to keep the pasta from sticking). Add onion and mushrooms. Cook, stirring frequently, 3 to 5 minutes, until tender.

Add tomatoes, tomato sauce, water, and spices to skillet. When mixture boils, stir in macaroni. Cover, reduce heat to medium-low, and cook 20 minutes. Stir mixture every 4 to 5 minutes while cooking.

Each serving provides:

310	Calories	60 g	Carbohydrate
11 g	Protein	341 mg	Sodium
4 g	Total fat (1 g Sat. fat)	0 mg	Cholesterol

Almost-Manicotti

My good friend and fellow cooking teacher, Pat Tabibian, came up with the brilliant idea of using egg roll wrappers in place of the usual manicotti. It sure saves time! Look for the packaged egg roll wrappers in the dairy or produce sections of most large grocery stores.

Makes 6 servings

2¹/₂   cups reduced-fat ricotta cheese
1   10-ounce package frozen, chopped spinach, thawed and
        drained well
3   tablespoons grated Parmesan cheese
1   teaspoon *each* dried basil and oregano
¹/₄   teaspoon garlic powder
¹/₈   teaspoon pepper
1   15¹/₂-ounce jar reduced-fat, meatless spaghetti sauce
12   egg roll wrappers
1   cup shredded reduced-fat mozzarella cheese (4 ounces)

Preheat oven to 375°.

Lightly oil a 9 × 13-inch baking pan or spray with a nonstick cooking spray.

In a large bowl, combine ricotta cheese, spinach, Parmesan cheese, and spices. Mix well.

Spread ¹/₂ cup of the spaghetti sauce in the bottom of the prepared pan.

Place ¹/₄ cup of the cheese filling along one edge of an egg roll wrapper. Roll up into a cylinder and place seam side down in pan. Continue with remaining filling and wrappers.

Spoon remaining sauce over rolls and spread with the back of a spoon, covering all of the rolls. Sprinkle evenly with mozzarella cheese.

Bake, uncovered, 20 to 25 minutes, until hot and bubbly.

Let stand 5 minutes before serving.

✦*Quick tip:* This dish can be completely assembled up to a day ahead, then removed from the refrigerator an hour before baking.

✧*Serve-again hint:* Freeze any leftovers in serving-size packages, then pop them (covered) into a toaster oven or microwave to reheat.

Each serving provides:

385	Calories	50 g	Carbohydrate
23 g	Protein	865 mg	Sodium
9 g	Total fat (5 g Sat. fat)	39 mg	Cholesterol

Tex-Mex Lasagne

Here's an interesting, delicious twist on an all-time favorite. Black beans and corn add color and salsa adds flavor to this delectable dish. Using uncooked noodles saves lots of time and makes the preparation easier.

Makes 8 servings

1	16-ounce jar salsa (hot or mild)
3	8-ounce cans salt-free (or regular) tomato sauce
3/4	cup water
1	15-ounce container reduced-fat ricotta cheese
1	tablespoon grated Parmesan cheese
1 1/2	cups shredded reduced-fat Cheddar cheese, or *half* Cheddar and *half* mozzarella (6 ounces)
1	8-ounce package lasagna noodles, uncooked
1	8-ounce can salt-free (or regular) corn, drained
1	cup canned black beans, rinsed and drained

Preheat oven to 350°.

Lightly oil a 9 × 13-inch baking pan or spray with nonstick cooking spray.

In a large bowl, stir together salsa, tomato sauce, and water.

In a small bowl, combine ricotta and Parmesan cheeses.

Set aside 1/4 cup of the Cheddar cheese for topping.

To assemble the lasagne, spread 1 cup of the sauce in the bottom of the prepared pan. Top with a *third* of the noodles, then 1/2 cup of the sauce. Spoon *half* of the ricotta cheese mixture over the noodles. Top with the corn, followed by *half* of the remaining Cheddar cheese. Top with another 1/2 cup of the sauce.

Place another *third* of the noodles on top, pressing them down firmly onto the filling. Follow with 1/2 cup of sauce, the remaining ricotta cheese, the black beans, the remaining Cheddar cheese, and another 1/2 cup of sauce. Top with remaining noodles, again pressing them down firmly.

Spoon remaining sauce over noodles, making sure the top noodles are covered with sauce.

Cover and bake 40 minutes. Uncover and spoon sauce from sides of pan over noodles. Sprinkle with reserved Cheddar cheese and continue to bake, uncovered, 30 minutes more.

Let stand 5 minutes before serving.

Note: If you're using a 1-pound can of black beans, you can put the remaining cup of beans in a food processor with a clove of garlic to make a quick, delicious sandwich spread.

Each serving provides:

312	Calories	42 g	Carbohydrate
18 g	Protein	895 mg	Sodium
8 g	Total fat (4 g Sat. fat)	28 mg	Cholesterol

Stuffed Shells with Broccoli and Cheese

Adding broccoli to an all-time favorite creates a dish with color, flavor, and an enhanced nutritional profile. Lovers of Italian food, behold!

Makes 6 servings
(4 shells each serving)

6	ounces jumbo pasta shells, uncooked (24 shells)
1	15-ounce container reduced-fat ricotta cheese (1^3/4 cups)
3	ounces shredded reduced-fat mozzarella cheese (^{3}/4 cup)
1	tablespoon grated Parmesan cheese
^{1}/2	teaspoon dried basil
^{1}/8	teaspoon garlic powder
^{1}/8	teaspoon pepper
1	10-ounce package frozen, chopped broccoli, thawed and drained
^{1}/4	cup thinly sliced green onion (green part only)
3	cups reduced-fat, meatless spaghetti sauce

Cook pasta shells according to package directions. Drain. Place them on wax paper in a single layer.

Preheat oven to 350°.

Lightly oil a 9 × 13-inch baking pan or spray with a nonstick cooking spray.

In a medium bowl, combine ricotta cheese, mozzarella, Parmesan, basil, garlic powder, and pepper. Mix well. Add broccoli and green onion, mixing well. Fill pasta shells with cheese mixture, using about 1^1/2 tablespoons for each shell.

Spread 1 cup of the sauce in the bottom of the pan. Place shells in pan, cheese side up. Spoon remaining sauce evenly over shells.

Cover tightly and bake 35 minutes.

	Each serving provides:		
307	Calories	38 g	Carbohydrate
19 g	Protein	582 mg	Sodium
9 g	Total fat (5 g Sat. fat)	27 mg	Cholesterol

Salsa-roni

Salsa plus macaroni equals salsa-roni. Quick and easy, you can mix this dish up in no time.

Makes 6 servings

8   ounces elbow macaroni, uncooked (about 1²/3 cups)
1   1-pound can salt-free (or regular) stewed tomatoes
1   16-ounce jar salsa, hot or mild
1   1-pound can black beans, rinsed and drained (or 2 cups of cooked beans)

Cook macaroni according to package directions. Drain.

Return macaroni to saucepan and add remaining ingredients. Heat through.

❖*Serve-again hint:* Leftovers make a delicious cold pasta salad. Serve on a bed of greens and garnish with black olives and sliced tomatoes, cucumbers, and avocado. It's also great to pack for lunch.

Each serving provides:

226	Calories	45 g	Carbohydrate
8 g	Protein	918 mg	Sodium
1 g	Total fat (0 g Sat. fat)	0 mg	Cholesterol

Mediterranean Pasta Sauce

Allspice and fennel are among the spices that, along with a few opened cans, make a pasta sauce that's thick, rich, and delicious. Like many sauces, this one is even better the next day. It also freezes beautifully.

Makes 12 servings
($2/3$ cup each serving)

2	teaspoons vegetable oil
1	cup chopped onions
1	28-ounce can crushed tomatoes
1	1-pound can salt-free (or regular) stewed tomatoes
1	15-ounce can salt-free (or regular) tomato sauce
1	6-ounce can tomato paste
1	tablespoon firmly packed brown sugar
2	teaspoons dried oregano
1	teaspoon dried basil
1	teaspoon fennel seeds, crushed slightly
$1/2$	teaspoon ground allspice
$1/2$	teaspoon garlic powder
$1/8$	teaspoon pepper
	Salt

Heat oil in a large saucepan over medium heat. Add onions. Cook, stirring frequently, until onions are tender, about 5 minutes. Add small amounts of water as necessary, about a tablespoon at a time, to prevent sticking.

Add remaining ingredients, mixing well. When mixture boils, reduce heat to medium-low, cover, and simmer 40 to 45 minutes.

Serve over your favorite pasta.

✦*Quick tip:* Look for a child-size wooden rolling pin in a toy store. It's great for crushing spices.

✧*Serve-again hint:* Reheat leftover sauce and spoon it over baked potatoes, steamed vegetables, or any cooked grain. It also adds zip to lasagne.

Each serving provides:			
66	Calories	13 g	Carbohydrate
2 g	Protein	235 mg	Sodium
1 g	Total fat (0 g Sat. fat)	0 mg	Cholesterol

Savory Eggplant Pasta Topping

This delectable pasta topping is not exactly a sauce. It's more like a pile of deliciously herbed vegetables smothered in a rich broth. What a wonderful way to top any type of pasta or grain.

Makes 6 servings
(2/3 cup each serving)

2	teaspoons olive oil
2	cups chopped red bell pepper
1	cup chopped onion
3	cups eggplant, peeled, cut into 1/4-inch to 1/2-inch pieces (about 12 ounces)
2	cups sliced mushrooms
5	cloves garlic, crushed
1	tablespoon dried basil
1	teaspoon dried rosemary, crumbled
1/2	teaspoon dried thyme
2	cups vegetable broth, or 2 cups of water and 2 teaspoons Vegetable Broth Mix (page 34)
2	tablespoons cornstarch
	Salt and pepper

Heat oil in a large nonstick skillet over medium heat. Add red pepper and onion. Cook 5 minutes, stirring frequently.

Add remaining vegetables and herbs to skillet. Cook, stirring frequently, 10 to 15 minutes, until eggplant is tender.

Combine broth and cornstarch in a small bowl. Stir to dissolve cornstarch. Add to skillet. Continue to cook, stirring, until mixture comes to a boil. Continue to cook and stir 1 minute.

Add salt and pepper to taste.

❖*Serve-again hint:* Turn a baked potato into a gourmet feast when you top it with the leftover sauce. If you like, you can add any type of cooked beans.

Each serving provides:

76	Calories		14 g	Carbohydrate
2 g	Protein		42 mg	Sodium
2 g	Total fat (0 g Sat. fat)		0 mg	Cholesterol

Mexicali Pasta Sauce

Perfect for a last-minute dinner, this easy sauce can be thrown together while the pasta cooks. All you need is a few cans and some spices to create a Mexican-style sauce that is also a great topper for rice or any other cooked grain.

Makes 6 servings
(3/4 cup each serving)

1	1-pound can salt-free (or regular) stewed tomatoes, undrained
1	1-pound can black beans, rinsed and drained (or 2 cups of cooked beans)
1	11-ounce can corn, drained, *or* one 10-ounce package frozen corn, thawed slightly
1	8-ounce can salt-free (or regular) tomato sauce
1¹/₂	to 2 teaspoons chili powder
³/₄	teaspoon ground cumin
1	teaspoon dried oregano
	Salt

Combine all ingredients in a medium saucepan. Bring to a boil over medium heat. Cover, reduce heat to medium-low, and simmer 10 to 15 minutes.

Spoon over pasta or any cooked grain.

❖*Serve-again hint:* For easy burritos, heat the leftovers and roll them in heated flour tortillas, along with shredded lettuce, chopped tomato, and shredded reduced-fat Cheddar cheese.

	Each serving provides:		
120	Calories	25 g	Carbohydrate
5 g	Protein	293 mg	Sodium
1 g	Total fat (0 g Sat. fat)	0 mg	Cholesterol

Tomato Curry Sauce

A real change of pace for pasta, this spicy sauce will make your taste buds tingle.

Makes 6 servings
(²/₃ cup each serving)

2	teaspoons vegetable oil
1	cup chopped onion
3	cloves garlic, finely chopped
8	ripe plum tomatoes, chopped into ¹/₄-inch to ¹/₂-inch pieces (about 1¹/₄ pounds)
2	teaspoons curry powder
¹/₄	teaspoon dried thyme
¹/₄	teaspoon salt
2	8-ounce cans salt-free (or regular) tomato sauce
	Fresh cilantro, chopped (optional)

Heat oil in a large saucepan over medium heat. Add onion and garlic. Cook 5 minutes, stirring frequently.

Stir in tomatoes, curry powder, thyme, and salt. Cook 5 minutes.

Add tomato sauce, mixing well. Reduce heat to medium-low and simmer, uncovered, 10 minutes.

Spoon sauce over pasta, rice, or noodles.

Top with a sprinkling of cilantro, if desired.

❖*Serve-again hint:* Leftover sauce can be reheated and spooned over a baked potato for a quick and easy lunch or dinner.

Each serving provides:

63	Calories	11 g	Carbohydrate
2 g	Protein	112 mg	Sodium
2 g	Total fat (0 g Sat. fat)	0 mg	Cholesterol

Pasta Sauce with Artichokes and Dill

The aromatic flavors of the Mediterranean blend to make this a truly memorable dish. Spoon it over pasta, add a tossed salad and a chunk of crusty bread, and serve it with pride to your family or guests.

Makes 6 servings
(2/3 cup each serving)

2	teaspoons olive oil
1	cup chopped onion
1	cup carrots, sliced crosswise into 1/8-inch slices
4	cloves garlic, crushed
1	1-pound can salt-free (or regular) tomatoes, chopped, undrained
1	8-ounce can salt-free (or regular) tomato sauce
1/4	cup dry white wine
1	teaspoon dill weed
	Salt and pepper
1	9-ounce package frozen artichoke hearts, thawed and drained

Heat oil in a medium saucepan over medium heat. Add onion, carrots, and garlic. Cook 10 minutes, stirring frequently. Add small amounts of water as necessary, about a tablespoon at a time, to prevent sticking.

Add tomatoes, tomato sauce, wine, dill weed, salt, and pepper. Bring mixture to a boil, then reduce heat slightly and simmer, uncovered, 10 minutes.

Add artichokes and continue to cook, uncovered, 10 minutes more. (You can cut the artichokes into smaller pieces if you wish, but be sure to cut them lengthwise to keep them from falling apart.)

◆*Quick tip:* Place the artichoke hearts in the refrigerator a day ahead and they will be thawed and ready for use, or they can be thawed quickly in the microwave.

Each serving provides:			
86	Calories	14 g	Carbohydrate
3 g	Protein	46 mg	Sodium
2 g	Total fat (0 g Sat. fat)	0 mg	Cholesterol

Pasta Sauce with Mushrooms and Red Wine

Turn an ordinary jar of pasta sauce into a gourmet meal with a few easy additions. Serve it over any type of pasta or use it in lasagne or over stuffed shells.

Makes 6 servings
(³/4 cup each serving)

1	teaspoon olive oil
1	pound mushrooms, sliced
3	cloves garlic, crushed
1	26-ounce jar reduced-fat, meatless spaghetti sauce
¹/2	cup dry red wine
1	teaspoon dried basil
¹/4	teaspoon pepper

Heat oil in a large saucepan over medium heat. Add mushrooms and garlic. Cook, stirring frequently, about 6 minutes, until mushrooms are tender.

Add remaining ingredients. Bring mixture to a boil, then reduce heat to medium-low and simmer, uncovered, 20 minutes. Stir occasionally while cooking and reduce heat if necessary to prevent splattering. (If you want a thicker sauce and have the time, cook it a little longer.)

Each serving provides:			
92	Calories	14 g	Carbohydrate
4 g	Protein	385 mg	Sodium
2 g	Total fat (0 g Sat. fat)	0 mg	Cholesterol

Sandwiches, Pizzas, Burritos, and Other Easy Fixin's

Hardly a day goes by in the life of a typical American in which a sandwich is not consumed. We eat sandwiches on biscuits for breakfast, on bread for lunch, on rolls for dinner. We toast them. We grill them. We eat them open-faced.

Have you ever wondered how all this came about? Where did this mainstay of our very existence get its start? According to historians, the fourth Earl of Sandwich, an English political leader in the 1700s, was directly responsible for the creation of the sandwich. Supposedly an avid gambler who didn't want to take time away from gambling to eat, he had his meat brought to him between two slices of bread. This way, he could stay at the gaming table without missing a meal. The idea caught on.

Probably the most versatile of meals, sandwiches can be made from an endless variety of ingredients. Even yesterday's leftovers can become a whole new meal. When creating sandwiches, always make nutrition count. Choose whole grain breads and rolls and garnish the fillings with lots of fresh vegetables. Also, choose lowfat or fat-free condiments, such as ketchup, mustard, barbecue sauce, and reduced-fat mayonnaise.

This section contains lots of ideas for stuffing, rolling, and wrapping tasty ingredients, turning them into delicious and quick sandwiches, pizzas, and burritos. Add a salad or a bowl of soup, and that's all you need for a quick and easy meal that's also tasty and nutritious.

Lentil Pitas with
Greek Olives and Roasted Peppers

Sound too good to be easy? Just chop a few ingredients while the lentils cook, and you have the fixings for a delicious, warm sandwich reminiscent of a Greek feast. Be sure to use the Greek black olives that are found in the deli department rather than canned olives.

Makes 6 servings

4	cups water
1	cup lentils, uncooked
8	Greek black olives, pitted, cut vertically into thin strips
1/2	cup green onions, thinly sliced (green and white parts)
1/3	cup roasted red bell peppers (half of an 8-ounce jar), cut into thin strips
2	teaspoons dried marjoram
3/4	teaspoon ground coriander
1/2	teaspoon dill weed
1/4	teaspoon *each* salt and pepper
2 1/2	tablespoons olive oil
1	tablespoon lemon juice
3	large (2-ounce) pita breads, cut in half crosswise

Bring water to a boil in a medium saucepan. Add lentils, cover, reduce heat to medium-low, and simmer 30 minutes, until lentils are tender (don't let them get mushy).

While lentils are cooking, in a medium bowl, combine olives, onions, roasted peppers, marjoram, coriander, dill weed, salt, and pepper. Mix well.

Drain lentils and add to olive mixture, mixing well.

In a small bowl, whisk oil and lemon juice together. Pour over lentils and mix well.

Divide warm lentil mixture and spoon into pitas.

❖*Serve-again hint:* Serve the leftovers cold atop a bed of greens or scoop it with (baked) tortilla chips or celery sticks.

	Each serving provides:		
254	Calories	36 g	Carbohydrate
12 g	Protein	369 mg	Sodium
7 g	Total fat (1 g Sat. fat)	0 mg	Cholesterol

Tofu Salad Sandwich with Tahini Sauce

This tasty salad can be made ahead and chilled, or it can be served right away at room temperature. Either way, it's a delicious blend of flavors and textures.

Makes 4 servings

1	teaspoon vegetable oil
1	pound firm tofu, cut into 2 × 1/4 × 1/4-inch strips, drained well between layers of towels
5	green onions, cut crosswise into 2-inch pieces, then each piece cut in half lengthwise (green and white parts)
1/2	cup coarsely shredded carrots
3	tablespoons tahini (sesame paste)
2	tablespoons reduced-sodium (or regular) soy sauce
2	tablespoons red wine vinegar
2	teaspoons sugar
1/4	teaspoon bottled hot sauce (or to taste)
1/4	teaspoon garlic powder
2	large (2-ounce) pita breads, cut in half crosswise
4	romaine or green leaf lettuce leaves

Heat oil in a large nonstick skillet over medium-high heat. Add tofu. Cook, stirring constantly with a tossing motion, until tofu is lightly browned on all sides.

Place tofu in a medium bowl. Add green onions and carrots. Toss to combine.

Place tahini in a small bowl. Gradually stir in soy sauce. Add vinegar, sugar, hot sauce, and garlic powder. Mix well. Add to tofu mixture. Toss until tofu is evenly coated.

Open each pita half and line with lettuce. Divide tofu mixture evenly and spoon into pitas.

❖*Serve-again hint:* Cold leftovers are terrific over a bed of greens as an appetizer or light lunch.

Each serving provides:			
284	Calories	27 g	Carbohydrate
17 g	Protein	494 mg	Sodium
13 g	Total fat (2 g Sat. fat)	0 mg	Cholesterol

No-Cook Falafel Sandwich

Here's all of the flavor of a Middle Eastern falafel sandwich without the traditional deep-frying. It makes an easy last-minute lunch or dinner.

Makes 4 servings

Falafel
1	1-pound can chickpeas (garbanzo beans), rinsed and drained (or 2 cups of cooked beans)
1/3	cup finely chopped red onion
2	tablespoons lemon juice
2	tablespoons plain nonfat yogurt
1/2	teaspoon *each* garlic powder, ground cumin, and ground coriander
1/4	teaspoon pepper
1/8	teaspoon salt

Cucumber Topping
1/2	cup coarsely shredded, peeled cucumber
1/4	cup plain nonfat yogurt
	Dash salt
	Freshly ground black pepper

Assembly
2	large (2-ounce) pita breads, cut in half crosswise
3/4	cup shredded romaine lettuce
1/2	cup chopped tomato

Place chickpeas in a medium bowl. Mash with a fork or potato masher. Add onion, lemon juice, yogurt, and spices. Mix well.

To make the cucumber topping, combine cucumber, yogurt, salt, and pepper in a small bowl.

The sandwiches can be assembled right away, or the chickpea and cucumber mixtures can be chilled for several hours or overnight (mix well before serving).

To assemble the sandwiches, in each pita half, place a quarter of the chickpea mixture. Top with shredded lettuce, chopped tomato, and 1¹/₂ tablespoons of the cucumber mixture.

✧*Serve-again hint:* The chickpea mixture makes a great spread for crackers, celery, or (baked) tortilla chips.

Each serving provides:

185	Calories	33 g	Carbohydrate
9 g	Protein	403 mg	Sodium
2 g	Total fat (0 g Sat. fat)	0 mg	Cholesterol

Greek Spinach Subs

Truly a spectacular treat, this easy sandwich is light yet filling, and it works well for lunch or dinner. My family raved about it.

Makes 4 servings

1	cup lowfat (1%) cottage cheese
1/3	cup crumbled feta cheese (2 ounces)
1/2	cup thinly sliced green onions (green and white parts)
1	large clove garlic, crushed
1/8	teaspoon pepper
1	10-ounce package frozen chopped spinach, thawed and drained well (squeeze out as much water as possible)
4	6-inch submarine rolls
1	medium cucumber, peeled, thinly sliced
1	large tomato, thinly sliced

In a medium bowl, combine cottage cheese, feta cheese, green onions, garlic, and pepper. Add spinach and mix well. (This can be used right away or refrigerated for a day or two.)

At serving time, preheat the broiler.

Split each roll lengthwise, but do not cut all the way through. Open the rolls and place on a baking sheet. Spread spinach filling on the top and bottom of each roll, using 1/2 cup of filling for each sandwich. Place sandwiches under the broiler until hot and bubbly. (Watch them carefully; if the bread browns too quickly, move the pan to a lower rack, reduce the oven temperature to 400°, and leave the sandwiches in the oven until heated through.)

Place cucumber and tomato slices on one half of each sandwich, close the rolls, and enjoy.

✦*Quick tip:* If you place the spinach in the refrigerator the night before, it will probably be thawed when you are ready for it. It also thaws nicely in the microwave.

✧*Serve-again hint:* Save any remaining filling to make more sandwiches or serve it cold on crackers or sliced veggies.

Each serving provides:

284	Calories	41 g	Carbohydrate
17 g	Protein	811 mg	Sodium
6 g	Total fat (3 g Sat. fat)	15 mg	Cholesterol

Curried Tofu Salad Sandwich

There's lots of color, flavor, and crunch in this easy, do-ahead salad, along with little bursts of sweetness from the raisins. Make it a day or two ahead and, when you're ready, just spread it between slices of whole grain toast, add lettuce and tomato, and enjoy.

Makes 4 servings

1	pound firm or medium tofu, sliced and drained well between layers of towels
1/4	cup finely chopped celery
1/4	cup finely chopped red bell pepper
1/4	cup raisins
2	tablespoons thinly sliced green onions (green and white parts)
2	tablespoons slivered almonds, lightly toasted
1/4	cup plain nonfat yogurt
1 1/2	teaspoons honey
1	teaspoon prepared yellow mustard
1	teaspoon curry powder
1/4	plus 1/8 teaspoon salt
1/8	teaspoon pepper
8	slices whole grain bread, toasted
4	romaine lettuce leaves
1	medium, ripe tomato, sliced

Place tofu in a large bowl and mash with a fork or potato masher. Add celery, red pepper, raisins, green onions, and almonds. Mix well.

In a small bowl, combine yogurt, honey, mustard, curry powder, salt, and pepper. Mix well. Add to tofu. Mix until well blended. Chill.

To serve, make four sandwiches by dividing tofu mixture evenly and placing it between slices of bread along with lettuce and tomato.

❖*Serve-again hint:* For an appetizer, this salad is delicious spread on melba toast rounds or stuffed into hollowed-out cherry tomatoes.

Each serving provides:			
314	Calories	41 g	Carbohydrate
19 g	Protein	513 mg	Sodium
10 g	Total fat (1 g Sat. fat)	0 mg	Cholesterol

Veggie Subs with Feta and Basil

The combined flavors of fresh basil and feta cheese make these mouth-watering sandwiches really special. You can vary the vegetables or add others if you like. Just be sure to cook them only until they are tender-crisp so they retain their crunch.

Makes 4 servings

2	teaspoons olive oil
1	large onion, sliced vertically into thin slices
1/2	large green bell pepper, sliced into thin strips
1/2	large red bell pepper, sliced into thin strips
3	cloves garlic, crushed
1	small zucchini, unpeeled, cut into strips, about 1/4 × 2 1/2 inches
1	small yellow summer squash, cut into strips (same size as the zucchini)
4	6-inch submarine rolls
1/3	cup crumbled feta cheese (2 ounces)
1/4	cup thinly sliced fresh basil (dried basil doesn't work well here)
	Salt and freshly ground black pepper

Heat oil in a large nonstick skillet over medium heat. Add onion, green and red peppers, and garlic. Cook, stirring frequently, 5 minutes.

Add zucchini and yellow squash. Continue to cook, stirring frequently, until vegetables are tender-crisp, about 5 minutes. Add small amounts of water as necessary, a few tablespoons at a time, to prevent sticking.

To assemble, cut a thin slice, lengthwise, off the top of each roll. Hollow out the rolls, leaving about a ¹/₂-inch shell. Divide feta and basil and sprinkle evenly into each roll. Spoon vegetables into rolls. Sprinkle with salt and pepper. Replace the top of the roll.

Serve right away.

❖*Serve-again hint:* Any leftover vegetables can be reheated in a toaster oven or microwave and served as a side dish, sprinkled with feta.

Each serving provides:

269	Calories	41 g	Carbohydrate
9 g	Protein	525 mg	Sodium
8 g	Total fat (2 g Sat. fat) 1	3 mg	Cholesterol

Artichoke-Bean Salad Pockets

Open a few jars, cut a pita in half, and enjoy. This tangy salad is ready in no time.

Makes 4 servings

1	6-ounce jar marinated artichoke hearts, drained
1	1-pound can Great Northern beans, rinsed and drained (or 2 cups of cooked beans)
1	2-ounce jar chopped pimientos, drained
1	tablespoon red wine vinegar
1	teaspoon dried basil
1/2	teaspoon ground cumin
	Freshly ground black pepper
6	1-ounce whole wheat pita breads
	Lettuce
	Sliced tomato

Coarsely chop artichoke hearts. Remove and discard any tough outer layers. Place artichokes in a large bowl and add beans, pimientos, vinegar, basil, cumin, and pepper. Mix well.

Cut pitas in half crosswise and split each half open. Line the inside of each half with lettuce and tomato, then fill with the salad.

Serve right away. (If you prefer, the salad can be made up to 2 days ahead and refrigerated, and the sandwiches can be made when needed.)

✧*Serve-again hint:* The salad can be mounded on a bed of lettuce and garnished with assorted fresh veggies, or used to top a tossed salad.

Each serving provides:

207	Calories	38 g	Carbohydrate
9 g	Protein	528 mg	Sodium
3 g	Total fat (0 g Sat. fat)	0 mg	Cholesterol

California Fruit and Veggie Sandwich

A specialty of my good friend, Roz Breslouer, this tasty sandwich takes only minutes to prepare. We love the sweet, refreshing burst of orange in every bite. The listed vegetable amounts are approximate.

Makes 2 servings

4	romaine lettuce leaves
1/2	medium, ripe tomato, sliced
1/2	small red onion, sliced
1/2	small cucumber, unpeeled, sliced (peel the cucumber if it has been waxed)
1	medium orange, peeled, sliced crosswise into 1/4-inch slices (discard outer white membrane)
1/2	small, ripe avocado, peeled, thinly sliced
4	slices whole wheat or multigrain bread, lightly toasted
2	teaspoons Dijon mustard
2	teaspoons honey

Layer the vegetables and fruit on 2 slices of the bread.

Combine mustard and honey in a small bowl or custard cup and mix well. Spread on the remaining 2 slices of bread. Place on top of fruit. Hold sandwiches together with toothpicks (be careful when eating).

Serve right away.

Each serving provides:

294	Calories	51 g	Carbohydrate
8 g	Protein	433 mg	Sodium
9 g	Total fat (1 g Sat. fat)	0 mg	Cholesterol

Mexican Lunch Muffins

Here's a quick and easy lunch and a change of pace from an ordinary grilled cheese sandwich.

Makes 4 servings

2	English muffins
1	cup reduced-fat Cheddar cheese (4 ounces)
3/4	cup chopped tomatoes
3	tablespoons thinly sliced green onion (green part only)
1	jalapeño pepper, finely minced, seeds and membranes discarded (optional)
1	teaspoon chili powder
1/4	teaspoon dried oregano
1/8	teaspoon garlic powder

Split muffins and toast them lightly.

While muffins are toasting, combine remaining ingredients, mixing well. Divide evenly and pile onto muffin halves.

Place under the broiler and broil 2 to 3 minutes, or until the cheese is melted and the topping is hot and bubbly.

Serve right away.

Each serving provides:			
158	Calories	15 g	Carbohydrate
12 g	Protein	362 mg	Sodium
6 g	Total fat (4 g Sat. fat)	20 mg	Cholesterol

Grilled Portobello Sandwich

Thick and meaty, portobello mushrooms are a natural for sandwiches. Adding lettuce, tomato, and mayonnaise lets you replace the fatty B.L.T. sandwich with the all-new P.L.T. Look for portobello mushrooms in the produce department of most large grocery stores (they look like giant mushrooms).

Makes 2 servings

2	teaspoons vegetable oil
1	teaspoon red wine vinegar
1	teaspoon reduced-sodium (or regular) soy sauce
1/4	teaspoon garlic powder
1	large portobello mushroom (about 7 ounces), sliced crosswise into 1/2-inch slices, stem removed and discarded
4	slices whole wheat bread
2	teaspoons reduced-calorie mayonnaise
	Sliced tomato
	Pepper
	Romaine lettuce

Preheat a broiler or grill.

In a small bowl or custard cup, combine oil, vinegar, soy sauce, and garlic powder. Mix well. Using *half* of the mixture, brush one side of each mushroom slice.

Place mushroom slices on a broiler pan, seasoned side up, and place under the broiler for about 2 minutes, until browned. (If grilling, place on a grill, seasoned side down.) Turn slices and brush the other side with the remaining mixture. Continue to broil or grill about 2 more minutes, until slices are tender and nicely browned.

While mushroom is cooking, toast the bread. Spread mayonnaise on 2 of the slices.

Make 2 sandwiches by placing mushrooms on bread and topping with tomato, pepper, and lettuce.

Each serving provides:

221	Calories	32 g	Carbohydrate
8 g	Protein	430 mg	Sodium
9 g	Total fat (1 g Sat. fat)	2 mg	Cholesterol

Grilled Spiced Eggplant Sandwich

The idea for this unique sandwich came from the popular Greek gyro sandwich. I've replaced the traditional meat with grilled eggplant and kept the tasty spice blend, creating a delicious sandwich that's perfect for lunch or dinner.

(Makes 4 servings)

Eggplant
Olive oil or nonstick cooking spray

1   small eggplant (about ³/₄ pound), unpeeled, cut crosswise into ¹/₂-inch slices

¹/₂   teaspoon ground allspice

¹/₂   teaspoon ground coriander

¹/₂   teaspoon garlic powder

¹/₂   teaspoon onion powder

Yogurt Sauce
¹/₂   cup plain nonfat yogurt

¹/₄   cup finely chopped cucumber, seeds removed (peel the cucumber if the skin has been waxed)

1   clove garlic, crushed

¹/₈   teaspoon salt

¹/₈   teaspoon pepper

Assembly
2   large (2-ounce) whole wheat pita breads

1   medium tomato, chopped

About 20 minutes before cooking, place eggplant slices on a baking sheet that has been lightly oiled or sprayed with a nonstick cooking spray. With your finger, lightly "paint" each slice with olive oil or spray with nonstick spray.

Combine spices in a small bowl and mix well. Using *half* of the mixture, sprinkle it evenly on the eggplant. Turn slices over and repeat on the other side using the remaining half of spice mixture. Let stand 20 minutes (or up to 1 hour).

Meanwhile, in a small bowl, combine all ingredients for yogurt sauce. Mix well and place in refrigerator until needed. (You can make this a day ahead, if you wish.)

Preheat broiler or grill.

Broil or grill eggplant about 5 minutes on each side, or until nicely browned.

To assemble the sandwiches, cut pitas in half crosswise. Divide eggplant evenly and place in pitas. Add chopped tomato. Divide yogurt sauce and spoon into pitas.

Serve right away.

Each serving provides:

146	Calories	26 g	Carbohydrate
6 g	Protein	248 mg	Sodium
3 g	Total fat (0 g Sat. fat)	1 mg	Cholesterol

Tofu Pitas with Salsa-Dijon

Stir-frying the tofu gives it a denser texture that is ideal for sandwiches. The unique sauce turns the normally bland tofu into a delicious, tangy feast.

Makes 4 servings

1/3	cup salsa (hot or mild)
1/4	cup plain nonfat yogurt
1/4	cup finely chopped celery
2	tablespoons Dijon mustard
1	tablespoon thinly sliced green onion (green and white parts)
1	teaspoon vegetable oil
1	pound firm tofu, cut into $2 \times 1/4 \times 1/4$-inch strips, drained well between layers of towels
2	large (2-ounce) pita breads, cut in half crosswise
4	romaine lettuce leaves
1	ripe tomato, thinly sliced

In a small bowl, combine salsa, yogurt, celery, mustard, and green onion. Mix well. Set aside.

Heat oil in a large nonstick skillet over medium-high heat. Add tofu. Cook, stirring constantly with a tossing motion, until tofu is lightly browned on all sides.

Place tofu in a large bowl and top with salsa mixture. Toss until well blended.

Open each pita half and line with lettuce and tomato. Divide tofu mixture evenly and spoon into pitas.

❖*Serve-again hint:* For a take-along lunch, fill a container with the tofu mixture and take along a pita. At lunch time, just spoon the filling into the pita and enjoy.

	Each serving provides:		
221	Calories	23 g	Carbohydrate
15 g	Protein	577 mg	Sodium
7 g	Total fat (1 g Sat. fat)	0 mg	Cholesterol

Oriental Bean Pitas

Pea pods, red pepper, and celery add lots of color and crunch to this tasty salad in a pita. Add lettuce, tomato, or onion to the sandwich, and you have a filling and nutritious meal-in-one.

Makes 4 servings

1	1-pound can Great Northern beans, rinsed and drained (or 2 cups of cooked beans)
$1/2$	cup canned crushed pineapple (packed in juice), drained
$1/3$	cup finely chopped red bell pepper
$1/3$	cup finely chopped snow peas
$1/4$	cup finely chopped celery
1	tablespoon reduced-sodium (or regular) soy sauce
1	tablespoon sesame seeds, lightly toasted
1	teaspoon sesame oil
$1/8$	teaspoon ground ginger
	Salt and pepper
2	large (2-ounce) whole wheat pita breads, cut in half crosswise

In a large bowl, combine all ingredients, *except* pita. Mix well. Chill thoroughly.

To serve, open up each pita and add lettuce and tomato, if desired. Mix bean salad, divide evenly, and pile into pitas.

❖*Serve-again hint:* Purée the leftovers in a food processor, and you have a delicious sandwich spread or dip for fresh veggies.

Each serving provides:

191	Calories	33 g	Carbohydrate
8 g	Protein	492 mg	Sodium
4 g	Total fat (0 g Sat. fat)	0 mg	Cholesterol

Veggie Hero

There are lots of variations of this tasty sandwich, and it can be made with virtually any combination of vegetables. This one is one of my family's favorites. It's colorful and crunchy and makes a perfect picnic sandwich or light supper.

Makes 4 servings

4	6-inch to 8-inch crusty submarine rolls
2	tablespoons coarse brown mustard
4	large romaine lettuce leaves
1	small red onion, very thinly sliced
4	large radishes, very thinly sliced
4	medium cauliflower flowerets, very thinly sliced
1/2	medium, red bell pepper, very thinly sliced
4	small dill pickles, very thinly sliced
2	medium tomatoes, sliced
2	mild pickled salad peppers, sliced (or hot ones, if you prefer)
1	medium carrot, coarsely shredded
1	cup shredded reduced-fat Cheddar cheese (4 ounces)
2	tablespoons fat-free Italian dressing

Split rolls lengthwise, but do not cut all the way through. Open carefully and hollow out each roll, leaving a 1/2-inch shell in each half. Spread the bottom half of each roll with mustard.

Layer the vegetables and cheese in the order listed. Drizzle with Italian dressing. Close sandwiches and secure with toothpicks. To serve, cut each sandwich in half and carefully remove the toothpicks.

◆*Quick tip:* You can slice all of the veggies ahead of time and assemble the sandwiches when needed, or prepare the sandwiches ahead, except for the Italian dressing, and wrap tightly until serving time. Add the dressing just before serving.

Each serving provides:

348	Calories	51 g	Carbohydrate
18 g	Protein	1691 mg	Sodium
8 g	Total fat (4 g Sat. fat)	20 mg	Cholesterol

Mediterranean Pizza Subs

You can make lots of variations of this tasty sandwich. Just chop any veggies you like, add pizza sauce, top with cheese, and voilà! The small, thin eggplants, about the size of a zucchini, are very tender and are a good choice for this dish.

Makes 4 servings

2	teaspoons olive oil
2	cups eggplant, peeled, chopped into 1/4-inch to 1/2-inch pieces
1	cup sliced mushrooms
1	cup sliced zucchini or yellow summer squash, 1/4-inch thick (or you can use some of each)
1/2	cup chopped onion
1/4	cup chopped green bell pepper
1/4	cup chopped red bell pepper
2	to 3 cloves garlic, finely chopped
1	cup bottled pizza sauce
4	6-inch submarine rolls, split open and toasted lightly
1	cup shredded reduced-fat mozzarella cheese (4 ounces)

Heat oil in a large nonstick skillet over medium heat. Add all of the vegetables and garlic. Cook, stirring frequently, 10 minutes, or until vegetables are tender.

Stir pizza sauce into vegetables. Reduce heat to medium-low, cover, and cook 5 minutes more.

Divide vegetables evenly and pile into the rolls. Top each with 1 ounce of cheese.

Close the rolls to form sandwiches.

Enjoy right away.

❖*Serve-again hint:* You can make delicious appetizers or snacks with the leftovers. Reheat the veggies and pile them onto crackers (be sure to choose fat-free crackers). Top with a little cheese and serve hot.

Each serving provides:			
313	Calories	43 g	Carbohydrate
15 g	Protein	769 mg	Sodium
9 g	Total fat (3 g Sat. fat)	10 mg	Cholesterol

Mushroom and Swiss Toasts

Sautéed mushrooms topped with Swiss cheese and accented with delicious honey-mustard make a truly exceptional sandwich. Add a tossed salad and a piece of fresh fruit, and you have a lunch with pizzazz.

Makes 4 servings

1 1/2	teaspoons Dijon mustard
1 1/2	teaspoons honey
4	cups sliced mushrooms
1/2	teaspoon garlic powder
	Salt and pepper
2	English muffins, split and lightly toasted
4	slices (1 ounce each) reduced-fat Swiss cheese

Combine mustard and honey in a small bowl or custard cup, mixing well. Set aside.

Heat a large nonstick skillet over medium-high heat. Add mushrooms. Cook 5 minutes, or until mushrooms begin to brown, stirring frequently. Remove from heat, sprinkle evenly with garlic powder, salt, and pepper, and mix well.

Spread honey-mustard on each muffin half. Top with mushrooms, then a slice of cheese.

Place sandwiches under the broiler for a few minutes, until cheese is melted. Serve hot.

Each serving provides:

176	Calories	19 g	Carbohydrate
13 g	Protein	230 mg	Sodium
5 g	Total fat (3 g Sat. fat)	15 mg	Cholesterol

Mexican Bean Burgers

These moist burgers are high in flavor, high in fiber, and very low in fat. Try them on a burger bun, topped with salsa, shredded lettuce, chopped onion, and tomato. What a feast!

Makes 8 burgers

1	1-pound can black beans, rinsed and drained (or 2 cups of cooked beans)
2	cups cooked brown rice, preferably warm
1/4	cup very finely minced onion
3	tablespoons ketchup
1	to 2 teaspoons chili powder
1	teaspoon dried oregano
1/2	teaspoon garlic powder
1/2	teaspoon ground cumin
	Salt and pepper

Combine all ingredients in a large bowl. Mash with a fork or potato masher until beans are mashed well and mixture is thoroughly combined.

Divide mixture evenly and form into 8 burgers, 1/2-inch to 3/4-inch thick. Wet your hands slightly if necessary, to avoid sticking.

Lightly oil a nonstick skillet or griddle or spray with a nonstick cooking spray. Preheat over medium heat. Place burgers in skillet and cook until browned on both sides, turning burgers several times.

✦*Quick tip:* Have cooked rice on hand in the freezer. Place it in a strainer, pour boiling water over it, drain, and it's ready to use.

✧*Serve-again hint:* Make sandwiches with the leftover burgers, refrigerate, and serve them cold, along with all the toppings.

Each burger provides:			
101	Calories	19 g	Carbohydrate
4 g	Protein	166 mg	Sodium
1 g	Total fat (0 g Sat. fat)	0 mg	Cholesterol

Eggplant Pizza Wheels

Slices of eggplant actually become the crust for these delicious pizzas. What a unique way to get kids to eat their vegetables! A side dish of pasta makes a perfect accompaniment, or serve the pizza wheels as a side dish for six people when pasta is the entree.

Makes 4 servings
(about 5 wheels each serving)

1	medium eggplant (1 to 1¹/₄ pounds), peeled, sliced crosswise into ¹/₄-inch slices
¹/₂	cup skim milk
³/₄	cup dry bread crumbs
1	1-pound can (or jar) pizza sauce
1	cup shredded reduced-fat mozzarella cheese (4 ounces)

Preheat oven to 450°.

Lightly oil a large baking sheet or spray with a nonstick cooking spray.

Dip each eggplant slice in the milk and then in the bread crumbs, coating both sides. Place eggplant on prepared baking sheet.

Bake 20 minutes.

Place a tablespoon of the sauce on each eggplant slice. Spread the sauce, staying about ¹/₂ inch away from the edges of the slices. Sprinkle cheese on each slice.

Bake 5 to 10 minutes more, until the cheese is melted and begins to brown.

❖*Serve-again hint:* Leftovers make a great snack, either hot or cold.

	Each serving provides:		
240	Calories	30 g	Carbohydrate
14 g	Protein	817 mg	Sodium
7 g	Total fat (2 g Sat. fat)	10 mg	Cholesterol

Mexican Tortilla Pizza

Too easy for words, this will become a favorite lunch dish when you're in a hurry and everyone's hungry. You can add other toppings if you like. Try sliced olives, finely chopped green pepper, chopped cilantro, jalapeño peppers, or whatever else you can imagine.

Makes 4 servings

4	8-inch flour tortillas
1	cup salsa (hot or mild)
1/2	cup shredded reduced-fat Cheddar cheese (2 ounces)
3	tablespoons thinly sliced green onions (green and white parts)

Preheat oven to 400°.

Have a large ungreased baking sheet ready.

Arrange tortillas in a single layer on the baking sheet. Spread 1/4 cup of salsa on each tortilla, staying about 1/2 inch away from the edges. Divide cheese evenly and sprinkle over salsa. Top with green onions.

Bake 6 to 8 minutes, until cheese is melted and edges of tortillas are crisp.

Cut into wedges to serve.

◆*Quick tip:* Use kitchen shears to cut the tortillas quickly and evenly.

Each serving provides:

175	Calories	24 g	Carbohydrate
8 g	Protein	918 mg	Sodium
5 g	Total fat (2 g Sat. fat)	10 mg	Cholesterol

Greek Tofu Patties with Yogurt-Tahini Sauce

This is a delicious contrast of flavors and textures. Tofu provides the perfect, mild background for these unique patties that combine the sweetness of dates, the crunch of nuts, and the fragrance of onions and dill. They're great topped with the yogurt-tahini sauce, but they also taste great with Chinese sweet and sour sauce.

Makes 4 servings

Tofu Patties

1	pound firm or medium tofu, sliced, drained well between layers of towels
5	medium dates, pitted, finely chopped
2^1/$_2$	tablespoons finely chopped walnuts
1/4	cup thinly sliced green onions (green part only)
1/4	cup dry bread crumbs
2	egg whites
1	tablespoon honey
2	teaspoons dill weed
1/4	teaspoon salt
1/8	teaspoon pepper

Yogurt-Tahini Sauce

1/4	cup tahini (sesame paste)
2	tablespoons lemon juice
1/4	teaspoon garlic powder
1/2	cup plain nonfat yogurt

Assembly

2	large (2-ounce) pitas, cut in half crosswise

Place tofu in a large bowl and mash well with a fork or potato masher. Add remaining patty ingredients and mix well.

Divide mixture evenly and shape into 8 patties, about 1/2-inch thick.

Lightly oil a large nonstick griddle or skillet or spray with a non-stick cooking spray. Preheat over medium heat. Place patties in skillet and cook until nicely browned on both sides, turning patties several times. Spray skillet again, if necessary, to prevent sticking.

While patties are cooking, prepare sauce by combining all sauce ingredients in a small bowl and mixing well.

To assemble, place 2 patties in each pita half and top with about 2 tablespoons of sauce.

✦*Quick tip:* Chopping the dates is easy with kitchen shears.

Each serving provides:

409	Calories	43 g	Carbohydrate
22 g	Protein	429 mg	Sodium
18 g	Total fat (2 g Sat. fat)	1 mg	Cholesterol

Veggie Pita Pizzas

Lots of spinach, mushrooms, and onions piled high turn each pita into a fill-
ing personal-size pizza. Add a salad or some soup, and you have a perfect
last-minute meal that kids and grown-ups will love.

Makes 4 servings

1	teaspoon vegetable oil
1	cup finely chopped onion
1	cup thinly sliced mushrooms
2	cloves garlic, finely chopped
1/2	teaspoon dried oregano
1/4	teaspoon fennel seeds, slightly crushed
1/8	teaspoon pepper
1	cup reduced-fat, meatless spaghetti sauce or pizza sauce
4	6-inch whole wheat pita breads (use the whole pitas—do not cut or split them)
1	10-ounce package frozen, chopped spinach, thawed and drained well
3/4	cup shredded reduced-fat mozzarella cheese (3 ounces)
1	teaspoon grated Parmesan cheese

Preheat oven to 375°.

Have an ungreased baking sheet ready (preferably a nonstick sheet).

Heat oil in a small nonstick skillet over medium heat. Add onion, mushrooms, and garlic. Cook, stirring frequently, 5 minutes, until tender. Remove from heat and stir in oregano, fennel seeds, and pepper.

Spread spaghetti sauce on pitas, staying 1/2 inch away from the edges. Divide spinach evenly and place on sauce, then divide mozzarella cheese and sprinkle over spinach. Divide onion mixture and arrange over cheese, then sprinkle with Parmesan cheese, using 1/4 teaspoon on each pita. Place the pitas on baking sheet.

Bake 15 minutes.

◆*Quick tip:* Keep spinach in the freezer so it's always handy. It thaws quickly in a microwave.

Each serving provides:

314	Calories	49 g	Carbohydrate
15 g	Protein	784 mg	Sodium
8 g	Total fat (2 g Sat. fat)	8 mg	Cholesterol

Veggie Fajitas

Simply stir-fry the veggies, then spoon them into tortillas with a few quick toppings. You can enjoy the delightful taste of Mexican food with very little fat or fuss.

Makes 6 servings

Fajitas

6	8-inch flour tortillas
2	teaspoons vegetable oil
1	cup onion, sliced vertically into thin slices
1	cup thinly sliced green bell pepper
1	cup thinly sliced red bell pepper
1	cup sliced mushrooms
1	cup zucchini, cut vertically into quarters, then thinly sliced
1	cup yellow summer squash, cut vertically into quarters, then thinly sliced
1¹/₂	teaspoons dried oregano
1	teaspoon chili powder
1	teaspoon ground cumin
¹/₂	teaspoon garlic powder
	Salt and pepper

Toppings

¹/₂	cup chopped tomato
³/₄	cup shredded reduced-fat Cheddar or Monterey Jack cheese (3 ounces)
¹/₂	medium avocado, thinly sliced
	Salsa

Preheat oven to 350°.

Stack tortillas and wrap them tightly in foil. Heat in oven for 10 minutes.

While tortillas are heating, prepare fajita filling. Heat oil in a large nonstick skillet over medium-high heat. Add onion and green and red peppers. Cook 3 minutes, stirring frequently. Add mushrooms, zucchini, yellow squash, and spices. Continue to cook, stirring frequently, 3 more minutes, until vegetables are tender-crisp.

Divide mixture evenly and place along the center of each tortilla. Top each one with tomato, cheese, avocado, and salsa. Roll tortilla around filling.

Serve right away.

◆*Quick tip:* Assembly is easy if you put the cooked veggies in the center of the table, surrounded by small bowls of the toppings, and let everyone make his/her own fajita.

Each serving provides:			
231	Calories	29 g	Carbohydrate
9 g	Protein	288 mg	Sodium
9 g	Total fat (3 g Sat. fat)	10 mg	Cholesterol

Veggie Quesadillas

Quesadillas (KAY-sa-DEE-yahs) are the Mexican version of sandwiches. If you like, you can place a few teaspoons of chopped tomato, green onion, or green chilies on top of the cheese before you fold the tortillas. Served with salsa, this makes a great appetizer or lunch dish.

Makes 4 servings

2	teaspoons vegetable oil
2	cups shredded cabbage
1	cup sliced mushrooms
1/2	cup chopped onion
1/2	cup chopped green bell pepper
1	teaspoon dried oregano
1	teaspoon chili powder
3/4	teaspoon ground cumin
1/2	teaspoon garlic powder
4	8-inch flour tortillas
1/2	cup shredded reduced-fat Cheddar cheese (2 ounces)
	Salsa

Heat oil in a large nonstick skillet over medium-high heat. Add cabbage, mushrooms, onion, and green pepper. Sprinkle with spices. Cook, stirring frequently, until vegetables are tender, about 5 minutes. Remove from heat.

Place tortillas on a flat surface. Divide vegetables evenly and place on one half of each tortilla. Top with cheese. Fold tortillas in half and press down gently.

Spray skillet lightly with nonstick cooking spray and reheat over medium heat. Place tortillas in skillet, two at a time. Heat tortillas, flipping them back and forth, until cheese is melted and tortillas are hot and crispy on both sides.

Serve right away, topped with salsa.

◆*Quick tip:* Shredded cabbage is available in most grocery stores, packed in plastic bags. You can use some for this recipe and make soup or cole slaw with the rest.

Each serving provides:			
205	Calories	26 g	Carbohydrate
9 g	Protein	292 mg	Sodium
8 g	Total fat (2 g Sat. fat)	10 mg	Cholesterol

Quick 'n' Spicy Tofu Burritos

A special thanks to my dear friend, Roz Breslouer, for the idea that led to the creation of this easy recipe. It only takes about 15 minutes from start to finish and can be made either mild or hot, depending on your "resistance."

Makes 6 burritos

1	pound firm or medium tofu, sliced and drained well between layers of towels
1	teaspoon chili powder
1	teaspoon dried oregano
1/2	teaspoon ground cumin
1/2	teaspoon garlic powder
1/8	teaspoon salt
1	8-ounce can salt-free (or regular) corn, drained
1	4-ounce can chopped green chilies (mild or hot), drained
6	8-inch flour tortillas
1	teaspoon vegetable oil
1	cup shredded reduced-fat Cheddar cheese (4 ounces)
	Salsa

Preheat oven to 350°.

Place tofu in a large bowl and mash with a fork or potato masher. Add spices and mix well. Stir in corn and chilies.

Wrap tortillas tightly in aluminum foil and place in oven to heat for 10 minutes.

While tortillas are heating, heat oil in a large nonstick skillet over medium heat. Add tofu mixture. Cook, stirring frequently, until mixture is heated through and is fairly dry, about 10 minutes.

Divide cheese evenly onto centers of tortillas. Top each one with ¹/₂ cup of tofu mixture. Fold in tops and bottoms of tortillas, then fold in the sides so that filling is enclosed. Turn burritos over and place on serving plate.

Serve with salsa.

✦*Quick tip:* You can keep both cheese and tortillas in the freezer so they'll always be on hand when you need them for a quick recipe.

	Each serving provides:		
272	Calories	28 g	Carbohydrate
18 g	Protein	490 mg	Sodium
10 g	Total fat (3 g Sat. fat)	13 mg	Cholesterol

Mushroom and White Bean Burritos

If you keep tortillas in your freezer and canned beans and salsa in the pantry, you can make this delicious south-of-the-border favorite in no time.

Makes 6 servings

Burritos

6	8-inch flour tortillas
2	teaspoons vegetable oil
1	cup onion, sliced vertically into thin slivers
1/2	cup finely chopped red bell pepper
3	cloves garlic, crushed
2	cups thinly sliced mushrooms
1/2	teaspoon ground cumin
1/2	teaspoon chili powder
1/3	cup water
1	teaspoon Vegetable Broth Mix (page 34)
1	1-pound can white kidney beans (cannellini) or Great Northern beans, rinsed and drained (or 2 cups of cooked beans)
1	cup shredded reduced-fat Cheddar cheese (4 ounces)

Toppings

Salsa (hot or mild)
Plain nonfat yogurt
Fresh cilantro, chopped (optional)

Preheat oven to 350°.

Place tortillas in a stack and wrap tightly in aluminum foil. Place in oven to heat for 10 minutes.

While tortillas are heating, heat oil in a large nonstick skillet over medium heat. Add onion, red pepper, and garlic. Cook 4 minutes, stirring frequently. Add mushrooms, cumin, and chili powder. Continue to cook, stirring frequently, 2 minutes. Add water, broth mix, and beans. Cook until mixture is hot and bubbly.

To assemble, place 1/2 cup of the bean mixture in the center of each tortilla. Top with 2 1/2 tablespoons of the cheese. Fold in tops and bottoms of tortillas, then fold in the sides so that filling is enclosed. Turn burritos over and place on serving plate.

Top each burrito with about 2 tablespoons of salsa and 1 tablespoon of yogurt. Sprinkle with cilantro, if desired.

✦*Quick tip:* Assembly of burritos is always easier if you put the beans and toppings in the center of the table, pass the tortillas, and let everyone make their own.

Each serving provides:			
332	Calories	46 g	Carbohydrate
16 g	Protein	537 mg	Sodium
10 g	Total fat (3 g Sat. fat)	13 mg	Cholesterol

Stuffed Baked Potatoes

Remember when your grandmother told you that potatoes are fattening? Fortunately, she was wrong. It isn't the potato that's the villain but rather the butter or other high-fat ingredient that is used to top the potato. A medium potato contains 95 calories and 0.1 grams of fat. Top it with just one tablespoon of butter, and you add 108 calories and 12 grams of fat. You can clearly see which one is the culprit!

Potatoes are high in carbohydrates and low in fat. They are also wonderful sources of protein, fiber, iron, potassium, vitamins B and C, and various minerals. Many of the nutrients are found in and just under the skin, so, whenever possible, leave the skin on.

A baked potato is an easy side dish and can also be turned into a filling entrée. In addition to the toppings offered in this section are many other dishes in this book that can be used as potato toppers. You can turn leftovers into a whole new dish by spooning them over a baked potato. For example, try topping your potato with one of the following:

- Mushroom-Bean Ragout (page 157)
- Three-Bean Chili (page 158)
- Bombay Kidney Beans (page 134)
- Butter Bean and Cheddar Casserole (page 123)
- Peachy Salsa Beans (page 117)
- Pumpkin and White Bean Stew (page 135)
- Savory Spiced Split Peas (page 137)
- Beans with Tomatoes and Feta (page 142)
- Zucchini in Tomato-Basil Sauce (page 318)
- Creamy Yellow Squash with Basil (page 319)
- Broccoli with Creamy Mustard Cheese Sauce (page 310)

Leftover steamed vegetables also make tasty potato toppers. Instead of butter, spoon vegetable broth over the potato before adding the vegetables. If you like sour cream on your potato, try nonfat yogurt instead and add a generous sprinkling of chopped chives and some freshly ground black pepper.

How to Bake Potatoes

Potatoes are easy to bake. Although they can be made in the microwave, the texture is just not the same as ones that have been baked in the oven. However, in a pinch, potatoes can be baked ahead of time and reheated in the microwave. To bake potatoes:

Choose a variety of potato suitable for baking, such as russet or Idaho.

Preheat oven to 375°.

Scrub the potatoes with a vegetable brush under running water. Remove any eyes. Pierce skin a few times with a fork or sharp knife to let the steam escape while baking.

Place potatoes directly on oven rack and bake for 1 hour or until tender to the touch (length of cooking time will depend on the size of the potatoes). Try not to place the potatoes too close together in the oven.

Note: For a crisper skin, rub the potato with a dash of oil before baking and increase oven temperature to 400°.

How to Bake Sweet Potatoes

For sweet potatoes, follow the above directions; however, it is best to place the sweet potatoes on a sheet of aluminum foil. They often drip while baking and can become quite messy and smoky in the oven. The foil makes oven cleanup much easier.

A quick and delicious fat-free topping is maple syrup with a sprinkling of cinnamon. In this section, you'll find other tantalizing fillings for sweet potatoes.

Portobello Potatoes

Enjoying a new popularity, portobello mushrooms make a tasty potato top-
ping with a true gourmet flavor. This delicious topping also tastes great with
mashed potatoes, creating a wonderful lowfat substitute for gravy.

Makes 4 servings

4	medium baking potatoes, 8 or 9 ounces each
2	teaspoons vegetable oil
1	cup finely chopped onion
4	portobello mushrooms, chopped into $1/4$-inch to $1/2$-inch pieces, stems removed and discarded (4 cups)
1	cup vegetable broth, or 1 cup of water and 1 teaspoon Vegetable Broth Mix (page 34)
$1/3$	cup dry red wine
$1/4$	teaspoon garlic powder
$1/8$	teaspoon salt
$1/8$	teaspoon pepper

Bake potatoes according to the directions on page 231.

While potatoes are baking, heat oil in a large nonstick skillet over medium heat. Add onion. Cook, stirring frequently, until onion is tender and begins to brown, about 5 minutes.

Add mushrooms to skillet. Cook, stirring frequently, 5 minutes.

Add remaining ingredients. When mixture boils, cook, stirring frequently, 7 to 8 minutes, until mushrooms are tender.

Cut a lengthwise slit in each potato. Push the ends of the potato together to open the potato.

Divide mushroom mixture evenly and spoon into potatoes. Spoon any remaining broth over mushrooms.

❖*Serve-again hint:* For a delicious side dish, heat the leftovers and toss with rice or noodles or add them to your favorite pasta sauce.

Each serving provides:

239	Calories	46 g	Carbohydrate
7 g	Protein	117 mg	Sodium
3 g	Total fat (0 g Sat. fat)	0 g	Cholesterol

Potatoes Parisienne

In French cooking, moirpoix *refers to the traditional mix of chopped carrots, onion, and celery that is sautéed and used in many dishes. I've turned it into a potato topper, creating a savory dish that's light, yet filling, and very tasty.*

Makes 4 servings

4	medium baking potatoes, 8 or 9 ounces each
2	teaspoons vegetable oil
1	cup finely chopped onion
1	cup finely chopped celery
1	cup finely chopped carrots
2	cups vegetable broth, or 2 cups of water and 2 teaspoons Vegetable Broth Mix (page 34)
1/2	cup chopped celery leaves
1	bay leaf
1/8	teaspoon dried thyme
1/8	teaspoon dill weed
	Salt and pepper

Bake potatoes according to the directions on page 231.

While potatoes are baking, heat oil in a medium saucepan over medium heat. Add onion, celery, and carrots. Cook 5 minutes, stirring frequently. Add small amounts of water as necessary, about a tablespoon at a time, to prevent sticking.

Add remaining ingredients, *except* salt and pepper. Mix well. When mixture boils, reduce heat slightly, cover, and simmer 10 to 15 minutes, until vegetables are just tender.

Remove and discard bay leaf.

Cut a lengthwise slit in each potato. Push the ends of the potato together to open the potato.

Divide the vegetables evenly and spoon into each potato. Divide broth and spoon over vegetables. Sprinkle with salt and pepper to taste.

Serve right away.

Each serving provides:

232	Calories	48 g	Carbohydrate
6 g	Protein	110 mg	Sodium
3 g	Total fat (0 g Sat. fat)	0 mg	Cholesterol

Potatoes with Onion and Mushroom Gravy

Who would have believed that you could enjoy a gravy-filled potato with only 2 grams of fat? This gravy is so thick and rich, you won't believe your taste buds. No one will guess that the secret ingredient is beans.

Makes 4 servings

4	medium baking potatoes, 8 or 9 ounces each
1	teaspoon vegetable oil
1/2	cup onion, sliced vertically into thin slivers
8	ounces mushrooms, sliced
1	1-pound can Great Northern beans, rinsed and drained (or 2 cups of cooked beans)
1/2	cup water
1 1/2	teaspoons reduced sodium (or regular) soy sauce
1	teaspoon Vegetable Broth Mix (page 34)
1/4	teaspoon garlic powder
1/8	teaspoon pepper

Bake potatoes according to the directions on page 231.

While potatoes are baking, heat oil in a medium saucepan over medium heat. Add onion and mushrooms. Cook 10 minutes, stirring occasionally.

In a blender container, combine remaining ingredients. Blend until smooth. Add to saucepan, mixing well. Heat through, stirring frequently.

Cut a lengthwise slit in each potato. Push the ends of the potato together to open the potato.

Divide the gravy evenly and spoon into each potato.

Serve right away.

❖*Serve-again hint:* Leftover gravy is scrumptious over rice or noodles. You may need to add a little water or vegetable broth, because the gravy tends to thicken as it stands.

Each serving provides:			
208	Calories	40 g	Carbohydrate
9 g	Protein	292 mg	Sodium
2 g	Total fat (0 g Sat. fat)	0 mg	Cholesterol

Veggie Potato Deluxe

The deluxe combination of broccoli, mushrooms, green onions, and sweet red pepper in a creamy sauce makes a delectable potato topping.

Makes 4 servings

4   medium baking potatoes, 8 or 9 ounces each
2   teaspoons vegetable oil
1   cup small broccoli flowerets
1   cup sliced mushrooms
1/2   cup red bell pepper, chopped
1/2   cup sliced green onions (green and white parts)
1   cup plain nonfat yogurt
1/2   cup skim milk
1   tablespoon plus 1 teaspoon cornstarch
2   teaspoons Dijon mustard
2   tablespoons grated Parmesan cheese
1/4   teaspoon garlic powder
       Salt and pepper
       Grated nutmeg (preferably freshly grated)

Bake potatoes according to the directions on page 231.

While potatoes are baking, heat oil in a medium saucepan over medium heat. Add broccoli, mushrooms, and red pepper. Cook 5 minutes, stirring frequently. Add green onions. Continue to cook, stirring, 1 minute.

In a small bowl, combine yogurt, milk, cornstarch, mustard, Parmesan cheese, and garlic powder. Mix well, stirring to dissolve cornstarch. Add mixture to saucepan. Bring to a boil, stirring constantly. Continue to cook, stirring, 1 to 2 minutes.

Cut a lengthwise slit in each potato. Push the ends of the potato together to open the potato.

Divide the topping evenly and spoon into each potato.

Serve right away. Sprinkle each potato with salt, pepper, and a dash of nutmeg.

Each serving provides:

276	Calories	50 g	Carbohydrate
12 g	Protein	192 mg	Sodium
4 g	Total fat (1 g Sat. fat)	4 mg	Cholesterol

Spicy Black Bean Potatoes

So quick and spicy, this easy filling, with its Mexican flair, can also be served over rice or noodles. Spooning hot vegetable broth over the potato before adding the filling makes the potato moist without the need for butter.

Makes 4 servings

4	medium baking potatoes, 8 or 9 ounces each
1	teaspoon vegetable oil
1¹/₂	cups sliced mushrooms
¹/₂	cup finely chopped onion
¹/₂	cup finely chopped green bell pepper
1¹/₂	teaspoons ground cumin
¹/₄	teaspoon garlic powder
1¹/₄	cups salsa (mild or hot)
1	1-pound can black beans, rinsed and drained (or 2 cups of cooked beans)
³/₄	cup hot vegetable broth, or ³/₄ cup of hot water and 1 teaspoon Vegetable Broth Mix (page 34)

Bake potatoes according to the directions on page 231.

While potatoes are baking, heat oil in a medium nonstick skillet over medium heat. Add mushrooms, onion, and green pepper. Sprinkle with cumin and garlic powder. Cook, stirring frequently, until vegetables are tender, about 5 minutes.

Stir in salsa and beans. Heat through.

Cut a lengthwise slit in each potato. Push the ends of the potato together to open the potato.

Spoon 3 tablespoons of the broth into each potato. Divide filling evenly and pile into potatoes.

Serve right away.

❖*Serve-again hint:* Heat the leftovers and roll them in a tortilla for a quick burrito, or pile them into taco shells and top with shredded lettuce and chopped tomatoes.

Each serving provides:			
289	Calories	58 g	Carbohydrate
10 g	Protein	1023 mg	Sodium
2 g	Total fat (0 g Sat. fat)	0 mg	Cholesterol

Swiss Spinach Potato

Swiss cheese and spinach, delicately laced with nutmeg, give a baked potato a true gourmet flavor. Instead of butter, milk is spooned over the potato, making it moist and tasty without adding extra fat.

Makes 4 servings

4	medium baking potatoes, 8 or 9 ounces each
3/4	cup skim milk
1	teaspoon onion powder
1	teaspoon Vegetable Broth Mix (page 34)
1/8	teaspoon ground nutmeg
	Salt and pepper
1	10-ounce package frozen chopped spinach, thawed and drained well
2	ounces reduced-fat Swiss cheese, cut into small pieces (1/2 cup)

Bake potatoes according to the directions on page 231.

While potatoes are baking, in a small nonstick skillet, combine milk, broth, and spices. Stir in spinach. Bring to a boil over medium heat, stirring frequently. Remove from heat and stir in cheese.

Cut a lengthwise slit in each potato. Push the ends of the potato together to open the potato.

Divide the spinach mixture evenly and spoon into each potato. Divide any remaining milk and spoon over spinach.

Serve right away.

◆*Quick tip:* In the morning, place the frozen spinach in the refrigerator to thaw and at dinner time, allow yourself the luxury of stopping at the nearest drive-in to pick up the baked potatoes. The rest is easy.

Each serving provides:

243	Calories	44 g	Carbohydrate
13 g	Protein	163 mg	Sodium
3 g	Total fat (1 g Sat. fat)	8 mg	Cholesterol

Luau Potatoes

Unusual, but with a wonderful flavor, this topping brings a new dimension to the baked potato. If you're skeptical, you just have to try this.

Makes 2 servings

2	medium potatoes, 8 or 9 ounces each
1	8-ounce can crushed pineapple (packed in juice), drained (reserve juice)
1/2	cup shredded reduced-fat Cheddar cheese (2 ounces)
3	tablespoons reserved pineapple juice
2	tablespoons finely chopped red bell pepper
2	tablespoons finely chopped green onion (green and white parts)
2	teaspoons reduced-sodium (or regular) soy sauce
1/8	teaspoon garlic powder

Bake potatoes according to the directions on page 231.

While potatoes are baking, combine remaining ingredients, mixing well.

Remove potatoes from oven and increase oven temperature to 375°.

Cut a lengthwise slit in each potato. Push the ends of the potato together to open the potato.

Divide pineapple mixture evenly and pile into each potato. Place potatoes on a baking sheet and place in oven for 5 to 10 minutes, until cheese is melted and topping is hot.

Each serving provides:

323	Calories	57 g	Carbohydrate
15 g	Protein	439 mg	Sodium
5 g	Total fat (4 g Sat. fat)	20 mg	Cholesterol

Tropical Sweet Potatoes and Bananas

Ripe bananas laced with orange and cinnamon add a sweet, tropical flavor to these delectable sweet potatoes. What a perfect match!

Makes 4 servings

4	medium sweet potatoes, 8 or 9 ounces each
2	medium, ripe (yet firm) bananas, cut into 1/4-inch pieces
3	tablespoons frozen orange juice concentrate, thawed
3	tablespoons maple syrup
1/4	teaspoon ground cinnamon
	Dash ground nutmeg

Bake sweet potatoes according to the directions on page 231.

While potatoes are baking, combine remaining ingredients in a small bowl.

Cut a lengthwise slit in each potato. Push the ends of the potato together to open the potato. Divide banana mixture evenly and spoon into potatoes.

◆*Quick tip:* If you put the frozen orange juice concentrate in the refrigerator in the morning, it will be thawed in time for dinner. Use the rest to make juice.

✧*Serve-again hint:* If you have any banana mixture left over, refrigerate it and serve over oatmeal for breakfast.

Each serving provides:

295	Calories		71 g	Carbohydrate
4 g	Protein		25 mg	Sodium
1 g	Total fat (0 g Sat. fat)		0 mg	Cholesterol

Fruit-Filled Sweet Potatoes

Oranges, pineapple, and cinnamon make a perfect topping, heightening the sugary flavor of the potatoes. The fruit juices add moisture, so no margarine is needed. In fact, there's no fat at all added to this filling dinner potato.

Makes 2 servings

2	medium sweet potatoes, 8 or 9 ounces each
1	8-ounce can crushed pineapple (packed in juice), drained (reserve juice)
1	medium orange, peeled and sectioned (discard white membrane)
2	tablespoons reserved pineapple juice
1	tablespoon firmly packed brown sugar
1/2	teaspoon ground cinnamon

Bake sweet potatoes according to the directions on page 231.

While potatoes are baking, combine remaining ingredients, mixing well.

Remove potatoes from oven and increase oven temperature to 375°.

Cut a lengthwise slit in each potato. Push the ends of the potato together to open the potato.

Divide the fruit mixture evenly and pile into each potato. Place potatoes on a baking sheet and place in oven for 10 minutes, until fruit is hot.

Each serving provides:

312	Calories		76 g	Carbohydrate
4 g	Protein		27 mg	Sodium
1 g	Total fat (0 g Sat. fat)		0 mg	Cholesterol

Quickbreads and Muffins

What can I say about quickbreads and muffins, except that they're easy, quick, nutritious, and delicious? The ease comes from the fact that no kneading is necessary. They're quick because they are made with the basic two-bowl method. The dry ingredients go into one bowl, the moist in another, both are mixed together, and baked. More nutritious than most lowfat breads and muffins, these homebaked gems contain wholesome ingredients such as whole grains, fruits, and fruit juices. They're an excellent source of fiber.

Instead of whole eggs, these recipes use only egg whites, thereby eliminating the cholesterol that is found only in the yolks. Several egg replacers are available that will also work. If you wish to eliminate the eggs entirely, a three-ounce piece of soft or medium tofu, blended until smooth, can be used to replace two egg whites or one whole egg.

You need only to break open a tender, hot muffin or spread jam on a slice of warm, freshly baked bread to see for yourself how delicious they are.

Bake extras and keep them in the freezer, where they're just a toaster oven away from becoming a delicious breakfast, lunch, dessert, or snack.

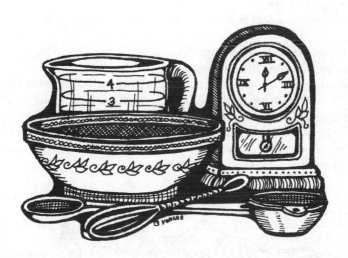

Chocolate-Raisin-Ginger Bread

Sweet enough to be served for dessert, this tangy bread has the terrific taste of chocolate and the sweetness of raisins along with the unmistakable bite of ginger. You'll make this one over and over again.

Makes 10 servings

3/4	cup whole wheat flour
3/4	cup all-purpose flour
1/4	cup cocoa (unsweetened)
1 1/2	teaspoons baking soda
1	tablespoon ground ginger
1	teaspoon ground cinnamon
1/3	cup raisins
1	cup applesauce (unsweetened)
1/4	cup skim milk
1/4	cup molasses
1/4	cup sugar
2	egg whites
2	tablespoons vegetable oil
1	teaspoon vanilla extract
1	teaspoon cider vinegar

Preheat oven to 350°.

Lightly oil a 4 × 8-inch loaf pan or spray with a nonstick cooking spray.

In a large bowl, combine both types of flour, cocoa, baking soda, and spices. Mix well. Stir in raisins.

In another bowl, combine remaining ingredients. Beat with a fork or wire whisk until blended. Add to dry mixture, stirring until all ingredients are moistened. Place in prepared pan.

Bake 45 to 50 minutes, until a toothpick inserted in the center of the bread comes out clean. Cool in pan on a wire rack for 5 minutes, then turn out onto rack to finish cooling.

✧*Serve-again hint:* You can make a stupendous dessert by lining a shallow bowl with the leftovers and topping with vanilla pudding (fat-free, of course), or layering cubes of the bread with pudding in parfait glasses.

Each serving provides:

173	Calories	33 g	Carbohydrate
4 g	Protein	208 mg	Sodium
4 g	Total fat (1 g Sat. fat)	0 mg	Cholesterol

Cinnamon-Raisin Beer Bread

A special thanks to my good friend and talented artist, Vonnie Crist, for her creative idea that led to this unique, sweet version of an easy favorite. It's delicious plain or toasted and is superb with a cup of hot coffee or tea.

Makes 10 servings

Topping
2	tablespoons firmly packed brown sugar
2	tablespoons chopped walnuts
1	teaspoon ground cinnamon

Bread
1¹/₄	cups all-purpose flour
1	cup whole wheat flour
2¹/₂	teaspoons baking powder
¹/₄	cup sugar
¹/₈	teaspoon salt
¹/₃	cup raisins
1	12-ounce can light beer, at room temperature
2	teaspoons vanilla extract

Preheat oven to 375°.

Lightly oil a 4 × 8-inch loaf pan or spray with a nonstick cooking spray.

In a small bowl, combine topping ingredients, mixing well. Set aside.

In a large bowl, combine both types of flour, baking powder, sugar, and salt. Mix well. Stir in raisins.

Add beer and vanilla, stirring until foam subsides and all ingredients are moistened.

Spoon *half* the batter in the prepared pan. Sprinkle evenly with *half* of the topping. Spoon in remaining batter and sprinkle with remaining topping.

Bake 45 minutes, or until a toothpick inserted in the center of the bread comes out clean.

Cool in pan on a wire rack for 5 minutes, then turn out onto rack to finish cooling.

❖*Serve-again hint:* Sliced thin, this bread makes the best peanut butter and jelly or peanut butter and banana sandwich.

Each serving provides:

162	Calories	34 g	Carbohydrate
4 g	Protein	155 mg	Sodium
2 g	Total fat (0 g Sat. fat)	0 mg	Cholesterol

Corn Bread

This basic corn bread can be served as is or used in the delectable Festive Cranberry–Corn Bread Stuffing (page 250). It can also be jazzed up by adding various optional ingredients.

Makes 12 servings

Corn Bread

1	cup yellow cornmeal
1	cup all-purpose flour
2	teaspoons baking powder
1/2	teaspoon salt
2	egg whites
2	tablespoons vegetable oil
2	tablespoons honey
1	cup plus 2 tablespoons skim milk

Optional Ingredients

1	cup of any of the following: finely chopped apples, pears, red and/or green peppers, shredded reduced-fat Cheddar cheese, *or* 2 tablespoons finely chopped jalapeño peppers or olives

Preheat oven to 425° (400° for glass pan).

Lightly oil a 9-inch square baking pan or spray with a nonstick cooking spray.

In a large bowl, combine cornmeal, flour, baking powder, and salt. Mix well.

In another bowl, combine remaining ingredients, including any optional ingredients, if using. Beat with a fork or wire whisk until

blended. Add to dry mixture, stirring just until all ingredients are moistened. Spoon into prepared pan.

Bake 20 minutes, or until a toothpick inserted in the center of the bread comes out clean.

Place pan on a wire rack. Cut into squares and serve warm for best flavor.

Each serving provides:

122	Calories	21 g	Carbohydrate
3 g	Protein	194 mg	Sodium
3 g	Total fat (0 g Sat. fat)	0 mg	Cholesterol

Festive Cranberry–Corn Bread Stuffing

You'll know why I call this stuffing festive when you see all the beautiful colors and textures. It takes a little more time to prepare than most of my recipes; however, my recipe testers urged me to include it, because it can be assembled in advance and simply heated when you're ready.

Makes 12 servings

1	recipe Corn Bread (page 248)
2	cups cranberries, fresh or frozen, coarsely chopped (if using frozen cranberries, there's no need to thaw)
1/4	cup sugar
2	teaspoons vegetable oil
2	cups chopped, peeled sweet potatoes, in 1/4-inch pieces (about 14 ounces)
1	cup chopped onion
1	cup thinly sliced celery
1	cup sliced mushrooms
1	tablespoon parsley flakes
2	teaspoons grated fresh orange peel
1	teaspoon ground ginger
3/4	teaspoon salt
1/4	teaspoon pepper
1	cup vegetable broth, or 1 cup of water and 1 teaspoon Vegetable Broth Mix (page 34)

Coarsely crumble corn bread into a large bowl.

In a small bowl, combine cranberries and sugar. Mix well and set aside.

Heat oil in a large nonstick skillet over medium heat. Add sweet potatoes, onion, celery, and mushrooms. Cook, stirring frequently, until vegetables are tender, about 10 minutes. Add small amounts of water as necessary, about a tablespoon at a time, to keep mixture from sticking.

Remove skillet from heat and sprinkle mixture with parsley flakes, orange peel, ginger, salt, and pepper. Mix well, making sure spices are evenly distributed. Stir in cranberries.

Add corn bread and broth alternately, about a quarter at a time, tossing until mixture is well combined. Add additional broth if necessary to completely moisten stuffing.

At this point, you can refrigerate or freeze the stuffing. This recipe makes a lot, so you may want to freeze half for a later time.

Preheat oven to 375°.

Lightly oil a 1-quart to 3-quart casserole (depending on how much of the stuffing you plan to serve) or spray with a nonstick cooking spray.

Spoon stuffing into prepared casserole.

Bake, covered, 30 minutes, or until heated through (cooking time will take a little longer if stuffing has been refrigerated).

◆*Quick tip:* Prepare the corn bread up to several months ahead and freeze it until needed. You can also purchase it from a bakery, or even use a package mix, but read the ingredients carefully and be sure to note the fat content.

	Each serving provides:		
191	Calories	35 g	Carbohydrate
4 g	Protein	353 mg	Sodium
4 g	Total fat (0 g Sat. fat)	0 mg	Cholesterol

Banana Corn Bread

This wonderful dense bread combines bananas and cornmeal for an unusual twist. It's at its best when served warm, right out of the pan, and it makes a nice light meal when served alongside a large salad.

Makes 12 servings

1	cup yellow cornmeal
1/2	cup all-purpose flour
1/2	cup whole wheat flour
1	tablespoon baking powder
1/2	teaspoon ground allspice
1/2	teaspoon ground cinnamon
2	egg whites
2	tablespoons vegetable oil
1/3	cup skim milk
3	tablespoons honey
1/2	teaspoon vanilla extract
1	teaspoon coconut extract
1	cup mashed, very ripe bananas (2 medium bananas)
2	teaspoons shredded coconut, unsweetened (optional)

Preheat oven to 375°.

Lightly oil an 8-inch square baking pan or spray with a nonstick cooking spray.

In a large bowl, combine cornmeal, both types of flour, baking powder, allspice, and cinnamon. Mix well.

In another bowl, combine egg whites, oil, milk, honey, and extracts. Beat with a fork or wire whisk until blended. Add bananas, beating until mixture is well blended.

Add banana mixture to dry ingredients, mixing just until all ingredients are moistened. Spoon into prepared pan. Sprinkle with coconut, if desired.

Bake 20 to 25 minutes, until a toothpick inserted in the center of the bread comes out clean.

Cool in pan on a wire rack. Cut into squares to serve.

✧*Serve-again hint:* A square of this bread, spread with peanut butter or your favorite jam, makes a quick, nutritious breakfast on the run.

Each serving provides:			
142	Calories	26 g	Carbohydrate
3 g	Protein 1	136 mg	Sodium
3 g	Total fat (0 g Sat. fat)	0 mg	Cholesterol

Orange Surprise Corn Bread

*The orange flavor is only one of the surprises in this unusual variation of a
popular bread. It's slightly sweet and makes a wonderful breakfast bread.*

Makes 12 servings

1	cup yellow cornmeal
2/3	cup all-purpose flour
1/3	cup whole wheat flour
1/4	cup sugar
1	tablespoon baking powder
1 1/2	cups skim milk
2	tablespoons vegetable oil
2	egg whites
1 1/2	teaspoons grated fresh orange peel
1/3	cup chocolate chips or carob chips (mini chips also work well)

Preheat oven to 400°.

Lightly oil an 8-inch square baking pan or spray with a nonstick
cooking spray.

In a large bowl, combine cornmeal, both types of flour, sugar, and
baking powder. Mix well.

In another bowl, combine remaining ingredients, *except* chocolate
chips. Beat with a fork or wire whisk until blended. Add to dry mixture, stirring just until all ingredients are moistened. Stir in chocolate
chips. Spoon mixture into prepared pan.

Bake 20 to 25 minutes, or until a toothpick inserted in the center of
the bread comes out clean.

Place pan on a wire rack. Cut bread into squares and serve warm
for best flavor.

(If you are not serving the bread right away, you can keep it moist by covering the hot bread with aluminum foil until serving time.)

✧*Serve-again hint:* Cut the bread in half horizontally and toast it in an oven or toaster oven until lightly browned. Serve it topped with applesauce and garnished with twists of orange peel.

Each serving provides:

155	Calories	26 g	Carbohydrate
4 g	Protein	148 mg	Sodium
4 g	Total fat (1 g Sat. fat)	1 mg	Cholesterol

Buttermilk Bread with Poppy Seeds and Nuts

This delicately flavored bread is loaded with poppy seeds and nuts and topped with a sweet brown sugar glaze. It's a cozy-time treat to serve with a steamy hot cup of tea.

Makes 10 servings

Bread

1	cup all-purpose flour
3/4	cup whole wheat flour
1 1/2	tablespoons poppy seeds
1	teaspoon baking powder
1/2	teaspoon baking soda
3	tablespoons chopped walnuts
2/3	cup firmly packed brown sugar
1	cup buttermilk
2	egg whites
1	tablespoon vegetable oil
2	teaspoons vanilla extract

Glaze

1/4	cup confectioners' sugar
2	tablespoons firmly packed brown sugar
1 1/2	teaspoons milk
1/8	teaspoon vanilla extract
	Chopped walnuts for garnish (optional)

Preheat oven to 350°.

Lightly oil a 4 × 8-inch loaf pan or spray with a nonstick cooking spray.

In a large bowl, combine both types of flour, poppy seeds, baking powder, and baking soda. Mix well. Stir in nuts.

In another bowl, combine remaining bread ingredients. Beat with a fork or wire whisk until blended. Add to dry mixture, mixing until all ingredients are moistened. Place in prepared pan.

Bake 40 to 45 minutes, until a toothpick inserted in the center of the bread comes out clean. Cool in pan on a wire rack for 5 minutes, then turn out onto rack to finish cooling.

When bread is cool, prepare glaze: In a small bowl, combine both types of sugar. Add milk and vanilla. Mix until you have the consistency of a glaze. (If mixture is too thick, add milk, a few drops at a time, until the desired consistency is reached. If too thin, add a little more confectioners' sugar.) Drizzle glaze over top of bread. Top with additional nuts, if desired.

Note: You can make your own buttermilk by placing 1 tablespoon of vinegar in a measuring cup and adding skim milk to equal 1 cup.

Each serving provides:

208	Calories	38 g	Carbohydrate
5 g	Protein	157 mg	Sodium
4 g	Total fat (1 g Sat. fat)	1 mg	Cholesterol

Lemon Cranberry Loaf

If you love the tangy tingle of lemons and cranberries, you'll love this tasty bread. It's delicious plain or toasted and also makes a great hostess gift.

Makes 10 servings

3/4	cup all-purpose flour
3/4	cup whole wheat flour
2	teaspoons baking powder
1/2	teaspoon baking soda
1/2	teaspoon ground cinnamon
1	cup lemon nonfat yogurt
1/4	cup sugar
2	tablespoons vegetable oil
2	egg whites
2	teaspoons grated fresh lemon peel
1	cup cranberries, coarsely chopped

Preheat oven to 350°.

Lightly oil a 4 × 8-inch loaf pan or spray with a nonstick cooking spray.

In a large bowl, combine both types of flour, baking powder, baking soda, and cinnamon. Mix well.

In another bowl, combine remaining ingredients, *except* cranberries. Beat with a fork or wire whisk until blended. Stir in cranberries. Add to dry mixture, mixing until all ingredients are moistened. Spoon into prepared pan.

Bake 35 minutes, until a toothpick inserted in the center of the bread comes out clean.

Cool in pan on a wire rack for 5 minutes, then turn out onto rack to finish cooling.

Each serving provides:

142	Calories	25 g	Carbohydrate
4 g	Protein	183 mg	Sodium
3 g	Total fat (0 g Sat. fat)	0 mg	Cholesterol

Multigrain Cheese Bread

This tender, moist bread is dotted with cheese and chives and has all of the flavor and nutrition of wheat, oats, and corn. Served warm, it's a perfect accompaniment to a salad and a bowl of soup or chili.

Makes 12 servings

2/3	cup oat bran, uncooked
2/3	cup whole wheat flour
1/3	cup yellow cornmeal
1/4	cup wheat germ
1/2	cup nonfat dry milk
2	teaspoons baking powder
1	teaspoon baking soda
1	teaspoon onion powder
1/4	teaspoon salt
2	cups water
2	tablespoons vegetable oil
3/4	cup shredded reduced-fat Cheddar cheese (3 ounces)
1	tablespoon dried chives

Preheat oven to 350°.

Lightly oil an 8-inch square baking pan or spray with a nonstick cooking spray.

In a large bowl, combine oat bran, flour, cornmeal, wheat germ, dry milk, baking powder, baking soda, onion powder, and salt. Mix well.

Add water and oil. Mix until all ingredients are moistened. (Mixture will be fairly loose.) Let mixture stand 5 minutes. Stir in cheese and chives. Place mixture in prepared pan.

Bake 30 to 35 minutes, until top is set and lightly browned.

Let stand 5 minutes before cutting into squares.

Serve warm for best flavor.

Each serving provides:

113	Calories	14 g	Carbohydrate
6 g	Protein	303 mg	Sodium
5 g	Total fat (1 g Sat. fat)	6 mg	Cholesterol

Toaster Oat Bread

This delicious, high-fiber bread owes its name to the oat flavor that is really enhanced by toasting. It's great with jam or alongside a hearty bowl of soup or stew.

Makes 14 servings

1	cup whole wheat flour
1	cup all-purpose flour
1	cup oat bran, uncooked
1	cup rolled oats
1	tablespoon sugar
2	teaspoons baking powder
1	teaspoon baking soda
1/2	teaspoon salt
1	tablespoon lemon juice
2	cups skim milk
1	tablespoon vegetable oil
1	tablespoon honey

Preheat oven to 375°.

Lightly oil a 5 × 9-inch loaf pan or spray with a nonstick cooking spray.

In a large bowl, combine both types of flour, oat bran, rolled oats, sugar, baking powder, baking soda, and salt. Mix well.

In a small bowl, combine lemon juice and milk. Let stand 1 minute. Stir in oil and honey and add to dry mixture, mixing until all ingredients are moistened.

Place mixture in prepared pan.

Bake 30 to 35 minutes, until top of bread is crusty and brown and a toothpick inserted in the center of the bread comes out clean.

Cool in pan on a wire rack for 5 minutes, then turn out onto rack and cool completely before slicing.

	Each serving provides:		
133	Calories	25 g	Carbohydrate
5 g	Protein	258 mg	Sodium
2 g	Total fat (0 g Sat. fat)	1 mg	Cholesterol

Carrot 'n' Spice Bran Bread

*My Mom came up with this delectable bread, and it is one of our all-time fa-
vorites. Sliced and spread with fat-free cream cheese, it's a perfect breakfast,
snack, or not-too-sweet dessert. You'll find bran available in health food
stores and most grocery stores.*

Makes 12 servings

1¹/₄	cups whole wheat flour
¹/₂	cup all-purpose flour
1	cup bran (wheat bran, not the processed bran cereal)
1	teaspoon baking soda
1¹/₂	teaspoons ground cinnamon
¹/₂	teaspoon ground nutmeg
¹/₈	teaspoon *each* ground allspice and ground cloves
¹/₂	cup raisins
3	tablespoons chopped walnuts
2	egg whites
1	cup plain nonfat yogurt
¹/₂	cup honey
¹/₄	cup skim milk
2	tablespoons vegetable oil
1¹/₂	teaspoons vanilla extract
1	cup finely shredded carrots

Preheat oven to 350°.

Lightly oil a 5 × 9-inch loaf pan or spray with a nonstick cooking
spray.

In a large bowl, combine both types of flour, bran, baking soda,
and spices. Mix well. Stir in raisins and walnuts.

In another bowl, combine remaining ingredients, *except* carrots.
Beat with a fork or wire whisk until blended. Stir in carrots. Add to

dry mixture, mixing until all ingredients are moistened. Place in prepared pan. Smooth the top lightly with the back of a spoon.

Bake 45 to 50 minutes, until a toothpick inserted in the center of the bread comes out clean.

Cool in pan on a wire rack for 5 minutes, then turn out onto rack to finish cooling.

Each serving provides:

191	Calories	36 g	Carbohydrate
5 g	Protein	137 mg	Sodium
4 g	Total fat (1 g Sat. fat)	0 mg	Cholesterol

Honey-Almond Grape Nuts Bread

The crunchy cereal nuggets give this bread a wonderful texture and flavor along with the benefits of a high-fiber, vitamin-rich cereal. It's delicious warm, spread with raspberry jam and fat-free cream cheese.

Makes 12 servings

3/4	cup whole wheat flour
3/4	cup all-purpose flour
2/3	cup Grape Nuts cereal
1	teaspoon baking powder
1	teaspoon baking soda
1 1/2	teaspoons ground cinnamon
1 1/3	cups skim milk
1	tablespoon plus 1 teaspoon lemon juice
2	egg whites
1/4	cup plus 2 tablespoons honey
2	tablespoons vegetable oil
2	teaspoons vanilla extract
1	teaspoon almond extract

Preheat oven to 350°.

Lightly oil a 5 × 9-inch loaf pan or spray with a nonstick cooking spray.

In a large bowl, combine both types of flour, Grape Nuts, baking powder, baking soda, and cinnamon. Mix well.

In another bowl, combine milk and lemon juice. Let stand a few minutes. Add remaining ingredients. Beat with a fork or wire whisk until blended. Add to dry mixture, stirring until all ingredients are moistened. Place in prepared pan.

Bake 35 to 40 minutes, until a toothpick inserted in the center of the bread comes out clean.

Cool in pan on a wire rack for 5 minutes, then turn out onto rack to finish cooling.

Each serving provides:

149	Calories	27 g	Carbohydrate
4 g	Protein	209 mg	Sodium
3 g	Total fat (0 g Sat. fat)	1 mg	Cholesterol

Orange-Ginger-Apple Loaf

Oh so moist, this egg-free, multigrain bread is sweet enough to be served as dessert. One of my recipe testers said she tops it with fat-free cream cheese, reminding her of the steamed brown bread she had as a child. You can find rye flour in most health food stores and many large grocery stores.

Makes 10 servings

1/2	cup whole wheat flour
1/2	cup rye flour
1/2	cup yellow cornmeal
1	teaspoon baking soda
1	teaspoon ground cinnamon
2	teaspoons ground ginger
1/4	teaspoon ground nutmeg
1/3	cup golden raisins
1	cup skim milk
1	tablespoon lemon juice
1/3	cup molasses
2	tablespoons vegetable oil
1	tablespoon firmly packed brown sugar
2	teaspoons grated fresh orange peel
1	teaspoon vanilla extract
1	large Golden Delicious apple, unpeeled, coarsely shredded (1 cup)

Preheat oven to 350°.

Lightly oil a 4 × 8-inch loaf pan or spray with a nonstick cooking spray.

In a large bowl, combine both types of flour, cornmeal, baking soda, and spices. Mix well. Stir in raisins.

In another bowl, combine milk and lemon juice. Let stand a few minutes. Add remaining ingredients, *except* apple. Beat with a fork or wire whisk until blended. Stir in apple. Add to dry mixture, mixing until all ingredients are moistened. Place in prepared pan.

Bake 35 minutes, until a toothpick inserted in the center of the bread comes out clean.

Cool in pan on a wire rack for 5 minutes, then turn out onto rack to finish cooling.

Each serving provides:

160	Calories	30 g	Carbohydrate
3 g	Protein	145 mg	Sodium
4 g	Total fat (0 g Sat. fat)	0 mg	Cholesterol

Chocolate Chip Banana Bread

Chocolate chips (or carob chips) add just the right touch to this delectable bread that's sweet enough to be served for dessert. The addition of maple syrup makes the bread sweet and moist without adding extra fat.

Makes 12 servings

1	cup whole wheat flour
1	cup all-purpose flour
2	teaspoons baking powder
$1/2$	teaspoon ground cinnamon
$1/3$	cup chocolate chips or carob chips (or $1/4$ cup of mini chips)
3	egg whites
$1/2$	cup maple syrup
$1/2$	cup skim milk
$1/4$	cup firmly packed brown sugar
2	tablespoons vegetable oil
1	teaspoon vanilla extract
1	cup mashed, very ripe bananas ($2^{1}/2$ medium bananas)

Preheat oven to 350°.

Lightly oil a 5 × 9-inch loaf pan or spray with a nonstick cooking spray.

In a large bowl, combine both types of flour, baking powder, and cinnamon. Mix well. Stir in chocolate chips.

In another bowl, combine remaining ingredients, *except* bananas. Beat with a fork or wire whisk until blended. Stir in bananas. Add to dry mixture, mixing until all ingredients are moistened. Spoon into prepared pan.

Bake 50 minutes, until a toothpick inserted in the center of the bread comes out clean.

Cool in pan on a wire rack for 5 minutes, then turn out onto rack to finish cooling.

❖*Serve-again hint:* Toast the leftover slices in a toaster oven. Yum.

Each serving provides:

196	Calories	37 g	Carbohydrate
4 g	Protein	104 mg	Sodium
4 g	Total fat (1 g Sat. fat)	0 mg	Cholesterol

Pineapple-Lemon-Nut Bread

Slice this bread and spread with raspberry jam for a taste so sweet, you'll bake this one over and over again. There's no oil in it at all, so I've allowed myself the luxury of adding walnuts. The moistness comes from the crushed pineapple and the orange juice.

Makes 12 servings

1¹/2	cups whole wheat flour
1¹/2	cups all-purpose flour
4¹/2	teaspoons baking powder
¹/2	teaspoon ground cinnamon
¹/3	cup chopped walnuts
³/4	cup orange juice
¹/3	cup sugar
1	8-ounce can crushed pineapple (packed in juice), undrained
2	egg whites
2	teaspoons vanilla extract
2	teaspoons grated fresh lemon peel

Preheat oven to 350°.

Lightly oil a 5 × 9-inch loaf pan or spray with a nonstick cooking spray.

In a large bowl, combine both types of flour, baking powder, and cinnamon. Mix well. Stir in walnuts.

In another bowl, combine remaining ingredients. Beat with a fork or wire whisk until blended. Add to dry mixture, mixing until all ingredients are moistened. Spoon into prepared pan.

Bake 45 to 50 minutes, until a toothpick inserted in the center of the bread comes out clean.

Cool in pan on a wire rack for 5 minutes, then turn out onto rack to finish cooling.

◆*Quick tip:* When lemons are on sale, buy lots and grate them, placing the peel in the freezer. That way, lemon peel is always handy and it can be used without thawing. (Make the Spiced Lemonade Tea on page 462 with the lemon juice and pulp.)

Each serving provides:

179	Calories	34 g	Carbohydrate
5 g	Protein	194 mg	Sodium
3 g	Total fat (0 g Sat. fat)	0 mg	Cholesterol

Apricot Brown Bread

Bits of golden apricots dot this easy version of an old-fashioned bread. There's no oil in it at all, making this moist delicacy almost fat-free. Spread with fat-free cream cheese, it makes a perfect teatime treat.

Makes 12 servings

1	cup whole wheat flour
1	cup all-purpose flour
1^1/$_2$	teaspoons baking soda
1	teaspoon ground cinnamon
^{1}/$_8$	teaspoon salt
^{2}/$_3$	cup chopped, dried apricots
1^1/$_4$	cups skim milk
1	tablespoon vinegar
^{3}/$_4$	cup molasses
2	tablespoons sugar
2	egg whites

Preheat oven to 350°.

Lightly oil a 5 × 9-inch loaf pan or spray with a nonstick cooking spray.

In a large bowl, combine both types of flour, baking soda, cinnamon, and salt. Mix well. Stir in apricots.

In a medium bowl, combine milk and vinegar. Let stand a few minutes. Add remaining ingredients. Beat with a fork or wire whisk until blended. Add to dry mixture. Mix until all ingredients are moistened. Place in prepared pan.

Bake 50 minutes, until a toothpick inserted in the center of the bread comes out clean.

Cool in pan on a wire rack for 5 minutes, then turn out onto rack to finish cooling.

◆*Quick tip:* Use kitchen shears to snip the apricots into small pieces. If you don't have the time, you can buy them already chopped. Golden raisins can be used to substitute all or part of the apricots.

	Each serving provides:		
167	Calories	37 g	Carbohydrate
4 g	Protein	212 mg	Sodium
1 g	Total fat (0 g Sat. fat)	1 mg	Cholesterol

Apple Bran Muffins

As moist as a muffin can be, these high-fiber treats make an ideal, nutrition-packed treat. They're sweet and "cinnamony" and freeze well, too, so you can always be just a toaster away from breakfast or dessert.

Makes 12 muffins

1¹/₄ cups bran (wheat bran, not the processed bran cereal)
1 cup all-purpose flour
²/₃ cup whole wheat flour
2¹/₄ teaspoons ground cinnamon
1¹/₂ teaspoons baking soda
2 cups skim milk
4 teaspoons lemon juice
2 egg whites
¹/₄ cup plus 2 tablespoons molasses
1¹/₂ tablespoons vegetable oil
1¹/₂ teaspoons vanilla extract
1 large, sweet apple, unpeeled, coarsely shredded (1 cup)

Preheat oven to 375°.

Lightly oil 12 muffin cups or spray with a nonstick cooking spray.

In a large bowl, combine bran, both types of flour, cinnamon, and baking soda. Mix well.

In a medium bowl, combine milk and lemon juice. Let stand 1 minute. Add remaining ingredients, *except* apple. Beat with a fork or wire whisk until blended. Stir in apple. Add to dry mixture, mixing until all ingredients are moistened.

Divide mixture evenly into prepared muffin cups.

Bake 20 to 25 minutes, until a toothpick inserted in the center of a muffin comes out clean.

Remove muffins to a rack to cool.

❖*Serve-again hint:* Split a muffin horizontally and spread with peanut butter and jelly for a delicious sandwich that makes a unique breakfast or lunchtime treat.

Each muffin provides:

149	Calories	28 g	Carbohydrate
5 g	Protein	193 mg	Sodium
3 g	Total fat (0 g Sat. fat)	1 mg	Cholesterol

Sticky Bun Muffins

Spoon the nuts and topping in first, add the muffin batter, and when you in-vert the baked muffins, you'll have surprisingly easy sticky buns. They taste best served hot, right from the oven, and they can also be reheated briefly in a microwave.

Makes 12 muffins

Topping

1/4	cup chopped walnuts
2	tablespoons firmly packed brown sugar
2 1/2	tablespoons maple syrup
1	tablespoon soft tub-style (not diet) margarine
1/4	teaspoon ground cinnamon

Muffins

1 1/4	cups all-purpose flour
1	cup whole wheat flour
2	teaspoons baking powder
1/2	teaspoon baking soda
2	teaspoons ground cinnamon
1/2	cup raisins
1	cup vanilla nonfat yogurt
1/3	cup skim milk
2	tablespoons vegetable oil
1/4	cup plus 2 tablespoons firmly packed brown sugar
3	egg whites
1 1/2	teaspoons vanilla extract

Preheat oven to 375°.

Lightly oil 12 muffin cups or spray with a nonstick cooking spray. Divide walnuts evenly and place in muffin cups.

Combine remaining topping ingredients in a small bowl or custard cup, mixing well. Divide evenly and spoon over walnuts in muffin cups (about 1 teaspoon per cup).

In a large bowl, combine both types of flour, baking powder, baking soda, and cinnamon. Mix well. Stir in raisins.

In another bowl, combine remaining ingredients. Beat with a fork or wire whisk until blended. Add to dry mixture, mixing until all ingredients are moistened.

Divide mixture evenly into muffin cups.

Bake 18 to 20 minutes, until a toothpick inserted in the center of a muffin comes out clean.

Cool muffins in pan on a wire rack for 5 minutes, then invert onto rack. Spoon any topping remaining in pan over muffins.

Each muffin provides:

222	Calories	38 g	Carbohydrate
5 g	Protein	183 mg	Sodium
6 g	Total fat (1 g Sat. fat)	1 mg	Cholesterol

Lemon Blueberry Muffins

The flavors of lemon and blueberries complement each other deliciously, so I added a triple dose of lemon to these tender, moist muffins.

Makes 12 muffins

1¹/₄	cups all-purpose flour
1	cup whole wheat flour
2	teaspoons baking powder
1	teaspoon baking soda
1	8-ounce container lemon nonfat yogurt
¹/₃	cup skim milk
2	tablespoons vegetable oil
¹/₄	cup plus 2 tablespoons sugar
3	egg whites
2	teaspoons grated fresh lemon peel
1¹/₂	teaspoons vanilla extract
1	teaspoon lemon extract
1	cup blueberries, fresh or frozen (if using frozen berries, do not thaw)

Preheat oven to 400°.

Lightly oil 12 muffin cups or spray with a nonstick cooking spray.

In a large bowl, combine both types of flour, baking powder, and baking soda. Mix well.

In another bowl, combine remaining ingredients, *except* blueberries. Beat with a fork or wire whisk until blended. Add to dry mixture, mixing until all ingredients are moistened. Stir in blueberries.

Divide mixture evenly into prepared muffin cups.

Bake 15 to 18 minutes, until muffins are golden and a toothpick inserted in the center of a muffin comes out clean.

Remove muffins to a wire rack. Serve warm for best flavor.

◆*Quick tip:* When blueberries are in season, wash them and spread them on a towel to dry, then freeze them in plastic bags so they'll always be ready when you want them.

Each muffin provides:

167	Calories		29 g	Carbohydrate
5 g	Protein		214 mg	Sodium
3 g	Total fat (0 g Sat. fat)		0 mg	Cholesterol

Multigrain Raisin Muffins

These superb, high-fiber muffins are just the right thing to serve with brunch. Serve them hot, pass the jam, and enjoy.

Makes 12 muffins

3/4   cup whole wheat flour
1/4   cup plus 2 tablespoons all-purpose flour
3/4   cup yellow cornmeal
3/4   cup rolled oats, uncooked
1/4   cup wheat germ
2   teaspoons baking powder
1   teaspoon baking soda
1   teaspoon ground cinnamon
1/2   cup raisins
13/4   cups skim milk
1/3   cup firmly packed brown sugar
2   tablespoons vegetable oil
2   egg whites
2   teaspoons vanilla extract

Preheat oven to 400°.

Lightly oil 12 muffin cups or spray with a nonstick cooking spray.

In a large bowl, combine both types of flour, cornmeal, oats, wheat germ, baking powder, baking soda, and cinnamon. Mix well. Stir in raisins.

In another bowl, combine remaining ingredients. Beat with a fork or wire whisk until blended. Add to dry mixture, mixing until all ingredients are moistened. Spoon batter into prepared muffin cups.

Bake 12 minutes, until a toothpick inserted in the center of a muffin comes out clean.

Remove muffins to a wire rack. Serve warm for best flavor.

Each muffin provides:			
186	Calories	33 g	Carbohydrate
6 g	Protein	218 mg	Sodium
4 g	Total fat (1 g Sat. fat)	1 mg	Cholesterol

Orange-Pineapple Muffins

The orange juice concentrate adds a delicious, deep flavor and the crushed pineapple adds just the right texture to these tender muffins.

Makes 12 muffins

Muffins

1¹/₄	cups whole wheat flour
1	cup all-purpose flour
2	teaspoons baking powder
¹/₂	teaspoon baking soda
1¹/₂	teaspoons ground cinnamon
2	egg whites
1	6-ounce can frozen orange juice concentrate, thawed
³/₄	cup skim milk
¹/₃	cup sugar
2	tablespoons vegetable oil
1¹/₂	teaspoons vanilla extract
1	teaspoon grated fresh orange peel
2	8-ounce cans crushed pineapple (packed in juice), drained very well (place pineapple in a large strainer and press out as much juice as possible)

Topping

2	teaspoons sugar
¹/₄	teaspoon ground cinnamon

Preheat oven to 400°.

Lightly oil 12 muffin cups or spray with a nonstick cooking spray.

In a large bowl, combine both types of flour, baking powder, baking soda, and cinnamon. Mix well.

In another bowl, combine remaining muffin ingredients, *except* pineapple. Beat with a fork or wire whisk until blended. Stir in pineapple. Add to dry mixture, mixing until all ingredients are moistened.

Divide mixture evenly into prepared muffin cups.

To make the topping, combine sugar and cinnamon. Sprinkle evenly over muffins.

Bake 18 to 20 minutes, until muffins are golden and a toothpick inserted in the center of a muffin comes out clean.

Remove muffins to a wire rack. Serve warm for best flavor.

Each muffin provides:			
193	Calories	37 g	Carbohydrate
4 g	Protein	153 mg	Sodium
3 g	Total fat (0 g Sat. fat)	0 mg	Cholesterol

Cranberry Oatmeal Muffins

Cranberry sauce provides the moistness for these delicious muffins. Each bite is dotted with juicy little pockets of cranberry sauce.

Makes 12 muffins

1	cup rolled oats
3/4	cup all-purpose flour
1/2	cup whole wheat flour
1	teaspoon baking powder
1/2	teaspoon baking soda
1/2	teaspoon ground cinnamon
1	cup jellied cranberry sauce
1/2	cup orange juice
1/4	cup plus 2 tablespoons honey
2	tablespoons vegetable oil
2	egg whites
1	teaspoon vanilla extract
1/2	teaspoon orange extract

Preheat oven to 400°.

Lightly oil 12 muffin cups or spray with a nonstick cooking spray.

In a large bowl, combine oats, both types of flour, baking powder, baking soda, and cinnamon. Mix well.

In another bowl, combine remaining ingredients. Beat with a fork or wire whisk until blended. Break up any large clumps of cranberry sauce (don't worry about the smaller ones--they will form the nice little pockets of flavor). Add to dry mixture, mixing until all ingredients are moistened.

Divide mixture evenly into prepared muffin cups.

Bake 18 to 20 minutes, until a toothpick inserted in the center of a muffin comes out clean.

Remove muffins to a wire rack. Serve warm for best flavor.

Each muffin provides:

175	Calories	33 g	Carbohydrate
3 g	Protein	110 mg	Sodium
4 g	Total fat (0 g Sat. fat)	0 mg	Cholesterol

Carrot-Raisin Corn Muffins

A spark is added to the traditional corn muffin with the texture of carrots and the sweetness of raisins. These easy, high-fiber favorites are at home with any meal and also make a nutritious after-school snack.

Makes 12 muffins

1	cup yellow cornmeal
1/2	cup all-purpose flour
1/2	cup whole wheat flour
2	teaspoons baking powder
1/4	cup sugar
1/2	teaspoon salt
1 1/2	cups skim milk
2	egg whites
2	tablespoons vegetable oil
1	cup finely shredded carrots
1/2	cup raisins (golden raisins are my first choice)

Preheat oven to 450°.

Lightly oil 12 muffin cups or spray with a nonstick cooking spray.

In a large bowl, combine cornmeal, both types of flour, baking powder, sugar, and salt. Mix well.

In another bowl, combine milk, egg whites, and oil. Beat with a fork or wire whisk until blended. Stir in carrots and raisins. Add to dry mixture, mixing until all ingredients are moistened. Spoon into prepared muffin cups.

Bake 13 to 15 minutes, until a toothpick inserted in the center of a muffin comes out clean.

Remove muffins to a wire rack. Serve warm for best flavor.

❖*Serve-again hint:* Packing a lunch? Peanut butter and jelly sandwiches are far from routine when made with these tender muffins.

Each muffin provides:			
157	Calories	28 g	Carbohydrate
4 g	Protein	202 mg	Sodium
3 g	Total fat (0 g Sat. fat)	1 mg	Cholesterol

Oat Bran–Fruit Muffins

If you're lucky enough to enjoy these muffins as soon as they come out of the oven, you're in for a real treat! Chock-full of fruit and with lots of oat bran, these are an excellent source of fiber.

Makes 12 muffins

2	cups oat bran, uncooked
1/2	cup whole wheat flour
2	teaspoons baking powder
1	teaspoon baking soda
1 1/2	teaspoons ground cinnamon
2/3	cup mixed, chopped dried fruit
3/4	cup skim milk
3/4	cup applesauce, unsweetened
1/4	cup firmly packed brown sugar
2	egg whites
2	tablespoons vegetable oil
1 1/2	teaspoons vanilla extract

Preheat oven to 400°.

Lightly oil 12 muffin cups or spray with a nonstick cooking spray.

In a large bowl, combine oat bran, flour, baking powder, baking soda, and cinnamon. Mix well. Stir in dried fruit.

In another bowl, combine remaining ingredients. Beat with a fork or wire whisk until blended. Add to dry mixture, mixing until all ingredients are moistened.

Divide mixture evenly into prepared muffin cups.

Bake 12 minutes, until a toothpick inserted in the center of a muffin comes out clean.

Remove muffins to a wire rack. Serve warm for best flavor.

Each muffin provides:

138	Calories	27 g	Carbohydrate
5 g	Protein	209 mg	Sodium
4 g	Total fat (1 g Sat. fat)	0 mg	Cholesterol

Surprise Orange-Spice Muffins

The surprise is tomato sauce! It adds moistness, flavor, and a pretty color to these spicy muffins.

Makes 12 muffins

1¹/₄	cups all-purpose flour
1	cup whole wheat flour
2	teaspoons baking powder
¹/₂	teaspoon baking soda
1	teaspoon ground cinnamon
¹/₂	teaspoon ground nutmeg
¹/₄	teaspoon ground cloves
¹/₈	teaspoon ground allspice
¹/₃	cup raisins
1	8-ounce can salt-free tomato sauce
¹/₂	cup orange juice
¹/₂	cup firmly packed brown sugar
2	tablespoons vegetable oil
2	egg whites
1	teaspoon vanilla extract
1	teaspoon orange extract

Preheat oven to 400°.

Lightly oil 12 muffin cups or spray with a nonstick cooking spray.

In a large bowl, combine both types of flour, baking powder, baking soda, and spices. Mix well. Stir in raisins.

In another bowl, combine remaining ingredients. Beat with a fork or wire whisk until blended. Add to dry mixture. Mix until all ingredients are moistened.

Divide mixture evenly into prepared muffin cups.

Bake 15 to 18 minutes, until a toothpick inserted in the center of a muffin comes out clean.

Remove muffins to a wire rack. Serve warm for best flavor.

Each muffin provides:			
173	Calories	32 g	Carbohydrate
4 g	Protein	152 mg	Sodium
3 g	Total fat (0 g Sat. fat)	0 mg	Cholesterol

Brown Sugar and Oat Tea Cakes

I call these tea cakes because they're slightly smaller than large muffins and are just the perfect size to have as a snack with tea. They're sweet and moist and are delicious served warm. Feeling blue? Take two with tea!

Makes 12 muffins

Muffins

1	cup rolled oats, uncooked
2/3	cup whole wheat flour
2/3	cup all-purpose flour
1	tablespoon baking powder
1	cup skim milk
2	egg whites
1/3	cup firmly packed brown sugar
2	tablespoons vegetable oil
1	tablespoon vanilla extract

Topping

2	teaspoons firmly packed brown sugar
1	teaspoon granulated sugar
1/4	teaspoon ground cinnamon

Preheat oven to 425°.

Lightly oil 12 muffin cups or spray with a nonstick cooking spray.

In a large bowl, combine oats, both types of flour, and baking powder. Mix well.

In another bowl, combine remaining muffin ingredients. Beat with a fork or wire whisk until blended. Add to dry mixture, mixing until all ingredients are moistened.

Divide mixture evenly into prepared muffin cups.

Combine topping ingredients and sprinkle evenly over muffins.

Bake 18 minutes, until a toothpick inserted in the center of a muffin comes out clean.

Remove muffins to a wire rack. Serve warm for best flavor.

	Each muffin provides:		
142	Calories	23 g	Carbohydrate
4 g	Protein	145 mg	Sodium
4 g	Total fat (0 g Sat. fat)	0 mg	Cholesterol

Grains

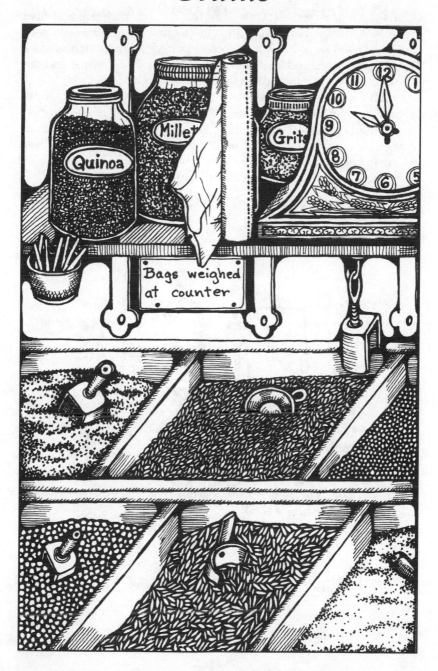

Grains provide a versatile, tasty way to add carbohydrates and fiber to meals. Available year-round and easy to store, they need only to be simmered in water or broth to become a perfect side dish or breakfast. Topped with beans and vegetables, they make a filling entrée and can even become the star ingredient in luscious desserts.

Be adventurous. Try a variety of grains. Start with the more popular ones, such as brown rice, millet, bulgur (cracked wheat), and barley. Visit a health food store and seek out the unusual ones such as triticale, amaranth, and teff. You'll find that each one has its own unique flavor and texture. A whole new world awaits you.

Be sure to read the "All About Grains" section on page 18.

Bulgur Pilaf with Golden Raisins and Ginger

Bulgur cooks quickly, making it a perfect last-minute grain. Combining the sweetness of raisins and crystallized ginger with the savory flavor of onions makes a side dish that goes with almost any entree. Look for bulgur wheat in most large grocery stores.

Makes 6 servings

1 1/2	cups water
1/2	cup orange juice
4	teaspoons Vegetable Broth Mix (page 34)
1	cup bulgur, uncooked
1/4	cup golden raisins
1/3	cup thinly sliced green onions (green and white parts)
1	heaping tablespoon finely chopped crystallized ginger

Combine water, orange juice, and broth mix in a medium saucepan. Bring to a boil. Stir in bulgur, then cover, reduce heat to medium-low, and cook 15 minutes, until liquid has been absorbed.

Fluff bulgur with a fork and stir in remaining ingredients.

Each serving provides:

124	Calories	29 g	Carbohydrate
3 g	Protein	62 mg	Sodium
0 g	Total fat (0 g Sat. fat)	0 mg	Cholesterol

Spiced Bulgur

This quick grain dish is delicious by itself, but it really comes to life when served with an Indian-style entree. For a truly spectacular dinner, serve it topped with the Curried Chickpeas and Spinach (page 141). It's definitely party fare!

Makes 6 servings

2	teaspoons vegetable oil
1/2	cup finely chopped onion
2	cloves garlic, crushed
2	cups water
1	bay leaf
1/4	teaspoon ground cloves
1/8	teaspoon salt
1/8	teaspoon pepper
1	cup bulgur, uncooked

Heat oil in a medium saucepan over medium heat. Add onion and garlic. Cook, stirring frequently, 2 to 3 minutes. Add remaining ingredients, *except* bulgur. Bring mixture to a boil. Stir in bulgur, cover, reduce heat to low, and simmer 15 minutes, until water has been absorbed.

Fluff with a fork before serving. Remove and discard bay leaf.

Note: For a pretty presentation, pack each serving into a half-cup measuring cup and invert it onto the plate.

Each serving provides:

101	Calories	19 g	Carbohydrate
3 g	Protein	51 mg	Sodium
2 g	Total fat (0 g Sat. fat)	0 mg	Cholesterol

Bulgur with Honeyed Apricots and Oranges

This hearty breakfast also travels well in a thermos, so even if you must have breakfast on the go, this one can go with you.

Makes 6 servings

Apricots and Oranges
3/4   cup dried apricots, cut into thin strips (measure after cutting)
1/3   cup boiling water
2   tablespoons honey
1/4   teaspoon vanilla extract
1/8   teaspoon ground cinnamon
2   medium oranges, peeled and sectioned, then cut into 1-inch pieces (discard white membranes)

Bulgur
2 1/4   cups apple juice
1   teaspoon honey
1   teaspoon vanilla extract
1/2   teaspoon ground cinnamon
1/8   teaspoon ground nutmeg
1   cup bulgur, uncooked

In a medium bowl, combine apricots, boiling water, and honey. Stir in vanilla and cinnamon. Stir in oranges. Set aside to soak.

While apricots are soaking, in a medium saucepan, combine apple juice with remaining ingredients, *except* bulgur. Bring to a boil. Stir in bulgur. Reduce heat to medium-low, cover, and simmer 15 minutes.

To serve, spoon the bulgur into serving bowls and top each serving with 1/4 cup of the apricot mixture.

◆*Quick tip:* To make morning preparation easier, cut the apricots and oranges the night before and set out all of the jars of spices.

Each serving provides:

214	Calories	52 g	Carbohydrate
4 g	Protein	9 mg	Sodium
1 g	Total fat (0 g Sat. fat)	0 mg	Cholesterol

Orange Rice Salad with Sesame and Ginger

This delicious salad makes a great addition to a backyard picnic and is also at home on a fancy dinner buffet. The ginger adds a spark to the delicate orange flavor, and the sesame seeds add a special crunch.

Makes 6 servings

2	cups cooked brown rice
3	medium oranges, peeled and sectioned (discard white membranes)
1/2	cup thinly sliced green onions (green and white parts)
1/3	cup golden raisins
1	tablespoon sesame seeds, lightly toasted*
1/3	cup orange juice
1 1/2	tablespoons vegetable oil
2	tablespoons reduced-sodium (or regular) soy sauce
1	teaspoon grated fresh ginger root
1/8	teaspoon sesame oil

In a medium bowl, combine rice, oranges, green onions, raisins, and sesame seeds. Mix gently.

In a small bowl, combine remaining ingredients, mixing well. Pour over rice. Mix gently until well combined.

Chill several hours to blend flavors.

◆*Quick tip:* If you keep leftover cooked rice in the freezer, it will always be handy for recipes such as this one.

*Spread sesame seeds on a sheet of aluminum foil and place in a 325° oven or toaster oven for a few minutes until the seeds are lightly toasted.

Each serving provides:			
183	Calories	33 g	Carbohydrate
3 g	Protein	206 mg	Sodium
5 g	Total fat (1 g Sat. fat)	0 mg	Cholesterol

Fragrant Indian Rice

Basmati rice, with its delectable nutty aroma and firm texture, is perfect for this dish. Check the grain aisle in your supermarket or health food store. It's definitely worth the effort. (Long-grain white rice will also work, but basmati definitely wins in the flavor test.)

Makes 4 servings

2	teaspoons vegetable oil
1	cup onion, sliced vertically into thin slivers
2	large cloves garlic, crushed
1¹/₂	teaspoons grated fresh ginger root
2	cups plus 2 tablespoons water
¹/₃	cup raisins
¹/₂	teaspoon salt
¹/₄	teaspoon ground cardamom
¹/₄	teaspoon ground cinnamon
¹/₄	teaspoon pepper
¹/₈	teaspoon ground cloves
1	cup basmati rice, uncooked

Heat oil in a medium saucepan over medium heat. Add onion. Cook, stirring frequently, 3 minutes. Add garlic and ginger root. Continue to cook, stirring frequently, 3 more minutes. Add small amounts of water as necessary, about a tablespoon at a time, to prevent sticking.

Add water, raisins, salt, and spices. When mixture boils, stir in rice. Cover, reduce heat to medium-low, and cook 20 minutes, until liquid has been absorbed. Remove from heat and let stand, covered, for 5 minutes.

Fluff rice with a fork before serving.

Each serving provides:

231	Calories	50 g	Carbohydrate
6 g	Protein	298 mg	Sodium
3 g	Total Fat (0 g Sat. Fat)	0 mg	Cholesterol

Spiced Raisin Rice

Mildly spiced with a pleasant flavor and aroma, this dish makes a perfect accompaniment to any spicy bean dish. A delicious addition is the burst of sweetness each time you bite into a raisin.

Makes 4 servings

2¹/₂	cups water
¹/₄	cup raisins
2¹/₂	tablespoons minced onion flakes
2	teaspoons parsley flakes
¹/₂	teaspoon ground sage
¹/₄	teaspoon ground cinnamon
1	cup brown rice, uncooked

In a medium saucepan, combine water, raisins, onion flakes, parsley flakes, and spices. Bring to a boil over medium heat.

Add rice. When water boils again, reduce heat to low, cover, and simmer 40 to 45 minutes, until rice is tender and most of the liquid has been absorbed.

Remove from heat, fluff rice with a fork, replace lid, and let stand 5 minutes before serving.

◆*Quick tip:* To cook this dish in a microwave, see "Cooking Brown Rice in the Microwave" on page 20. It only saves about 10 minutes, but it's an easier and neater cooking method.

Each serving provides:

206	Calories	45 g	Carbohydrate
4 g	Protein	5 mg	Sodium
1 g	Total fat (0 g Sat. fat)	0 mg	Cholesterol

Orange Rice Pilaf

The oranges blend well with the onions and lend a delicate sweetness to this unusual rice dish. It's a perfect complement to any entrée.

Makes 4 servings

2	teaspoons vegetable oil
1	cup chopped onion
1¹/₄	cups orange juice
1¹/₄	cups water
1	3-inch cinnamon stick
6	whole cloves
1	cup brown rice, uncooked
2	medium oranges, peeled and sectioned (discard the white membranes)
¹/₄	cup raisins

Heat oil in a medium saucepan over medium heat. Add onion. Cook, stirring frequently, 5 minutes.

Add orange juice, water, cinnamon stick, and cloves. When mixture boils, stir in rice. Cover, reduce heat to medium-low, and simmer 40 to 45 minutes, until rice is tender and most of the liquid has been absorbed.

Remove from heat and stir in orange sections and raisins. Replace lid, and let stand 5 minutes, then fluff rice with a fork. Remove and discard the cinnamon sticks and cloves.

Each serving provides:

304	Calories	64 g	Carbohydrate
5 g	Protein	7 mg	Sodium
4 g	Total fat (1 g Sat. fat)	0 mg	Cholesterol

Risotto Milanese

This classic Italian rice dish has a delightful flavor and a lovely golden color. And, due to the unique qualities of the arborio rice, it has a firm yet creamy texture all its own. It's a bit of a time-consuming dish, because it needs your undivided attention for 20 to 25 minutes, but it's very special and definitely worth the effort. Look for arborio rice in specialty stores and in many large grocery stores.

Makes 6 servings

5	cups vegetable broth, or 5 cups of water and 5 teaspoons Vegetable Broth Mix (page 34)
1/4	teaspoon saffron
2	teaspoons olive oil
1	cup finely chopped onions
1	clove garlic, finely minced
1 1/2	cups arborio rice, uncooked (other types of rice don't work well in this dish)
1/2	cup dry white wine
2	tablespoons grated Parmesan cheese
	Freshly ground black pepper

Bring the broth to a simmer in a medium saucepan over medium heat. Place the saffron in a small bowl or custard cup. Add 1/2 cup of the hot broth and set aside. Keep remaining broth warm over low heat.

Heat oil in a large nonstick skillet over medium heat. Add onions and garlic. Cook, stirring frequently, 3 to 4 minutes, until onions are tender.

Add the rice to the skillet. Cook 1 minute, stirring. Add the wine and cook until most of it is evaporated. Add the saffron in its broth. Then add 1/2 cup of broth and continue cooking, stirring constantly, until the rice has absorbed the liquid. Continue to add broth, 1/2 cup at a time, stirring constantly. Continue to cook and stir for 1 minute after the last addition of broth. The finished consistency should be creamy, yet the texture of the rice should still be firm. (The whole process will take about 20 minutes.)

Remove skillet from heat and stir in Parmesan cheese. Spoon into a serving bowl and top with lots of freshly ground pepper.

Serve right away. (If you can't serve it right away, undercook the dish by 5 minutes; just before serving, complete the cooking process.)

Each serving provides:

226	Calories	46 g	Carbohydrate
5 g	Protein	124 mg	Sodium
2 g	Total fat (1 g Sat. fat)	1 mg	Cholesterol

Broccoli-Millet Timbales

Timbales are made by simply pressing the cooked grain into a large mold or individual molds, then inverting it onto a plate. It's a quick yet elegant side dish that looks like you've fussed for hours.

Makes 4 servings

1 1/2   cups water
1/2   cup millet, uncooked
1   teaspoon vegetable oil
1/2   cup chopped onion
2   cloves garlic, finely minced
1   10-ounce package frozen, chopped broccoli, thawed
1/4   teaspoon salt
1/8   teaspoon pepper
      Grated Parmesan cheese

Lightly oil 4 custard cups or spray with a nonstick cooking spray.

Bring water to a boil in a small saucepan over medium heat. Stir in millet. Cover, reduce heat to medium-low, and cook 20 minutes, or until the water has been absorbed.

While millet is cooking, heat oil in a medium nonstick skillet over medium heat. Add onion and garlic. Cook, stirring frequently, until onion is tender and begins to brown, about 4 to 5 minutes. Add broccoli, salt, and pepper. Cook, stirring frequently, 5 minutes. Remove skillet from heat and stir in cooked millet. Mix well.

Pack mixture firmly into prepared custard cups. Invert onto a serving plate. Sprinkle lightly with Parmesan cheese.

Serve right away.

Each serving provides:

143	Calories	24 g	Carbohydrate
5 g	Protein	154 mg	Sodium
4 g	Total fat (0 g Sat. fat)	0 mg	Cholesterol

Millet with Butternut Squash

This delicious grain and vegetable combo, with its lively color and wonderful texture, adds flair to any entree. It's also a great source of fiber and beta carotene.

Makes 6 servings

1	teaspoon vegetable oil
1/2	cup chopped onion
3	cups vegetable broth, or 3 cups of water and 3 teaspoons Vegetable Broth Mix (page 34)
2	cups butternut squash, peeled, cut into 1/2-inch cubes
1	bay leaf
1/4	teaspoon salt
1	cup millet, uncooked
	Freshly ground black pepper

Heat oil in a medium saucepan over medium heat. Add onion. Cook, stirring frequently, 3 minutes, or until onion is tender and starts to brown. Add small amounts of water as necessary, about a tablespoon at a time, to prevent sticking.

Add broth, squash, bay leaf, and salt. When mixture boils, stir in millet. Reduce heat to medium-low, cover, and simmer 25 minutes, until squash is tender and liquid has been absorbed.

Fluff millet with a fork before serving. Remove and discard bay leaf.

Sprinkle each serving with pepper to taste.

Each serving provides:

168	Calories	33 g	Carbohydrate
5 g	Protein	148 mg	Sodium
2 g	Total fat (0 g Sat. fat)	0 mg	Cholesterol

Cinnamon-Scented Barley with Raspberries

Barley is a nutritious, high-fiber grain that is often forgotten. The puffy little kernels add a unique crunch to this delicious dish that can be served for breakfast, as a snack, or as a not-too-sweet dessert. If you freeze raspberries when they are in season or on special, they'll always be handy when you want them.

Makes 8 servings

1	cup barley, uncooked
4	cups skim milk
1/3	cup sugar
1	teaspoon ground cinnamon
1	teaspoon ground cardamom
2	teaspoons vanilla extract
1	teaspoon almond extract
1	cup raspberries, fresh or frozen (if using frozen berries, choose the ones that are unsweetened or in light syrup and thaw them only enough to be able to separate the berries)

Preheat oven to 350°.

Lightly oil a 9-inch square baking pan or spray with a nonstick cooking spray.

In a medium saucepan, combine barley, milk, sugar, cinnamon, and cardamom. Bring to a boil over medium heat, stirring occasionally. Reduce heat slightly and simmer 5 minutes, stirring frequently. Remove from heat and stir in vanilla and almond extracts.

Place mixture in prepared pan and stir to evenly distribute the barley. Cover tightly with aluminum foil.

Bake 40 to 45 minutes, until most of the milk has been absorbed.

Remove pan from oven and let stand, covered, 10 minutes.

Uncover and stir in raspberries.

Serve warm.

❖*Serve-again hint:* I love it cold, but my family reheats it in the microwave, then pours a little milk over it. It's a great after-school snack.

Each serving provides:

176	Calories	34 g	Carbohydrate
7 g	Protein	67 mg	Sodium
1 g	Total fat (0 g Sat. fat)	2 mg	Cholesterol

Italian Barley with Tomatoes and Cheese

Just throw everything into one pot and let it cook while you prepare the rest of the dinner. Barley takes about 45 minutes to cook, but this plump, high-fiber grain is well worth the wait. Although this is a hearty side dish for four people, the first time I made it, Harry and I ate the whole bowlful as an entree. It's delicious—a lot like pasta.

Makes 4 servings

1	1-pound can salt-free (or regular) tomatoes, chopped, undrained
1	cup water
1	cup finely chopped onion
$1/2$	cup barley, uncooked
1	teaspoon dried oregano
$1/4$	teaspoon garlic powder
$1/8$	teaspoon *each* salt and pepper
2	tablespoons grated Parmesan cheese

In a medium saucepan, combine all ingredients, *except* Parmesan cheese. Bring to a boil over medium heat, stirring occasionally. Reduce heat to medium-low, cover, and simmer 45 minutes, until barley is tender and liquid has been absorbed. Stir several times while cooking. Toward the end of cooking, be sure to stir several times and reduce heat if necessary to prevent sticking.

To serve, spoon barley into a shallow serving bowl. Sprinkle evenly with Parmesan cheese.

❖*Serve-again hint:* Spoon leftovers into hollowed-out tomatoes and heat in a microwave or 350° oven or toaster oven until hot.

Each serving provides:

133	Calories	26 g	Carbohydrate
5 g	Protein	135 mg	Sodium
2 g	Total fat (1 g Sat. fat)	2 mg	Cholesterol

Quinoa with Feta and Mint

Quinoa (pronounced KEEN-wah) is a relatively quick-cooking grain that's very high in protein and an excellent source of minerals. It has a fluffy texture and a light, subtle flavor that make it a great change of pace from rice.

Makes 6 servings

1	teaspoon vegetable oil
1/2	cup finely chopped onion
2	cups vegetable broth, or 2 cups of water and 2 teaspoons Vegetable Broth Mix (page 34)
1	cup quinoa, uncooked
2	ounces feta cheese, rinsed and crumbled (1/3 cup)
2	tablespoons (packed) fresh mint leaves, finely chopped
1/4	teaspoon pepper

Heat oil in a medium saucepan over medium heat. Add onion. Cook, stirring frequently, 3 minutes.

Carefully add broth and bring mixture to a boil. Stir in quinoa, reduce heat to medium-low, cover, and simmer 15 minutes. Remove from heat and let stand 10 minutes without opening lid.

Fluff quinoa with a fork and place in a serving bowl. Stir in feta, mint, and pepper.

✦*Quick tip:* The best way to chop fresh mint is to snip it with kitchen shears. As with any fresh herb, it's also best to snip it just before using.

Each serving provides:

149	Calories	22 g	Carbohydrate
5 g	Protein	160 mg	Sodium
4 g	Total fat (2 g Sat. fat)	8 mg	Cholesterol

Nutty Kasha Pilaf

Kasha (buckwheat groats) is a high-fiber grain with a delectable nutty flavor and aroma. It's available in most large grocery stores and can usually be found in two sizes, or granulations. Look for the smaller size (fine granulation), because it cooks faster than the larger size.

Makes 6 servings

1	teaspoon vegetable oil
1	cup finely chopped onion
1	cup kasha, uncooked
1/4	cup chopped walnuts
2	teaspoons dried parsley flakes
2	teaspoons Vegetable Broth Mix (page 34)
1	teaspoon dried basil
1/4	teaspoon dried thyme
1/4	teaspoon salt
1/8	teaspoon pepper
1/8	teaspoon garlic powder
2 1/2	cups boiling water

Heat oil in a medium nonstick skillet over medium heat. Add onion. Cook, stirring frequently, until onion is tender and begins to brown, about 5 minutes.

Add kasha to skillet. Cook, stirring frequently, until kasha is lightly toasted and fragrant. Reduce heat to medium-low.

Stir walnuts and remaining ingredients into water in a bowl. Carefully stir into skillet. Cover and cook 3 to 5 minutes, until the liquid has been absorbed.

Fluff with a fork before serving.

❖*Serve-again hint:* Leftover kasha makes a delicious filling for turnovers. Simply roll refrigerator biscuits into 4-inch circles, fill with kasha, fold biscuits in half, and crimp the edges. Bake in a 400° oven until golden.

Each serving provides:

169	Calories	29 g	Carbohydrate
5 g	Protein	122 mg	Sodium
5 g	Total fat (0 g Sat. fat)	0 mg	Cholesterol

Tex-Mex Grits

A Southern favorite takes on a brand new flavor in my favorite grits dish. I usually serve it as an accompaniment to a bean dish, but it's also great for brunch. In case you haven't tried grits, it's made from coarsely ground white corn and is a favorite breakfast food in the South.

Makes 6 servings

1¹/₂   cups water (approximately)
1   1-pound can salt-free (or regular) tomatoes, chopped, drained (reserve liquid)
¹/₂   cup quick grits (not the instant variety)
1   teaspoon ground cumin
¹/₄   teaspoon garlic powder
¹/₈   teaspoon pepper
       Salt
¹/₂   cup shredded reduced-fat Cheddar cheese (2 ounces)
¹/₄   cup thinly sliced green onions (green part only)

Add water to reserved tomato liquid to equal 2 cups. Place in a medium saucepan, add tomatoes, and bring to a boil over medium heat.

In a separate bowl, combine grits, cumin, garlic powder, pepper, and salt to taste. Stir into boiling liquid. Reduce heat to medium-low, cover, and cook 5 to 7 minutes, until mixture has thickened. Stir occasionally while cooking.

Remove saucepan from heat, stir in cheese and green onions, cover, and let stand 5 minutes.

Serve hot.

❖*Serve-again hint:* For a quick, change-of-pace breakfast, place leftovers in a bowl, cover, and heat in a microwave. Or, fill a burrito with hot grits and top with salsa.

Each serving provides:			
88	Calories	13 g	Carbohydrate
5 g	Protein	84 mg	Sodium
2 g	Total fat (1 g Sat. fat)	7 mg	Cholesterol

Polenta

Many nationalities have their own version of this cornmeal "pudding." In Italy, it's known as polenta *and is usually served cut into wedges and topped with either tomato sauce or grated cheese. I like it best topped with pasta sauce. Try any of the sauces in the "Pasta and Pasta Sauces" chapter or use a commercial, reduced-fat sauce. This is a nice change of pace from pasta.*

Makes 6 servings

4¹/₂   cups water
1¹/₂   cups yellow cornmeal
¹/₂   teaspoon salt

Lightly oil a 9-inch pie pan or spray with a nonstick cooking spray.

Place 3 cups of the water in a medium saucepan and bring to a boil over medium heat. Place cornmeal and salt in a small bowl and gradually add remaining water. Mix well and stir into boiling water. When water boils again, reduce heat to low and cook, stirring frequently, 25 to 30 minutes, until mixture is very thick. (Italian cooks strongly recommend stirring with a wooden spoon.) Spread mixture evenly in prepared pan.

Let stand for 5 minutes, then invert onto a serving plate, cut into wedges, and serve. Top each serving with your favorite sauce.

◆*Quick tip:* There's a quick-cooking polenta available in most health food stores that greatly reduces the cooking time. Just follow the package directions.

Each serving provides:

133	Calories	27 g	Carbohydrate
3 g	Protein	183 mg	Sodium
1 g	Total fat (0 g Sat. fat)	0 mg	Cholesterol

Savory Grain and Vegetable Casserole

Barley and bulgur, together with lots of veggies, make a delicious side dish casserole with wonderful flavor and texture.

Makes 6 servings

1	cup coarsely shredded carrots
1	cup finely chopped zucchini, unpeeled
1	cup finely chopped mushrooms
1/4	cup finely chopped onion
1/2	cup barley, uncooked
1/4	cup bulgur, uncooked
1 1/2	cups vegetable broth, or 1 1/2 cups of water and 1 1/2 teaspoons Vegetable Broth Mix (page 34)
1/4	teaspoon garlic powder
1/4	teaspoon salt
1/8	to 1/4 teaspoon pepper
1/2	cup shredded reduced-fat Cheddar cheese (2 ounces)

Preheat oven to 350°.

Lightly oil a 1 3/4-quart casserole or spray with a nonstick cooking spray.

Combine vegetables and grains in prepared casserole. Stir in broth and spices.

Cover tightly and bake 1 hour, stirring once halfway through cooking time.

Fluff with a fork, add cheese and toss.

❖*Serve-again hint:* Fill scooped-out tomatoes with leftover grains. Heat and serve.

Each serving provides:

129	Calories	20 g	Carbohydrate
6 g	Protein	201 mg	Sodium
3 g	Total fat (1 g Sat. fat)	7 mg	Cholesterol

Breakfast Grains with Apples and Grapes

Grains aren't just for dinner. They make a very nutritious and filling high-fiber breakfast. So, dig your Crock-Pot out of the basement and treat your family members to a delicious hot breakfast that's ready when they are. And, boy the house smells good!

Makes 6 servings

1/4	cup barley, uncooked
1/4	cup bulgur, uncooked
1/4	cup brown rice, uncooked
1/4	cup millet, uncooked
2	cups water
1	cup apple juice
1	medium Golden Delicious apple, unpeeled, chopped (1 cup)
1	cup seedless red grapes, cut in half (measure *after* cutting)
1	teaspoon ground cinnamon
1	teaspoon vanilla extract
	Maple syrup or brown sugar

Combine all ingredients, *except* maple syrup, in a Crock-Pot. Mix well.

Cover and cook on low setting 7 to 8 hours. Stir before serving. If a thinner consistency is desired, stir in a little water or apple juice.

Drizzle each serving with maple syrup or sprinkle with brown sugar. Sprinkle with additional cinnamon if desired.

✧*Serve-again hint:* Leftovers can be reheated quickly in a micro-wave, making this a great way for a small family to enjoy a hot break-fast for several days.

Each serving provides:

160	Calories	35 g	Carbohydrate
3 g	Protein	5 mg	Sodium
1 g	Total fat (0 g Sat. fat)	0 mg	Cholesterol

Vegetable Side Dishes

Vegetables, packed with vitamins, minerals, and fiber, are absolutely essential to a healthful, balanced diet. Health professionals recommend that we include a wide variety of vegetables in our diet, allowing us to benefit from the different nutrients that each one has to offer. If you are one of the many people who tend to prepare the same few vegetables over and over again, this section contains lots of easy recipes that will help you break out of the rut and explore the delicious world of vegetables.

When cooking vegetables, it is best to cook them until just tender-crisp and, for added fiber, to leave the skin on whenever possible. It is also important, in recipes that call for cooking vegetables in oil, to use a minimal amount of oil and to choose a monounsaturated oil such as canola oil or olive oil. When sautéing vegetables, a nonstick skillet is best, allowing you to keep the use of oil to a minimum.

Even though these recipes are for side dishes, it is possible to break out of the mold and create a delicious, healthful meal consisting entirely of an array of side dishes. We really don't need an entree such as that giant cut of meat that used to take center seat in the typical American meal.

Enjoy the vast array of flavors and textures that vegetables have to offer. For more information, read "All About Fruits and Vegetables" on page 21.

Stir-Fried Asparagus with Garlic and Ginger

This easy stir-fry really showcases the best qualities of fresh asparagus.

Makes 4 servings

2   tablespoons reduced-sodium (or regular) soy sauce
1¹/₂   teaspoons grated fresh ginger root
1   large clove garlic, crushed
2   teaspoons sesame oil
1   pound asparagus, cut diagonally into 1¹/₂-inch to 2-inch pieces, ends trimmed
2   tablespoons water

Combine soy sauce, ginger root, and garlic in a small bowl or custard cup.

Heat oil in a large skillet over medium-high heat. Add asparagus and soy mixture. Cook, stirring constantly, 3 minutes.

Reduce heat to medium, stir in water, cover, and steam 2 to 3 minutes, until asparagus is just tender-crisp.

Each serving provides:

47	Calories	5 g	Carbohydrate
3 g	Protein	302 mg	Sodium
2 g	Total fat (0 g Sat. fat)	0 mg	Cholesterol

Lemon-Parmesan Green Beans with Peppers

So simple and yet so delicious, this festive dish is right at home at a family meal or even at the fanciest of dinner parties.

Makes 4 servings

1	pound green beans, ends trimmed and strings removed
1	yellow or red bell pepper, cut vertically into 1/4-inch strips
1	tablespoon grated Parmesan cheese
1	teaspoon grated fresh lemon peel
1/4	teaspoon garlic powder
	Salt and pepper

Place a steamer rack in the bottom of a medium saucepan. Add enough water to come almost up to the bottom of the rack. Place saucepan over medium heat. When water boils, add green beans, cover saucepan, and cook 10 minutes. Add peppers and continue to cook 10 more minutes, or until green beans are tender.

Transfer beans and peppers to a serving bowl. Sprinkle evenly with remaining ingredients. Toss and serve.

◆*Quick tip:* Beans and peppers can be cut a day ahead and stored overnight in a plastic bag in the refrigerator.

Each serving provides:

43	Calories	9 g	Carbohydrate
3 g	Protein	30 mg	Sodium
1 g	Total fat (0 g Sat. fat)	1 mg	Cholesterol

Herbed Green Beans and Tomatoes

Fresh green beans and ripe, red tomatoes are a perfect backdrop for the herbs in this easy vegetable combo. It's a great dish for a summer barbecue, when vegetables are at their best.

Makes 6 servings

1	pound green beans, ends trimmed and strings removed
1	teaspoon dried basil
1	teaspoon dried oregano
1/2	teaspoon garlic powder
2	large, ripe tomatoes, coarsely chopped (about 2 cups)

Place a steamer rack in the bottom of a medium saucepan. Add enough water to come almost up to the bottom of the rack. Place saucepan over medium heat. When water boils, add green beans, cover saucepan, and cook 10 to 15 minutes, or until green beans are just tender (the length of cooking time will depend on the size and age of the beans). Drain. Remove steamer rack and discard cooking water.

Return beans to saucepan. Sprinkle with basil, oregano, and garlic powder. Stir to evenly distribute the herbs. Add tomatoes. Mix well.

Cover saucepan and heat over medium-low heat 5 minutes, or until hot.

❖*Serve-again hint:* Toss the leftovers with a small amount of reduced-fat Italian dressing and chill to make a delicious cold bean salad.

Each serving provides:			
35	Calories	8 g	Carbohydrate
2 g	Protein	10 mg	Sodium
0 g	Total fat (0 g Sat. fat)	0 mg	Cholesterol

Broccoli with Orange Dijonette

Dijonette is my own fancy word for Dijon vinaigrette. In this unique side dish, the broccoli is stir-fried and then quickly glazed with the tangy orange sauce. It adds a bright spark to any meal.

Makes 4 servings

1/3	cup orange juice
2	tablespoons red wine vinegar
1	tablespoon Dijon mustard
2	teaspoons cornstarch
1/2	teaspoon sugar
2	teaspoons vegetable oil
4	cups broccoli, cut into small flowerets

In a small bowl, combine orange juice, vinegar, mustard, cornstarch, and sugar. Mix until cornstarch is dissolved and mixture is smooth. Set aside.

Heat oil in a large nonstick skillet over medium heat. Add broccoli. Cook, stirring frequently, until broccoli is bright green, about 3 minutes.

Stir orange juice mixture and pour over broccoli. Cook, stirring, for about 30 seconds, until broccoli is evenly coated and sauce is thick.

Each serving provides:

81	Calories	11 g	Carbohydrate
5 g	Protein	121 mg	Sodium
3 g	Total fat (0 g Sat. fat)	0 mg	Cholesterol

Broccoli with Creamy Mustard Cheese Sauce

The scrumptious cheese sauce can also be used to top other veggies, such as cauliflower or Brussels sprouts, and it is wonderful over a baked potato.

Makes 6 servings
(3 tablespoons cheese sauce each serving)

6	cups broccoli flowerets
2	tablespoons all-purpose flour
2	tablespoons water
1	cup evaporated skim milk
2	tablespoons grated onion
1	tablespoon prepared yellow mustard
1	teaspoon prepared horseradish
1/2	cup shredded reduced-fat Cheddar cheese (2 ounces)
	Salt and pepper

Place a steamer rack in the bottom of a medium saucepan. Add enough water to come almost up to the bottom of the rack. Place saucepan over medium heat. When water boils, add broccoli, cover saucepan, and cook 8 to 10 minutes, or until broccoli is tender-crisp (length of cooking time will depend on the size of the flowerets). Drain.

While broccoli is cooking, place flour in a small saucepan. Gradually stir in water, mixing briskly to avoid lumps. Then gradually stir in milk, onion, and mustard. Cook, stirring constantly, until mixture comes to a boil. Continue to cook 1 to 2 minutes, until mixture has thickened and is hot and bubbly. Remove from heat and stir in horseradish, cheese, and salt and pepper to taste. (If a thinner sauce is desired, stir a little more milk into the sauce.)

Spoon over broccoli.

❖*Serve-again hint:* If you have cheese sauce left over, make a simple meal consisting of a salad and baked potatoes. Reheat the sauce and spoon it over the potatoes and sprinkle with fresh or dried chives.

	Each serving provides:		
112	Calories	15 g	Carbohydrate
11 g	Protein	187 mg	Sodium
2 g	Total fat (1 g Sat. fat)	8 mg	Cholesterol

Broiled Tomatoes Dijon

Broiled tomatoes make a nice extra accompaniment to almost any meal. They're easy to prepare and can even be made on the broiler cycle of a toaster oven—quickly and with very little fuss.

Makes 4 servings

2	teaspoons Dijon mustard
2	large, ripe tomatoes, cut in half crosswise (preferably at room temperature)
1	tablespoon dry bread crumbs
1	teaspoon grated Parmesan cheese
1/4	teaspoon dried basil
1/4	teaspoon dried oregano
	Salt and pepper
	Nonstick cooking spray

Spread 1/2 teaspoon of mustard on the cut side of each tomato half.

In a small bowl or custard cup, combine remaining ingredients, except nonstick cooking spray. Mix well and sprinkle evenly over tomatoes. Spray tomatoes lightly with nonstick cooking spray.

Broil 5 to 7 minutes, until tops of tomatoes are nicely browned. (Watch them carefully to prevent burning.)

Serve hot.

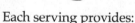

Each serving provides:

32	Calories		6 g	Carbohydrate
1 g	Protein		91 mg	Sodium
1 g	Total fat (0 g Sat. fat)		0 mg	Cholesterol

Swiss Chard with Garlic

One of my favorite greens, this quick-cooking vegetable is greatly enhanced by the flavor of garlic and the splash of soy sauce. It looks like a huge mountain of raw greens at first, but it cooks down dramatically.

Makes 4 servings

1½	pounds Swiss chard
2	teaspoons vegetable oil
6	to 8 cloves garlic, finely chopped
2	teaspoons soy sauce

Wash Swiss chard and remove the stems and large center veins. Tear each leaf into 3 to 4 pieces. (The water clinging to the leaves will aid in cooking.)

Heat oil in a large nonstick skillet or wok over medium-high heat. Add garlic. Cook 30 seconds. Add *half* of the Swiss chard, tossing it with the garlic. Add remaining greens and soy sauce and toss. Cover and cook 1 minute. Toss greens one more time and add a few tablespoons of water if mixture is too dry or if greens are sticking to the pan. Cover and cook 1 to 2 minutes more, until greens are tender.

Each serving provides:

59	Calories	8 g	Carbohydrate
3 g	Protein	506 mg	Sodium
3 g	Total fat (0 g Sat. fat)	0 mg	Cholesterol

Carrots and Apricots

Shredded carrots only need to cook for a few minutes. In this easy sauté, apricots lend a wonderful sweet flavor and blend deliciously with the carrots and onion.

Makes 4 servings

2	teaspoons vegetable oil
1	large onion, cut vertically into thin slivers
1	pound carrots, coarsely shredded
1/2	cup dried apricot halves, cut into thin strips (measure after cutting)
1/2	cup vegetable broth, or 1/2 cup of water and 1/2 teaspoon Vegetable Broth Mix (page 34)
1	teaspoon red wine vinegar
	Salt and pepper

Heat oil in a large nonstick skillet over medium heat. Add onion. Cook, stirring frequently, until onion is nicely browned, about 8 minutes.

Add carrots and apricots. Cook, stirring constantly, 2 minutes.

Stir in broth, reduce heat slightly, cover, and cook 5 minutes. Uncover and continue to cook for 1 to 2 minutes, stirring several times.

Stir in vinegar. Add salt and pepper to taste.

♦*Quick tip:* To make the preparation time quicker, shred the carrots in a food processor and cut the apricots with kitchen shears.

Each serving provides:

132	Calories	27 g	Carbohydrate
2 g	Protein	57 mg	Sodium
3 g	Total fat (0 g Sat. fat)	0 mg	Cholesterol

Gingered Carrots

These carrots, simmered in orange juice and spices, add an exotic touch to any meal. Kids like this dish because it's sweet. It's also nutritious, packed with beta carotene and vitamin C.

Makes 4 servings

2	cups carrots, sliced diagonally into 1/4-inch slices
2/3	cup orange juice
1/3	cup water
1/4	cup sugar or honey
1	teaspoon Vegetable Broth Mix (page 34)
1/2	teaspoon ground ginger
1/2	teaspoon grated fresh lemon peel
5	whole cloves

In a small saucepan, combine all ingredients. Bring to a boil over medium heat. Cook, stirring occasionally, until carrots are tender, about 30 minutes.

Remove and discard cloves before serving.

✦*Quick tip:* Frozen sliced carrots will also work.

✧*Serve-again hint:* Leftovers are good cold and can be eaten alone or spooned over lowfat cottage cheese.

Each serving provides:

93	Calories	23 g	Carbohydrate
1 g	Protein	40 mg	Sodium
1 g	Total fat (0 g Sat. fat)	0 mg	Cholesterol

Savory Carrot Casserole with Peas

Old-fashioned peas and carrots were never like this! Bright green peas dot the casserole, making this a festive as well as very tasty dish. The preparation is quick, however, the casserole bakes for an hour, so put it in the oven first; by the time you prepare the meal and eat your salad, it will be ready.

Makes 6 servings

1	pound carrots, grated or finely shredded
1	small onion, grated
1/3	cup all-purpose flour
1/2	cup water
2	egg whites
2	tablespoons dry sherry
1	teaspoon Vegetable Broth Mix (page 34)
1/8	teaspoon pepper
1	cup frozen peas

Preheat oven to 375°.

Lightly oil an 8-inch square baking pan or spray with a nonstick cooking spray.

In a large bowl, combine carrots, onion, and flour. Mix well.

In a small bowl, combine remaining ingredients, *except* peas. Beat with a fork or wire whisk until blended. Add to carrots, mixing well. Stir in peas.

Spoon mixture into prepared pan. Smooth the top with the back of a spoon.

Cover and bake 20 minutes.

Uncover and continue to bake 40 minutes more.

✦*Quick tip:* A food processor, using the steel blade, grates the carrot and onion in no time.

Each serving provides:

97	Calories	18 g	Carbohydrate
4 g	Protein	86 mg	Sodium
1 g	Total fat (0 g Sat. fat)	0 mg	Cholesterol

Orange-Ginger Mushrooms

Sautéing mushrooms in orange juice, with garlic and ginger, infuses them with the flavors of the Orient.

Makes 4 servings

1/3   cup orange juice
2   tablespoons reduced-sodium (or regular) soy sauce
1/2   teaspoon grated fresh orange peel
1/4   teaspoon garlic powder
1/4   teaspoon ground ginger
12   ounces mushrooms, sliced (about 4 cups)

In a large nonstick skillet, combine all ingredients *except* mushrooms. Mix well and bring to a boil over medium-high heat. Add mushrooms.

Cook, stirring frequently, until most of the liquid has cooked out, about 7 to 8 minutes.

◆*Quick tip:* Look for sliced mushrooms in packages or at the salad bar in most large grocery stores.

✧*Serve-again hint:* The refrigerated leftovers are delicious in a sandwich or a salad.

Each serving provides:

36	Calories	7 g	Carbohydrate
2 g	Protein	304 mg	Sodium
0 g	Total fat (0 g Sat. fat)	0 mg	Cholesterol

Baked Mushroom Packets

Just season the mushrooms, seal the foil, and bake. This easy dish is perfect to serve with baked potatoes. Everything can go directly on the oven rack at the same temperature, and there are no pots to wash. To serve two or three people, just cut the recipe in half and make one packet.

Makes 6 servings

1	pound mushrooms, ends of stems trimmed
2	tablespoons very finely minced onion
2	teaspoons dried parsley flakes
1/4	teaspoon salt
1/8	teaspoon pepper
1	tablespoon dry sherry

Preheat oven to 350°.

Cut two 15-inch sheets of aluminum foil.

Place half the mushrooms in the center of each piece of foil. Sprinkle evenly with onion, parsley flakes, salt, and pepper. Drizzle sherry over mushrooms.

Bring the edges of the foil up over the mushrooms, fold, and seal. (Make sure all of your seams are on the top of the packet, to prevent leaking.) Place packets directly on oven rack.

Bake 40 minutes.

❖*Serve-again hint:* Leftovers make a great topping for veggie burgers or a gourmet addition to a cracker topped with fat-free cream cheese.

Each serving provides:

20	Calories	4 g	Carbohydrate
2 g	Protein	93 mg	Sodium
0 g	Total fat (0 g Sat. fat)	0 mg	Cholesterol

Zucchini in Tomato-Basil Sauce

When my Mom and I fell in love with this dish in a restaurant, we came home determined to re-create it. This is our delicious version. It's quick and easy and makes good use of those abundant summer zucchini.

Makes 6 servings

2	teaspoons olive oil
1	cup chopped onion
3	cloves garlic, finely chopped
1	1-pound can salt-free (or regular) tomatoes, chopped, undrained
1	8-ounce can salt-free (or regular) tomato sauce
1	tablespoon sugar
2	teaspoons dried basil
1	teaspoon Vegetable Broth Mix (page 34)
	Salt and pepper
3	medium zucchini, unpeeled, sliced crosswise into 1/4-inch slices (4 cups)

Heat oil in a large saucepan over medium heat. Add onion and garlic. Cook 5 minutes, stirring frequently.

Add remaining ingredients, *except* zucchini. When mixture boils, reduce heat slightly and simmer, uncovered, 10 minutes, stirring occasionally.

Add zucchini. When mixture returns to a boil, cover and simmer 10 to 12 minutes, stirring several times, until zucchini is tender-crisp.

❖*Serve-again hint:* Add the leftovers to vegetable broth, and you have a delicious soup.

Each serving provides:

76	Calories	14 g	Carbohydrate
3 g	Protein	35 mg	Sodium
2 g	Total fat (0 g Sat. fat)	0 mg	Cholesterol

Creamy Yellow Squash with Basil

One of my favorite uses for yellow summer squash, this delicious dish is ready in minutes. It's rich and creamy and makes a great side dish any time of the year.

Makes 4 servings

1/4	cup plain nonfat yogurt
1	teaspoon grated Parmesan cheese
1	pound yellow summer squash (2 medium squash), unpeeled, coarsely shredded (about 4 cups)
2	teaspoons vegetable oil
1 1/2	teaspoons dried basil
1/4	teaspoon garlic powder
1/4	teaspoon salt
1/8	teaspoon pepper
2	teaspoons all-purpose flour

In a small bowl, combine yogurt and Parmesan cheese. Mix well and set aside.

In a large bowl, combine squash, oil, and spices. Mix well.

Heat a medium nonstick skillet over medium heat. Add squash mixture, cover, and cook 5 minutes, stirring occasionally. Uncover and sprinkle flour over squash. Continue to cook, stirring constantly, 2 to 3 more minutes, or until all liquid has cooked out.

Place squash in a serving bowl and stir in yogurt mixture.

Serve right away.

❖*Serve-again hint:* The reheated leftovers make a delectable topping for baked potatoes.

Each serving provides:

58	Calories	7 g	Carbohydrate
2 g	Protein	156 mg	Sodium
3 g	Total fat (0 g Sat. fat)	1 mg	Cholesterol

Green and Gold Squash Casserole

This savory pudding-like dish of zucchini and yellow squash is right at home for family dinners, and it also goes well on a fancy buffet table.

Makes 9 servings

2	teaspoons vegetable oil
1	cup onion, sliced vertically into thin slivers
2	medium zucchini (12 ounces total), unpeeled, cut into 1/2-inch pieces
2	medium yellow summer squash (12 ounces total), unpeeled, cut into 1/2-inch pieces
1/4	cup all-purpose flour
1/4	cup yellow cornmeal
1	teaspoon baking powder
3/4	teaspoon garlic powder
1/2	teaspoon salt
1/8	teaspoon pepper, or more to taste
3/4	cup evaporated skim milk
2	egg whites
1	tablespoon Dijon mustard
3/4	cup shredded reduced-fat Cheddar cheese (3 ounces)

Heat oil in a large nonstick skillet over medium-high heat. Add onion, zucchini, and yellow squash. Cook, stirring frequently, until vegetables are tender, about 8 minutes.

Preheat oven to 350°.

Lightly oil an 8-inch square baking pan or spray with a nonstick cooking spray.

In a large bowl, combine flour, cornmeal, baking powder, garlic powder, salt, and pepper. Mix well.

In a small bowl, combine milk, egg whites, and mustard. Beat with a fork or wire whisk until blended. Stir in cheese. Add to dry mixture,

mixing until all ingredients are moistened. Stir in zucchini mixture. Spoon into prepared pan.

Bake, uncovered, 30 to 35 minutes, until lightly browned.

Cut into squares to serve.

✧*Serve-again hint:* Reheat leftovers and top with meatless spaghetti sauce. It can easily serve as a light entree.

Each serving provides:

109	Calories	13 g	Carbohydrate
7 g	Protein	328 mg	Sodium
3 g	Total fat (1 g Sat. fat)	8 mg	Cholesterol

Cabbage and Red Pepper
with Sweet 'n' Sour Sauce

In this easy side dish, the sauce can be made in minutes while the cabbage steams. It's a brand new way to enjoy cabbage, which is a very nutritious vegetable.

Makes 6 servings

Vegetables

1	medium (2 pound) cabbage, cut into 6 wedges (cut the cabbage vertically through the core; do not remove the core, as it will keep the cabbage from falling apart)
1	large red bell pepper, cut into 1/2-inch strips

Sauce

1/3	cup firmly packed brown sugar
1/4	cup water
1	tablespoon cornstarch
1/4	cup red wine vinegar
2	teaspoons reduced-sodium (or regular) soy sauce
1	teaspoon Vegetable Broth Mix (page 34)
1/4	teaspoon garlic powder
1/8	teaspoon ground ginger

Place a steamer rack in the bottom of a large saucepan. Add enough water to come almost up to the bottom of the rack. Place saucepan over medium heat. When water boils, add cabbage, cover saucepan, and cook 5 minutes. Add red pepper, cover, and continue to cook 10 minutes more, or until cabbage is tender.

While vegetables are cooking, combine all sauce ingredients in a small saucepan. Stir to dissolve cornstarch. Bring mixture to a boil over medium heat, stirring constantly. Continue to cook, stirring, 1 minute.

To serve, place a cabbage wedge and a few red pepper strips on each plate and top with the sauce. (Each person will get about one tablespoon plus one teaspoon of the sauce.)

✧*Serve-again hint:* The cabbage reheats quickly in a microwave, and so does the sauce.

Each serving provides:

95	Calories	23 g	Carbohydrate
2 g	Protein	113 mg	Sodium
0 g	Total fat (0 g Sat. fat)	0 mg	Cholesterol

Cheesy Cauliflower

Easier than preparing a cheese sauce and much, much lower in fat, this quick dish turns cauliflower into an elegant affair.

Makes 6 servings

4   cups cauliflower, cut into small flowerets
³/₄   cup shredded reduced-fat Swiss *or* Cheddar cheese (3 ounces)
        Salt and pepper
1   tablespoon Italian-style bread crumbs

Place a steamer rack in the bottom of a medium saucepan. Add enough water to come almost up to the bottom of the rack. Place saucepan over medium heat. When water boils, add cauliflower, cover saucepan, and cook 8 to 10 minutes, or until cauliflower is tender-crisp. Drain.

Place cauliflower in a shallow serving bowl and sprinkle with cheese, salt, and pepper. Toss gently. Sprinkle with bread crumbs and serve.

✧*Serve-again hint:* To make a nutritious lunch, fill a whole wheat pita with the leftovers, add a little Dijon mustard, wrap the sandwich in foil, and heat in a microwave or toaster oven.

Each serving provides:

61	Calories	5 g	Carbohydrate
5 g	Protein	103 mg	Sodium
3 g	Total fat (2 g Sat. fat)	6 mg	Cholesterol

Sesame Cabbage Stir-Fry

Cabbage is often neglected as a side dish. Other than in cole slaw, many people forget how delicious this crunchy vegetable can be. In this dish, the touch of hoisin sauce (available in Asian food stores and in the imported foods section of many large supermarkets) at the end really adds a lively spark to this versatile vegetable.

Makes 6 servings

1	teaspoon vegetable oil
1	teaspoon sesame oil
2	cloves garlic, crushed
1	teaspoon grated fresh ginger root
5	cups finely shredded cabbage (about 1 1/4 pounds)
2	teaspoons sesame seeds
2	tablespoons hoisin sauce
	Pepper

Heat both oils in a large nonstick skillet over medium-high heat. Add garlic and ginger root. Cook 10 seconds.

Add cabbage and sesame seeds to skillet. Mix well, distributing the garlic and ginger root throughout the mixture. Cook, stirring constantly with a tossing motion, 3 to 4 minutes, or until cabbage starts to brown. Remove from heat and place cabbage in a serving bowl. Add hoisin sauce and mix well. Sprinkle with pepper to taste.

◆*Quick tip:* Many large grocery stores carry ready-to-use bags of shredded cabbage. They can really make life easy.

Each serving provides:

59	Calories	9 g	Carbohydrate
1 g	Protein	112 mg	Sodium
2 g	Total fat (0 g Sat. fat)	0 mg	Cholesterol

Stir-Fried Jicama and Peppers

If you haven't tried jicama (HEE-kah-mah), here's a perfect way to take the plunge (also see the recipe for Southwest Jicama Salad in the "Salads and Salad Dressings" chapter). It has a delicate flavor and crunchy texture similar to water chestnuts. It's often eaten raw, in salads and for dipping, and it makes a wonderful addition to any stir-fried dish. Look for jicama in the produce section of most large grocery stores.

Makes 6 servings

2	teaspoons vegetable oil
1/2	cup onion, sliced vertically into thin slivers
2	medium, red or yellow bell peppers, cut into thin strips
1	jicama (about 1/2 pound), peeled, cut into 2 × 1/4 × 1/2-inch strips
11/2	teaspoons grated fresh ginger root
3	cloves garlic, finely chopped
2	tablespoons reduced-sodium (or regular) soy sauce
1	teaspoon sugar
1/2	teaspoon sesame oil

Heat oil in a large nonstick skillet over medium-high heat. Add onion, peppers, jicama, ginger root, and garlic. Cook, stirring constantly with a tossing motion, 2 minutes.

Add soy sauce and sugar. Continue to cook, stirring constantly, for 2 more minutes, or until vegetables are just tender-crisp.

Remove from heat and sprinkle with sesame oil. Toss and serve.

Each serving provides:

49	Calories		8 g	Carbohydrate
1 g	Protein		203 mg	Sodium
2 g	Total fat (0 g Sat. fat)		0 mg	Cholesterol

Summer Garden Stir-Fry

Inspired by bountiful summer gardens that are often filled with squash and tomatoes (sometimes too many!), this easy stir-fry is colorful and delicious.

Makes 6 servings

2¹/₂	tablespoons reduced sodium (or regular) soy sauce
1	teaspoon cornstarch
¹/₂	teaspoon garlic powder
¹/₄	teaspoon ground ginger
2	teaspoons vegetable oil
1	cup onion, sliced vertically into thin slices
1	medium zucchini (about 8 ounces), unpeeled, sliced crosswise into ¹/₈-inch slices
1	medium yellow summer squash (about 8 ounces), unpeeled, sliced crosswise into ¹/₈-inch slices
2	medium tomatoes, each cut vertically into 8 wedges

In a small bowl or custard cup, combine soy sauce, cornstarch, garlic powder, and ginger. Stir to dissolve cornstarch. Set aside.

Heat oil in a large nonstick skillet over medium-high heat. Add onion. Cook, stirring constantly with a tossing motion, 1 minute. Add zucchini and yellow squash. Cook, stirring, 2 minutes. Add tomatoes. Cook, stirring, 30 seconds.

Stir soy mixture and add to skillet. Cook, stirring, 30 seconds, or until mixture is hot and evenly glazed.

Each serving provides:

51	Calories	8 g	Carbohydrate
2 g	Protein	256 mg	Sodium
2 g	Total fat (0 g Sat. fat)	0 mg	Cholesterol

Scalloped Corn with Pimientos and Herbs

Not your usual scalloped corn, this one is filled with flavorful herbs and topped with delicate, cheesy crumbs. It's quick enough for a family meal and elegant enough for a dinner party. It even makes a tasty and unique brunch dish.

Makes 6 servings

Vegetables

3	egg whites
1/4	cup skim milk
1	1-pound salt-free (or regular) cream-style corn
1	1-pound can salt-free (or regular) whole kernel corn, drained
1/2	cup thinly sliced green onions (green part only)
1	2-ounce jar chopped pimientos, drained
1/2	teaspoon dried basil
1/4	teaspoon dill weed
1/4	teaspoon pepper
	Salt

Topping

1	tablespoon wheat germ
1	tablespoon grated Parmesan cheese

Preheat oven to 350°.

Lightly oil a 1 1/2-quart shallow casserole or spray with a nonstick cooking spray.

In a large bowl, combine egg whites and milk. Beat with a fork or wire whisk until blended. Whisk in cream-style corn.

Add remaining ingredients, *except* topping ingredients, mixing well. Pour mixture into prepared casserole.

Combine wheat germ and Parmesan cheese and sprinkle evenly over casserole.

Bake, uncovered, 45 minutes, until set and lightly browned.
Let stand 5 minutes before serving.

✧*Serve-again hint:* For a quick sandwich, spoon any type of cooked
beans into the leftover corn, then heat and roll in a tortilla.

Each serving provides:

130	Calories	27 g	Carbohydrate
6 g	Protein	54 mg	Sodium
2 g	Total fat (0 g Sat. fat)	1 mg	Cholesterol

Southern Corn and Tomato Casserole

Similar to the Scalloped Corn with Pimientos and Herbs recipe (page 328), but with a slightly different flavor, this easy dish only takes 5 minutes to throw together. Then, just pop it in the oven and let it bake. It's rich and delicious and makes a perfect dish for a holiday buffet.

Makes 4 servings

1	1-pound can salt-free (or regular) tomatoes, chopped and drained
1	8-ounce can corn, drained
1	8-ounce can cream-style corn
2	egg whites
2	tablespoons all-purpose flour
1	tablespoon grated Parmesan cheese
1¹/2	teaspoons onion powder
1	teaspoon sugar
¹/4	teaspoon pepper
¹/4	teaspoon garlic powder
2	tablespoons wheat germ

Preheat oven to 350°.

Lightly oil an 8-inch square baking pan or spray with a nonstick cooking spray.

In a large bowl, combine all ingredients, *except* wheat germ, mixing well. Place in prepared pan. Sprinkle with wheat germ.

Bake, uncovered, 45 to 50 minutes, or until set and lightly browned.

If you prefer a crusty top, place the casserole under the broiler for a few minutes before serving.

❖*Serve-again hint:* Heat leftovers in a microwave and roll them in flour tortillas, along with salsa, plain nonfat yogurt, and a sprinkling of sliced green onions. It makes a great lunch or dinner.

Each serving provides:

168	Calories	33 g	Carbohydrate
7 g	Protein	382 mg	Sodium
3 g	Total fat (1 g Sat. fat)	1 mg	Cholesterol

Mashed Yukon Gold Potatoes and Garlic

Yukon Gold potatoes have a golden flesh and sweet flavor, making them increasingly popular. They're available in most large grocery stores, but if you can't find them, white potatoes will also work in this recipe. If the bits of potato skin that will be in the finished product bother you, you can peel the potatoes. I like the texture and additional fiber that the skin adds.

Makes 8 servings

3	pounds Yukon Gold potatoes, unpeeled, cut into 1-inch cubes
4	large cloves garlic, peeled
1/2	cup skim milk
1/2	teaspoon salt
1/4	teaspoon pepper

Place potatoes and garlic in 2 inches of boiling water in a large saucepan. Cover and cook over medium heat 15 minutes, or until potatoes are tender. Drain. (Save the liquid to add to a future vegetable broth.)

Place potatoes and garlic in a large bowl. Add remaining ingredients. Mash with a potato masher until smooth, adding a little more milk if necessary to moisten the potatoes. Mix well to evenly distribute the garlic throughout the potatoes.

Add additional salt and pepper to taste.

❖*Serve-again hint:* Cold leftovers can be formed into patties and cooked on a lightly oiled griddle until brown.

Each serving provides:

151	Calories	32 g	Carbohydrate
4 g	Protein	158 mg	Sodium
1 g	Total fat (0 g Sat. fat)	0 mg	Cholesterol

Spiced Potato and Vegetable Kugel

This kugel, or pudding, is moist and spicy, with just a hint of sweetness. It's a delicious side dish that can also be the main part of the meal when served with a variety of other vegetable dishes.

Makes 6 servings

Kugel

2	medium potatoes, unpeeled (1 pound total)
1	large carrot
1	medium zucchini, unpeeled (7 to 8 ounces)
1	egg white
1 1/2	tablespoons vegetable oil
1 1/2	tablespoons sugar
1/3	cup whole wheat flour
1/2	teaspoon ground cinnamon
1/4	teaspoon salt
1/8	teaspoon ground ginger
1/8	teaspoon pepper
1/16	teaspoon ground cloves

Topping

1	tablespoon dry bread crumbs
1/2	teaspoon sugar
1/4	teaspoon ground cinnamon

Preheat oven to 350°.

Lightly oil a 1-quart baking dish or spray with a nonstick cooking spray.

Finely shred the potatoes, carrot, and zucchini into a large bowl. Add remaining ingredients, *except* topping ingredients, and mix well. Place mixture in prepared dish and smooth the top with the back of a spoon.

Combine topping ingredients, mixing well. Sprinkle evenly over pudding.

Bake, uncovered, 45 to 50 minutes, until kugel is set and nicely browned.

Serve hot.

✦*Quick tip:* If you have a food processor with a fine shredding blade, the most time-consuming part can be done in no time.

Each serving provides:

149	Calories	25 g	Carbohydrate
4 g	Protein	122 mg	Sodium
4 g	Total fat (1 g Sat. fat)	0 mg	Cholesterol

Two-Color Party Spuds

This dish is great for parties, especially since it can be prepared ahead of time. It does take a little bit more time than most of my dishes, but it's so easy—and so unusual. The potato skins are stuffed half with white potatoes and half with sweet potatoes. It's a great Thanksgiving dish, too.

Makes 6 servings

3	medium baking potatoes, 8 or 9 ounces each
3	medium sweet potatoes (equal to the total weight of the baking potatoes)
1¹/₂	teaspoons vegetable oil
¹/₄	cup skim milk
1	teaspoon dried basil
¹/₄	teaspoon salt
¹/₈	teaspoon pepper
2	tablespoons orange juice
1	tablespoon honey
¹/₂	teaspoon orange extract
	Fresh herbs for garnish (optional)

Preheat oven to 375°.

Pierce the white potatoes and sweet potatoes each several times with a sharp knife and bake until tender, about 1 hour.

Cut white potatoes in half lengthwise and carefully scoop out the pulp, leaving a ¹/₄-inch shell. Place the pulp in a large bowl and add oil, milk, basil, salt, and pepper. Mash with a fork or potato masher until mixture is smooth. Add additional milk if mixture is too dry.

Cut sweet potatoes in half and scoop the pulp into another bowl. Add orange juice, honey, and orange extract. Mash until mixture is smooth.

Stuff the two mixtures into the potato skins, placing the white potato mixture along one side and the sweet potato mixture along the other side, creating a two-tone potato.

Place potatoes on a baking sheet that has been lightly sprayed with a nonstick cooking spray. Bake 20 minutes, or until potatoes are hot and lightly browned. (If you are making them in advance for a later serving, refrigerate the potatoes and bring them to room temperature before baking.)

If desired, just before serving, place a few sprigs of fresh herbs along the center line between the two potatoes.

Note: The sweet potato skins are usually too soft to stuff and they are not needed in this recipe, so I just drizzle them with honey, sprinkle with cinnamon, and enjoy them as a snack.

❖*Variation:* Instead of stuffing the potato skins, you can place the mashed potatoes in a casserole, half on each side, and bake until hot.

Each serving provides:

210	Calories	45 g	Carbohydrate
4 g	Protein	115 mg	Sodium
2 g	Total fat (0 g Sat. fat)	0 mg	Cholesterol

Potato and Zucchini Pan-Cake

Shredded potatoes and zucchini are cooked in a skillet, then broiled until brown and crisp. This really doesn't need a topping, but if you're like my family, you'll enjoy them with a little ketchup or salsa.

Makes 6 servings

2	teaspoons vegetable oil
1	cup finely chopped onion
3	cups coarsely shredded potato, unpeeled (1$^{1}/_{2}$ pounds)
2	cups coarsely shredded zucchini, unpeeled (12 ounces)
1$^{1}/_{2}$	teaspoons dried basil
$^{1}/_{2}$	teaspoon garlic powder
$^{1}/_{2}$	teaspoon salt
$^{1}/_{8}$	teaspoon pepper

Heat 1 teaspoon of the oil in a 10-inch cast-iron skillet. Add onion and cook until onion begins to brown, about 5 minutes, stirring frequently.

In a large bowl, combine potato, zucchini, and spices. Mix well.

Add the remaining oil to the skillet and add potato mixture. Cook, stirring, for 5 minutes, then flatten mixture down into a cake, reduce heat to medium-low, and cook 15 minutes.

While mixture is cooking, preheat broiler and place the rack 5 inches away from the heat source. Place skillet under the broiler for 5 to 8 minutes, until potatoes are brown and crisp.

Cut into wedges to serve.

Each serving provides:

117	Calories	23 g	Carbohydrate
4 g	Protein	193 mg	Sodium
2 g	Total fat (0 g Sat. fat)	0 mg	Cholesterol

Sweet Potato "Fries"

For years I've baked my French "fries" instead of frying them. When it was suggested to me that I try the same thing using sweet potatoes, I was skeptical. What a pleasant surprise when they turned out to be so delicious! Enjoy them plain or serve with ketchup or whatever you like on regular fries.

Makes 4 servings

2   large sweet potatoes (2 pounds total)
      Salt and pepper

Preheat oven to 450°.

Lightly oil a baking sheet or spray with a nonstick cooking spray.

Cut sweet potatoes into strips to resemble French fries. Place on prepared baking sheet in a single layer. Spray lightly with nonstick cooking spray. Sprinkle with salt and pepper to taste.

Bake 10 minutes, then stir potatoes and bake 10 minutes more, or until done to taste.

Each serving provides:

242	Calories	55 g	Carbohydrate
4 g	Protein	30 mg	Sodium
1 g	Total fat (0 g Sat. fat)	0 mg	Cholesterol

Five-Spice Sweet Potatoes

Five favorite spices, along with apricot jam and maple syrup, give this sweet potato casserole gourmet flair, yet it's incredibly easy to prepare. Sweet potatoes are high in fiber and beta carotene and are simply delicious. They're always a welcome treat.

Makes 6 servings

Sweet Potatoes
1	18-ounce can sweet potatoes (vacuum-packed)
1/4	cup maple syrup
1/4	cup fruit-only apricot spread
1/4	teaspoon *each* ground nutmeg, cinnamon, cloves, allspice, and cardamom

Topping
1	tablespoon fruit-only apricot spread
1/2	teaspoon water

Preheat oven to 375°.

Lightly oil a 1-quart baking dish or spray with a nonstick cooking spray.

Place sweet potatoes in a large bowl. Mash with a fork or potato masher. Add remaining ingredients, *except* topping ingredients. Mash again and mix well. Place in prepared pan. Smooth the top with the back of a spoon.

Combine topping ingredients in a small bowl or custard cup. Mix well, then spread over sweet potatoes.

Bake, uncovered, 30 minutes.

Each serving provides:

155	Calories	36 g	Carbohydrate
1 g	Protein	47 mg	Sodium
1 g	Total fat (0 g Sat. fat)	0 mg	Cholesterol

Acorn Squash with Pecans and Molasses

This delicious dish bakes for 50 to 60 minutes, but it only takes a few minutes to throw together, so you can put it in the oven first, then proceed with the rest of the meal. It's a great company dish because it looks so fancy and tastes so good.

Makes 4 servings

2	medium acorn squash, cut in half lengthwise, seeds and stringy parts removed and discarded
1/3	cup molasses
1/4	cup chopped pecans
2	teaspoons grated fresh orange peel
1/8	teaspoon salt

Preheat oven to 375°.

Lightly oil a large shallow baking pan or spray with a nonstick cooking spray.

Place squash halves cut side down in prepared pan. Bake, uncovered, 30 minutes.

In a small bowl, combine 3 tablespoons of the molasses with remaining ingredients. Mix well.

Turn baked squash over and divide molasses mixture evenly into cavities. (Before filling the squash, you may need to slice a tiny bit off the bottom of each half to keep the squash from tipping over.) Drizzle remaining molasses over squash. Return pan to oven and continue to bake 20 minutes more, or until squash is tender.

Each serving provides:

176	Calories	32 g	Carbohydrate
1 g	Protein	83 mg	Sodium
6 g	Total fat (1 g Sat. fat)	0 mg	Cholesterol

Steamed Apples and Butternut Squash

Simple and straightforward, this easy dish consists of apples and squash that are simmered in apple juice, then piled high and topped with a cinnamon-nut topping.

Makes 6 servings

Apples and Squash

1	small butternut squash (1¹/₂ pounds), peeled, seeded, cut into 1-inch pieces (3 cups)
²/₃	cup apple juice
1	teaspoon vanilla extract
1	tablespoon sugar
3	large Golden Delicious apples, peeled, cut into 1-inch pieces

Topping

2	tablespoons finely chopped walnuts
2	teaspoons sugar
¹/₂	teaspoon ground cinnamon

Place squash in a large saucepan. It's important to use a large saucepan (3 to 4 quarts) so that most of the squash will be sitting in the juice. Combine apple juice and vanilla extract and pour over squash. Sprinkle with sugar. Bring to a boil over medium heat, then cover, reduce heat to medium-low, and cook 7 or 8 minutes, until squash is slightly tender.

Add apples and mix well. Cover and continue to cook another 7 or 8 minutes, until apples and squash are tender. (Do not let them get mushy.)

Combine all topping ingredients in a small bowl or custard cup and set aside.

Drain squash mixture and pile into a 9-inch pie pan or other similar-sized shallow serving bowl. (Reserve the juice to use with leftovers—see below.)

Sprinkle evenly with topping and serve right away.

✧*Serve-again hint:* Purée the cooked squash and apples (hot or cold), along with topping, in a blender container or food processor. Add just enough reserved juice to make it blend smoothly. Serve cold as a delicious alternative to applesauce.

Each serving provides:

130	Calories	30 g	Carbohydrate
1 g	Protein	5 mg	Sodium
2 g	Total fat (0 g Sat. fat)	0 mg	Cholesterol

Bombay Stuffed Squash

A fruit and vegetable filling combined with tangy Indian spices makes a delightful side dish that's pretty as well as nutritious and very tasty.

Makes 4 servings

2	medium acorn squash, about 10 to 12 ounces each (or 1 large squash, about 1 1/2 pounds)
1	teaspoon vegetable oil
1/2	cup chopped onions
1	large Golden Delicious apple, unpeeled, chopped into 1/2-inch pieces
2	tablespoons raisins
2	tablespoons chopped pecans or walnuts
1	tablespoon firmly packed brown sugar
1	teaspoon curry powder
1/2	teaspoon ground cumin
1/2	teaspoon ground cinnamon
	Salt

Cut squash in half, lengthwise. Remove and discard seeds. Slice a thin piece off the bottom of each half to keep them from tipping over.

Heat oil in a small nonstick skillet over medium heat. Add onions and apple. Cook, stirring frequently, until tender, about 5 minutes. Add small amounts of water as necessary, about a tablespoon at a time, to prevent sticking. Remove skillet from heat and stir in raisins, nuts, and brown sugar. Sprinkle spices evenly over mixture, then mix well.

Preheat oven to 375°.

Place squash halves cut side up in a 9 × 13-inch baking pan. Divide onion mixture and pile it into squash, mounding it if necessary.

Pour hot water in pan around squash to a depth of 1/2 inch.

Cover tightly and bake 45 minutes, or until squash is tender. (If you are baking 1 large squash, it will take about 1 hour.)

	Each serving provides:		
143	Calories	29 g	Carbohydrate
2 g	Protein	7 mg	Sodium
4 g	Total fat (0 g Sat. fat)	0 mg	Cholesterol

Fruits

As appetizers, salads, desserts, or snacks, fruits are extremely versatile. With health professionals recommending that we have four to five servings of fruits and vegetables daily, what more delicious way is there to meet these guidelines? Fruits are a valuable source of carbohydrates, are practically fat-free, and supply us with vitamins and minerals. They are also a valuable source of fiber.

Fresh fruits are available in most areas all year long. The varieties may vary with the growing season, and frozen fruits (unsweetened) can easily take their place in most recipes. If you have a freezer, take advantage of the fruits that are in season and freeze them for later enjoyment.

If you choose the sweetest varieties of fruits, you can usually reduce the amount of sugar needed in a recipe. Also, very ripe fruit is generally sweeter than fruit that is less ripe. In preparing these and other recipes, always try to leave the skin on fruit whenever possible. If the fruit has been waxed, remove the skin.

Be creative and try different combinations of fruits. They are colorful, versatile, and delicious. They are truly Nature's Desserts.

Tropical Fruits with Banana Dressing

Mango and papaya reflect the cool taste of the tropics, with bananas adding just the right touch. This one is at home as a simple appetizer or as a dessert for a fancy dinner party. Prepare the easy dressing ahead so it will be nice and cold for serving.

Makes 4 servings

Banana Dressing

1   medium, very ripe banana
1   tablespoon firmly packed brown sugar
1   teaspoon lemon juice
1/2   cup vanilla nonfat yogurt

Fruit

1   ripe mango, peeled, sliced or cut into chunks,
     center seed removed
1   ripe papaya, peeled, sliced or cut into chunks,
     seeds removed

To prepare dressing, in a blender container, combine banana, brown sugar, and lemon juice. Blend until smooth. Spoon into a small bowl and add yogurt. Mix well.

Chill.

At serving time, arrange fruit in four individual serving bowls. (Champagne glasses make a nice presentation.) Divide dressing evenly and spoon over fruit.

Serve right away.

◆*Quick tip:* Refrigerate the banana ahead of time, and the dressing will get cold much faster.

Each serving provides:

128	Calories	31 g	Carbohydrate
3 g	Protein	25 mg	Sodium
0 g	Total fat (0 g Sat. fat)	1 mg	Cholesterol

Fruit Salad with Poppy-Lime Dressing

Fresh fruit always hits the spot after a filling meal or it can be a nutritious way to start the day. If you want to make this luscious medley more than a few hours ahead, refrigerate the dressing and each fruit separately, then assemble the salad and add the dressing at the last minute.

Makes 8 servings

Dressing

3	tablespoons honey
2	tablespoons lime juice
1/2	teaspoon poppy seeds
1/4	teaspoon grated fresh lime peel
	Dash ground nutmeg, preferably freshly grated

Fruit

2	cups cantaloupe melon, cut into small balls
1	cup blueberries
1	cup strawberries, cut vertically into quarters (measure after cutting)
2	medium, ripe peaches *or* nectarines, unpeeled, thinly sliced
2	ripe kiwis, peeled, cut in half vertically, then sliced 1/4-inch thick

To prepare dressing, combine all dressing ingredients in a small bowl. Chill several hours, or up to a few days.

Up to an hour before serving, toss fruit together in a large bowl.

Just before serving, stir dressing and pour over fruit. Toss and serve.

❖*Serve-again hint:* Leftovers become very juicy and make delicious parfaits when layered in tall glasses with angel food cake and lowfat vanilla ice cream.

Each serving provides:			
82	Calories	21 g	Carbohydrate
1 g	Protein	7 mg	Sodium
0 g	Total fat (0 g Sat. fat)	0 mg	Cholesterol

Yogurt and Fruit Bowl

This is such a pretty presentation for what might have been a simple bowl of fruit and yogurt. A straight-sided, clear glass bowl really helps to showcase the attractive layers.

Makes 6 servings

2	medium, ripe kiwis, peeled, cut in half lengthwise, and then crosswise into thin slices
2	cups vanilla nonfat yogurt
1/4	cup plus 2 tablespoons firmly packed brown sugar
1	cup thinly sliced strawberries
1	large, fresh peach, unpeeled, cut into very thin slices

Arrange kiwi slices, overlapping slightly, in the bottom of a 1-quart bowl. Top with 2/3 cup of the yogurt, spreading it evenly over the fruit. Sprinkle 2 tablespoons of the brown sugar evenly over the yogurt.

Arrange strawberry slices over the yogurt. Top with another 2/3 cup of the yogurt, followed by another 2 tablespoons of the brown sugar.

Arrange peach slices over the yogurt, then top with remaining yogurt and brown sugar.

Chill thoroughly.

❖*Serve-again hint:* On the second day, the mixture tends to become slightly watery. Take advantage of this and spoon it over angel food cake or fat-free pound cake.

Each serving provides:

153	Calories	34 g	Carbohydrate
5 g	Protein	60 mg	Sodium
0 g	Total fat (0 g Sat. fat)	2 mg	Cholesterol

Brandied Fruit

Any combination of dried fruit can be used in this rich, "imbibed" version of an all-time favorite. It's delicious by itself and can also be spooned over cottage cheese or lowfat vanilla ice cream or frozen yogurt. It also makes a great holiday or housewarming gift.

Makes 12 servings
(1/2 cup each serving)

1	32-ounce bottle apple juice
1/2	cup firmly packed brown sugar
2	3-inch cinnamon sticks
2	cups dried figs, cut in half (about 12 ounces)
2 1/2	cups dried apricot halves, cut in half (about 12 ounces)
2	cups pitted prunes, cut in half (about 12 ounces)
1/2	cup raisins
1 1/2	teaspoons whole cloves
1/4	cup brandy

In a large saucepan, combine apple juice, brown sugar, cinnamon sticks, figs, apricots, prunes, and raisins.

Place cloves in a tea strainer or tie them in cheesecloth to make a spice bag. Add to saucepan. Bring mixture to a boil over medium heat, stirring occasionally. Reduce heat to low, cover, and simmer 15 minutes. Remove from heat and stir in brandy.

Remove and discard cinnamon sticks and spice bag.

Serve hot or cold. Refrigerate leftovers. (If possible, make this dish ahead; the flavor develops and becomes richer after the fruit has been refrigerated for a few days.)

Each serving provides:

312	Calories	77 g	Carbohydrate
3 g	Protein	14 mg	Sodium
1 g	Total fat (0 g Sat. fat)	0 mg	Cholesterol

Cranberry-Pecan-Pear Relish

Cranberries are not only for Thanksgiving. This easy fruit relish is cool and refreshing in the summertime, too. Serve it as a meal accompaniment or a delicious light snack or dessert. Be sure to freeze plenty of cranberries when they are in season. They thaw quickly at room temperature and are ready to use in no time.

Makes 8 servings
(1/2 cup each serving)

3	cups cranberries
2	medium, ripe pears, unpeeled, coarsely chopped
2	oranges, peeled and sectioned (discard white membranes)
1/4	cup raisins
2	ounces pecan halves (about 24 halves)
1/4	cup plus 2 tablespoons sugar
2	teaspoons lemon juice

Combine all ingredients in a food processor. Using the steel blade, process until mixture is chopped, but not pureed. (A blender will also work, but you will need to blend the mixture in small batches to prevent it from becoming pureed.)

Spoon mixture into a bowl.

Chill thoroughly.

❖*Serve-again hint:* For a perfect take-along lunch, fill a container with lowfat cottage cheese and top it with this tangy relish.

Each serving provides:

159	Calories	30 g	Carbohydrate
1 g	Protein	1 mg	Sodium
5 g	Total fat (0 g Sat. fat)	0 mg	Cholesterol

Autumn Fruit Compote

You can, of course, make this delicious fruit medley any time of year, however, it really warms your heart on a crisp fall day. It's superb topped with the Creamy Sweet Cheese on page 44, and since this recipe makes a lot, you'll have plenty of leftovers to enjoy.

Makes 12 servings
(1/2 cup each serving)

3	cups mixed dried fruits (any mixture of prunes, apricots, pears, apples, peaches, or other dried fruit)
2	medium Golden Delicious apples, peeled, sliced 1/8-inch to 1/4-inch thick
1/2	cup water
1/2	cup orange juice
1	tablespoon lemon juice
3	21/2-inch cinnamon sticks
1/2	teaspoon ground cloves
2	medium pears, peeled, sliced 1/8-inch to 1/4-inch thick
3	medium oranges, peeled, sliced crosswise into 1/4-inch slices (discard white membranes)
1	cup seedless red grapes, cut in half (measure after cutting)

In a large saucepan, combine dried fruits, apples, water, orange juice, lemon juice, cinnamon sticks, and cloves. Bring to a boil over medium heat, stirring several times. Cook 5 minutes, stirring occasionally.

Add pears. Continue to cook, stirring occasionally, 5 more minutes, until apples and pears are just tender. Remove from heat and add orange slices and grapes. Mix gently.

Remove and discard cinnamon sticks.

Serve warm or cold.

Each serving provides:

153	Calories	40 g	Carbohydrate
1 g	Protein	8 mg	Sodium
1 g	Total fat (0 g Sat. fat)	0 mg	Cholesterol

Mixed Fruits in Lemon Sauce

So fresh and cool, this fruit medley is a brand new twist on the old fruit salad. Use any combination of fruits you like, substituting whatever is fresh and in season. A beautiful way to serve it is to pile the chilled fruit into parfait glasses and top with vanilla nonfat yogurt.

Makes 6 servings

Fruit

1/2	cup peaches, peeled, cut into 1/2-inch pieces (measure after cutting)
1/2	cup apricots, unpeeled, cut into 1/2-inch pieces (measure after cutting)
1/2	cup strawberries, sliced or quartered (measure after cutting)
1/2	cup blueberries
1/2	cup seedless red grapes, halved
1/2	cup seedless green grapes, halved

Lemon Sauce

1	cup water
3	tablespoons sugar
1	tablespoon plus 1 teaspoon cornstarch
1 1/2	tablespoons lemon juice
1/2	teaspoon grated fresh lemon peel
1/2	teaspoon vanilla extract

Mix fruit together in a bowl.

In a small saucepan, combine all sauce ingredients, *except* lemon peel and vanilla extract. Mix until cornstarch is dissolved. Bring to a boil over medium heat, stirring constantly. Continue to cook, stirring, 1 minute. Remove from heat and stir in lemon peel and vanilla. Let cool 15 minutes, then stir and pour over fruit. Mix well.

Chill thoroughly.

Each serving provides:			
75	Calories	19 g	Carbohydrate
1 g	Protein	2 mg	Sodium
0 g	Total fat (0 g Sat. fat)	0 mg	Cholesterol

Almond-Scented Cherries and Bananas

Turn a can of cherries and a few bananas into a delicious layered fruit compote. The flavors blend so naturally, making an irresistible dish.

Makes 6 servings

1	1-pound can pitted, unsweetened red tart cherries, undrained
1/2	cup sugar
2	tablespoons cornstarch
1	teaspoon almond extract
1/2	teaspoon ground cinnamon
2	medium, ripe bananas, sliced crosswise into 1/8-inch slices

Have a 1-quart bowl ready. (A clear glass bowl with straight sides shows the dish off best.)

In a small saucepan, combine cherries (with liquid), sugar, and cornstarch. Stir to dissolve cornstarch. Bring to a boil over medium heat, stirring constantly. Continue to cook, stirring, 1 minute. Remove from heat and stir in almond extract and cinnamon, mixing well.

Spoon *half* of the cherries in the bottom of the bowl. Top with bananas, making several overlapping layers. Spoon remaining cherries over bananas.

Serve warm or chill for later serving.

❖*Serve-again hint:* Cut angel food cake or fat-free pound cake into small cubes and fold them into the leftovers.

Each serving provides:			
140	Calories	35 g	Carbohydrate
1 g	Protein	6 mg	Sodium
0 g	Total fat (0 g Sat. fat)	0 mg	Cholesterol

Apricot Baked Bananas

This quick and easy dessert can be made while you're clearing the dinner dishes from the table. It's delicious by itself and is absolutely scrumptious over ice cream.

Makes 4 servings

1/4   cup fruit-only apricot spread
1/4   cup orange juice
1/4   teaspoon ground cinnamon
3   medium, ripe bananas, thinly sliced
4   teaspoons slivered almonds

Preheat oven to 400°.

Lightly oil 4 custard cups or spray with a nonstick cooking spray.

In a small bowl, combine apricot spread, orange juice, and cinnamon. Mix well.

Divide bananas evenly and place in prepared custard cups. Spoon apricot mixture over bananas. Top each one with 1 teaspoon of the almonds.

Bake 10 to 12 minutes, until hot and bubbly.

Serve hot.

❖*Serve-again hint:* Cold leftovers can turn an ordinary bowl of oatmeal into an exciting breakfast.

Each serving provides:

155	Calories	33 g	Carbohydrate
2 g	Protein	1 mg	Sodium
3 g	Total fat (0 g Sat. fat)	0 mg	Cholesterol

Papaya with Raspberry-Lime Sauce

So sweet, so simple, so elegant! This is a versatile dish that can be served as an appetizer or as a dessert. It's also delicious made with mangoes in place of the papayas. You'll have sauce left over, so be creative and spoon it over other fruits, angel food cake, lowfat brownies, lowfat ice cream . . .

Makes 4 servings

1	10-ounce package frozen raspberries, unsweetened or in light syrup, thawed, undrained
1	tablespoon lime juice
1	tablespoon sugar
2	ripe papayas, cut in half lengthwise, seeds removed and discarded

In a blender container, combine raspberries, lime juice, and sugar. Blend until pureed. Strain mixture and discard seeds.

Place papaya halves on individual serving plates. (Slice a tiny bit off the bottom of each one to keep them from rolling around.) Spoon 3 tablespoons of sauce into each half.

Serve right away.

Note: Sauce can be made up to 2 days ahead and refrigerated until needed. Papayas can either be chilled or served at room temperature.

Each serving provides:

111	Calories	28 g	Carbohydrate
2 g	Protein	5 mg	Sodium
1 g	Total fat (0 g Sat. fat)	0 mg	Cholesterol

Currant Apple Sauté

Serve this delectable dish warm over lowfat vanilla ice cream or angel food cake, or serve chilled, topped with a dollop of vanilla fat-free yogurt. Of course, it's also delicious by itself.

Makes 4 servings

4	medium Golden Delicious apples, peeled, cored, and thinly sliced
$1/4$	cup firmly packed brown sugar
2	tablespoons water
$1/2$	teaspoon grated fresh lemon peel
$1/2$	teaspoon ground cinnamon
$1/4$	cup currant jelly (other flavors will work, but be sure to use jelly rather than jam)
$1/2$	teaspoon vanilla extract

Combine apples, brown sugar, water, lemon peel, and cinnamon in a large nonstick skillet. Mix well. Place over medium heat, cover, and cook 5 minutes.

Add jelly to skillet and continue to cook, uncovered, 3 more minutes, stirring frequently.

Remove from heat and stir in vanilla.

❖*Serve-again hint:* Mix part-skim ricotta cheese with a little sugar and vanilla and layer it in parfait glasses or dessert bowls with the leftovers. You'll have delicious desserts that taste like apple cheesecake.

Each serving provides:

179	Calories	46 g	Carbohydrate
0 g	Protein	12 mg	Sodium
0 g	Total fat (0 g Sat. fat)	0 mg	Cholesterol

French Apples and "Cream"

*This delectable dessert was inspired by a recipe for a fancy French apple tart.
By eliminating the buttery crust and replacing the cream with milk, I was
able to come up with a much more sensible dessert that is still extremely delicious. For an elegant gourmet touch, top each serving with a scoop of the
Cinnamon Ice Cream on page 435.*

Makes 8 servings

6	medium, Golden Delicious apples, peeled, cut into 1/2-inch chunks
1/2	cup sugar
1	tablespoon ground cinnamon
1/2	cup raisins
1/4	cup chopped walnuts
1	cup evaporated skim milk
1	tablespoon all-purpose flour

Preheat oven to 400°.

Lightly oil a 10-inch pie pan or spray with a nonstick cooking
spray.

Place the apples in a large bowl. Add *half* the sugar, the cinnamon,
raisins, and walnuts. Toss until apples are evenly coated. Place in prepared pan.

Bake, uncovered, 20 minutes.

While apples are baking, combine evaporated skim milk with flour
and remaining sugar. Beat with a fork or wire whisk until combined.

Spoon milk mixture evenly over apples and return to oven for 10
more minutes.

Serve warm for best flavor, scooping apples from the bottom of the
pan to make sure there is "cream" with each serving.

Each serving provides:

190	Calories	40 g	Carbohydrate
3 g	Protein	38 mg	Sodium
3 g	Total fat (0 g Sat. fat)	1 mg	Cholesterol

Baked Apples with Lemon and Ginger

If you like the bite of ginger, this one's for you. The vanilla ice cream adds just the right mellow touch to the exciting flavors of lemon and ginger. Served in tall-stemmed sherbet glasses, this makes an impressive dessert.

Makes 8 servings

4	medium apples, such as Golden Delicious, McIntosh, Winesap (or other all-purpose or baking apples), peeled, cored, cut in half vertically
1/3	cup firmly packed brown sugar
1/4	cup maple syrup
1	tablespoon lemon juice
1	teaspoon ground ginger
3/4	teaspoon grated fresh lemon peel
1/2	teaspoon vanilla extract
	Lowfat vanilla ice cream or frozen yogurt

Preheat oven to 375°.

Lightly oil a 7 × 11-inch baking pan or spray with a nonstick cooking spray.

Place apples cut side down in prepared pan.

In a small bowl, combine remaining ingredients except ice cream, mixing well. Spoon mixture over apples.

Bake, uncovered, 20 minutes, or until apples are tender, basting every 5 minutes. (Length of cooking time will depend on variety of apples used.)

Turn apples over, baste again, and continue to bake 5 minutes more.

Serve warm.

For each serving, place an apple half in an individual serving bowl. Top with a scoop of ice cream or yogurt, then spoon some of the sauce over the top.

Each serving provides:			
104	Calories	25 g	Carbohydrate
0 g	Protein	5 mg	Sodium
1 g	Total fat (0 g Sat. fat)	0 mg	Cholesterol

Lemon-Amaretto Apples

Thinly sliced apples cook quickly and soak up so much of the sweet, sweet flavor in this easy dish. Serve it as a snack or dessert and, either way, you'll love its delectable taste. I prefer to use Golden Delicious apples, but any variety will work. Just watch the cooking time, because some varieties of apples cook quickly and tend to become mushy if overcooked.

Makes 6 servings

1/4	cup amaretto (or other almond-flavored liqueur)
1/4	cup water
1	tablespoon sugar
1	teaspoon grated fresh lemon peel
1	2 1/2-inch cinnamon stick
1/4	teaspoon almond extract
4	medium Golden Delicious apples, peeled, cored, sliced 1/8-inch thick

In a medium saucepan, combine amaretto, water, sugar, lemon peel, and cinnamon stick. Bring to a boil over medium heat. Stir in almond extract and apples. Reduce heat slightly, cover, and cook, stirring occasionally, 5 minutes, or until apples are just tender.

Serve warm or cold. Before serving, stir apples and discard cinnamon stick.

Each serving provides:

85	Calories	18 g	Carbohydrate
0 g	Protein	0 mg	Sodium
0 g	Total fat (0 g Sat. fat)	0 mg	Cholesterol

Microwave Applesauce

You'll love this applesauce — not only is it tasty, but it's also quick and delicious and there's no messy pot to wash. You can cook, store, and serve it all in the same bowl. For the best flavor, use a combination of apple varieties. A tasty mix is Golden Delicious, Winesap, Granny Smith, and Rome Beauty.

Makes 8 servings
(1/2 cup each serving)

3	pounds apples, peeled, cored, cut into chunks
1/4	cup water
1	teaspoon vanilla extract
1	tablespoon sugar or honey
1	tablespoon firmly packed brown sugar
1	teaspoon ground cinnamon
1/8	teaspoon ground nutmeg

Place apple chunks in a large microwave-safe bowl. Add water and vanilla extract. Sprinkle sugar, brown sugar, cinnamon, and nutmeg evenly over apples.

Cover tightly with a lid or plastic wrap. (If using plastic wrap, be sure the bowl is large enough so that the plastic is not touching the fruit, and make several slits in the wrap with a sharp knife to let the steam escape.)

Microwave on high speed for a total of 15 minutes, stopping to stir the apples every 5 minutes.

Stir the apples with a fork to desired consistency.

Serve warm or cold.

Each serving provides:

98	Calories	25 g	Carbohydrate
0 g	Protein	1 mg	Sodium
0 g	Total fat (0 g Sat. fat)	0 mg	Cholesterol

Crock-Pot Applesauce

For an easy cooking method, dig your Crock-Pot out of the basement and try making applesauce this way. The ingredients are exactly the same as the recipe for Microwave Applesauce. However, you can turn this one on at night and have wonderful, hot applesauce to spoon over your morning oatmeal. Again, for the best flavor, use a combination of apple varieties, such as Golden Delicious, Winesap, Granny Smith, and Rome.

Makes 8 servings
(1/2 cup each serving)

3	pounds apples, peeled, cored, cut into chunks
1/4	cup water
1	teaspoon vanilla extract
1	tablespoon sugar or honey
1	tablespoon firmly packed brown sugar
1	teaspoon ground cinnamon
1/8	teaspoon ground nutmeg

Place apple chunks in an electric Crock-Pot. Add water and vanilla extract. Sprinkle sugar, brown sugar, cinnamon, and nutmeg over apples. Stir the apples to evenly distribute the spices.

Cover and cook on low setting 7 to 8 hours, or overnight.

Stir the apples with a fork to desired consistency.

Serve warm or cold.

Each serving provides:

98	Calories	25 g	Carbohydrate
0 g	Protein	1 mg	Sodium
0 g	Total fat (0 g Sat. fat)	0 mg	Cholesterol

Orange-Spice Marinated Pears

So simple yet so delicious. You just slice the pears and let them sit in the easy sauce for several hours or overnight. It makes a very sweet, refreshing dessert or snack.

Makes 4 servings

2	large, ripe pears, unpeeled, seeds and core removed, sliced into paper-thin slices
3/4	cup orange juice
2	tablespoons honey
1/2	teaspoon vanilla extract
1/4	teaspoon ground cinnamon
1/16	teaspoon ground allspice

Spread pear slices in slightly overlapping rows in a 9 × 13-inch baking pan or other large, shallow pan.

Combine remaining ingredients in a small bowl. Mix well. Pour over pears. Cover and chill several hours, or overnight. Tilt the pan back and forth several times while chilling to redistribute the sauce.

After marinating, the pears can be transferred to a bowl.

❖*Serve-again hint:* Another delicious topping for lowfat vanilla ice cream!

Each serving provides:

117	Calories	30 g	Carbohydrate
1 g	Protein	1 mg	Sodium
0 g	Total fat (0 g Sat. fat)	0 mg	Cholesterol

Frozen Cranberry-Pineapple Loaf

My dear friend, Lynda Bell, has served this luscious frozen fruit mold as an appetizer or dessert many times, and she always receives rave reviews. It keeps well in the freezer and can be sliced as needed. It also makes a cool summer fruit snack. The lowfat yogurt used in the recipe is just slightly creamier than nonfat yogurt and works a little better.

Makes 10 servings

1   1-pound can whole berry cranberry sauce
1   8-ounce can crushed pineapple (packed in juice), drained well
1   8-ounce container lemon lowfat yogurt

Line a 4 × 8-inch loaf pan with plastic wrap.

In a medium bowl, combine all ingredients, mixing well. Spoon into prepared pan. Cover tightly and place in freezer until solid.

To serve, remove from freezer and let stand 10 minutes, then invert onto a serving plate, slice, and serve. (If only serving part of the mold, invert first, cut off as much as you will need, and return remaining mold to freezer. Just let the part you are serving stand at room temperature for the 10 minutes.)

✧*Serve-again hint:* Place a slice of the mold between graham crackers and enjoy a new dimension in frozen treats.

Each serving provides:

105	Calories	26 g	Carbohydrate
1 g	Protein	27 mg	Sodium
0 g	Total fat (0 g Sat. fat)	1 mg	Cholesterol

Peaches with Cinnamon and Rum

Nectarines will also work in this easy, spiced fruit dish. It can be served warm or cold and is delicious spooned over lowfat vanilla ice cream or topped with a dollop of vanilla nonfat yogurt.

Makes 4 servings

2   tablespoons firmly packed brown sugar
2   teaspoons lemon juice
1   teaspoon rum extract
1/4   teaspoon plus 1/8 teaspoon ground cinnamon
1/8   teaspoon ground allspice
4   medium, ripe peaches, peeled, sliced 1/4-inch thick

In a medium saucepan, combine brown sugar, lemon juice, rum extract, and spices. Heat over medium heat, stirring frequently, until mixture boils.

Add peaches. Cook, stirring frequently, until mixture boils again. Continue to cook, stirring occasionally, about 3 minutes, or until peaches are tender.

Serve warm or cold.

✦*Quick tip:* Thawed frozen peaches will also work. You may have to adjust the cooking time according to their firmness.

Each serving provides:

88	Calories	22 g	Carbohydrate
1 g	Protein	3 mg	Sodium
0 g	Total fat (0 g Sat. fat)	0 mg	Cholesterol

Peaches à l'Orange

This easy dish is a must when fresh peaches are in season. There are so many possibilities for serving it—over lowfat vanilla ice cream or frozen yogurt, as a topper for angel food cake, spooned over fresh berries, and even over oatmeal for breakfast. It can be served warm or cold and is equally tasty both ways.

Makes 6 servings

2/3	cup orange juice
3	tablespoons firmly packed brown sugar
1 1/2	teaspoons cornstarch
1	teaspoon grated fresh orange peel
6	whole cloves
6	whole allspice
3	cups peaches, peeled and thinly sliced

In a small saucepan, combine all ingredients, *except* peaches. Mix well, stirring until cornstarch is dissolved. Stir in peaches.

Bring mixture to a boil over medium heat, stirring frequently. Reduce heat slightly and continue to cook, stirring constantly, for 3 minutes.

Remove and discard cloves and allspice.

Each serving provides:

78	Calories	20 g	Carbohydrate
1 g	Protein	3 mg	Sodium
0 g	Total fat (0 g Sat. fat)	0 mg	Cholesterol

Orange-Date Combo

This delightful, fiber-rich fruit combo is especially tasty when made with fresh navel oranges. It can be served as either an appetizer, a snack, or a cool, refreshing dessert.

Makes 4 servings

4	medium oranges, peeled and sectioned (discard white membranes)
4	large pitted dates, sliced crosswise into very thin slices
1	tablespoon lemon juice, preferably fresh
6	almonds, coarsely chopped
1	teaspoon powdered sugar
1/2	teaspoon ground cinnamon

In a small bowl, combine oranges and dates. Drizzle with lemon juice and stir gently.

Toast almond pieces lightly by placing them in a 350° oven or a toaster oven for 2 to 3 minutes, or until they just begin to brown. Add to orange mixture and toss gently.

This salad can be served right away or chilled for later servings.

To serve, divide orange mixture evenly into 4 individual serving bowls. Sprinkle with powdered sugar and cinnamon just before serving.

❖*Serve-again hint:* Layer the leftovers in parfait glasses with vanilla nonfat yogurt. Sprinkle with a dusting of cinnamon.

Each serving provides:

111	Calories	27 g	Carbohydrate
2 g	Protein	1 mg	Sodium
1 g	Total fat (0 g Sat. fat)	0 mg	Cholesterol

Sherry-Minted Melon Balls

This cool, refreshing treat, with an unusual flavor combination, makes use of the abundant warm-weather cantaloupe. It's a make-ahead dish, which means no fuss at serving time. Serve it for breakfast, as a snack, or as a delectable, light dessert. (Look for fresh mint leaves in the produce section of most large grocery stores.)

Makes 6 servings

1/4	cup honey
3	tablespoons water
1/4	teaspoon ground cardamom
3	tablespoons orange juice
2	tablespoons lemon juice
2	tablespoons dry sherry
1	tablespoon finely chopped fresh mint leaves
1/4	teaspoon grated fresh orange peel
1	medium, ripe cantaloupe melon, cut into balls (about 3 cups)

In a small saucepan, combine honey, water, and cardamom. Bring to a boil over medium heat, then reduce heat slightly and simmer, uncovered, 5 minutes. Remove from heat and stir in remaining ingredients, *except* cantaloupe. Let mixture cool to lukewarm.

Place cantaloupe balls in a large bowl. Add honey mixture and mix well.

Chill several hours or overnight.

❖*Serve-again hint:* Purée the leftover fruit and marinade in a blender and serve as a delicious fruit soup or beverage. Garnish with fresh mint leaves.

Each serving provides:

82	Calories	20 g	Carbohydrate
1 g	Protein	9 mg	Sodium
0 g	Total fat (0 g Sat. fat)	0 mg	Cholesterol

Mango-Berry Combo

Fresh mangoes and strawberries complement each other deliciously in this easy fruit mixture. As a meal starter or light dessert, this dish is as refreshing as they come.

Makes 4 servings

1	medium, ripe mango, peeled, cut into 1/2-inch to 1-inch pieces, center seed removed
1 1/2	cups quartered strawberries
1/3	cup vanilla nonfat yogurt
1/16	teaspoon ground cinnamon
	Few drops vanilla extract

Toss mango and strawberries together in a medium bowl.

Combine yogurt, cinnamon, and vanilla and add to fruit, mixing gently.

Chill thoroughly.

❖*Serve-again hint:* Add a chopped, ripe banana to the leftovers just before serving. The taste is different and deliciously tropical.

Each serving provides:

68	Calories		16 g	Carbohydrate
2 g	Protein		15 mg	Sodium
0 g	Total fat (0 g Sat. fat)		1 mg	Cholesterol

Fresh Pineapple in Citrus Marinade

Be sure to choose a ripe pineapple for this refreshing dish. Look for one with a rich, yellow color and a fragrant aroma. If the pineapple is not ripe enough and is too tart, add a little sugar or honey to the juice mixture before cooking it.

Makes 6 servings

1	medium, ripe pineapple, peeled, cored, cut into 1-inch chunks (4 cups)
1/2	cup orange juice
1	tablespoon lime juice
1/2	teaspoon grated fresh lemon peel
1/8	teaspoon ground allspice
1/4	teaspoon rum extract
1/8	teaspoon orange extract

Arrange pineapple chunks in a single layer in an 8-inch square baking pan or shallow bowl.

In a small saucepan, combine orange juice, lime juice, lemon peel, and allspice. Bring to a boil over medium heat. Remove from heat and stir in extracts. Pour over pineapple.

Cover and chill several hours or overnight. Stir several times while marinating.

Serve cold.

✦*Quick tip:* Fresh pineapple chunks are often available at grocery store salad bars. They cost a little more, but they're really handy when you're in a hurry.

Each serving provides:

62	Calories	15 g	Carbohydrate
1 g	Protein	2 mg	Sodium
0 g	Total fat (0 g Sat. fat)	0 mg	Cholesterol

Baked Desserts

Everyone loves dessert! And, happily, embarking on a healthy lifestyle doesn't mean you have to forgo favorite delicacies such as cakes and pies. They can all be made with healthful ingredients and can provide nutritional benefits while still satisfying that sweet tooth. Whole grain flours, fruits, and fruit juices are among the star ingredients in the luscious desserts found in this section. The oils have been greatly reduced, replaced in part with applesauce, yogurt, honey, and other fat-free moist ingredients.

Aside from providing tasty endings to any meal, most of these desserts can double as a delicious breakfast and provide a more nutritional way to satisfy that morning sweet craving for anyone who usually starts the day with a doughnut.

So, take the time to bake some homemade goodies. They're easy and can be frozen in individual servings, creating treats that are ready in no time when you feel like having a special treat.

Applesauce Gingerbread

Served warm and topped with lowfat vanilla ice cream, this slimmed-down version of an old-time favorite has retained all of the wonderful, spicy flavor of the original.

Makes 12 servings

1	cup whole wheat flour
1/3	cup all-purpose flour
1	teaspoon baking soda
1 1/2	teaspoons ground ginger
1	teaspoon ground cinnamon
1	cup applesauce, unsweetened
1/3	cup molasses
2	egg whites
3	tablespoons skim milk
2	tablespoons vegetable oil
2	tablespoons sugar
1	teaspoon vanilla extract

Preheat oven to 350°.

Lightly oil an 8-inch square baking pan or spray with a nonstick cooking spray.

In a large bowl, combine both types of flour, baking soda, ginger, and cinnamon. Mix well.

In another bowl, combine remaining ingredients. Beat with a fork or wire whisk until blended. Add to dry mixture, mixing until all ingredients are moistened. Place in prepared pan.

Baked 30 to 35 minutes, until a toothpick inserted in the center of the cake comes out clean.

Cool in pan on a wire rack. Cut into squares and serve warm for best flavor.

◆*Quick tip:* Keep a few jars of unsweetened applesauce in the pantry. They come in handy as a replacement for most of the oil in baked goods.

	Each serving provides:		
114	Calories	21 g	Carbohydrate
2 g	Protein	121 mg	Sodium
3 g	Total fat (0 g Sat. fat)	0 mg	Cholesterol

Lemon Crumb Cake

One simple mix makes both the cake and the crumb topping, so this moist, lemony cake comes together in no time.

Makes 12 servings

1¹/₃	cups all-purpose flour
²/₃	cup whole wheat flour
¹/₂	cup sugar
¹/₄	cup firmly packed brown sugar
2	teaspoons grated fresh lemon peel
³/₄	teaspoon ground cinnamon
1¹/₃	cups lemon nonfat yogurt
3	tablespoons vegetable oil
2	egg whites
1	teaspoon vanilla extract
1	teaspoon baking powder
1	teaspoon baking soda

Preheat oven to 325°.

Lightly oil a 9-inch square glass baking pan or spray with a non-stick cooking spray.

In a large bowl, combine both types of flour, sugar, brown sugar, lemon peel, and cinnamon. Mix well.

Place ¹/₃ cup of the yogurt in a small bowl. Whisk in oil. (Mixture will not be smooth.) Add to dry mixture. Mix with a fork until dry ingredients are evenly moistened and mixture resembles coarse crumbs. Set aside 1 cup of this mixture for topping.

In a small bowl, combine remaining ingredients, mixing with a fork or wire whisk until blended. Add to crumb mixture, beating on medium speed of an electric mixer until combined. Beat on high speed 1 minute.

Spread batter in prepared pan. Sprinkle reserved crumb mixture evenly over the top. Bake 40 minutes, until a toothpick inserted in the center of the cake comes out clean.

Place pan on a wire rack to cool. Cut cake into squares and serve warm for best flavor.

(If not serving cake right away, let cool, then cover with foil or plastic wrap.)

❖*Serve-again hint:* Make a delectable blueberry shortcake by cutting the cake in half horizontally and filling with blueberries and topping with either vanilla or lemon nonfat yogurt.

Each serving provides:

183	Calories	33 g	Carbohydrate
4 g	Protein	170 mg	Sodium
4 g	Total fat (1 g Sat. fat)	0 mg	Cholesterol

Molasses Oat Squares

Chewy and moist, with lots of crunchy oats on top, these delectable squares are best when served warm and are great with a cup of coffee or tea.

Makes 12 servings

Cake
1¹/₃   cups rolled oats
³/₄   cup whole wheat flour
¹/₂   teaspoon baking soda
¹/₂   teaspoon *each* ground ginger and cinnamon
¹/₈   teaspoon ground allspice
¹/₂   cup raisins
¹/₃   cup molasses
¹/₃   cup firmly packed brown sugar
2   tablespoons vegetable oil
2   egg whites
1¹/₄   cups skim milk

Topping
2   teaspoons sugar
¹/₄   teaspoon ground cinnamon

Preheat oven to 350°.

Lightly oil an 8-inch square baking pan or spray with a nonstick cooking spray.

In a large bowl, combine oats, flour, baking soda, and spices. Mix well. Stir in raisins.

In another bowl, combine remaining cake ingredients. Beat with a fork or wire whisk until blended. Add to dry mixture, mixing until all ingredients are moistened. Pour into prepared pan.

Combine topping ingredients and sprinkle evenly over top of cake.
Bake 35 minutes, until a toothpick inserted in the center of the cake comes out clean.

Place pan on a wire rack to cool. Cut cake into squares and serve warm for best flavor.

❖*Serve-again hint:* Spread with jam or nonfat cream cheese, these squares make a super-delicious breakfast on the go.

Each serving provides:

163	Calories	30 g	Carbohydrate
4 g	Protein	82 mg	Sodium
3 g	Total fat (0 g Sat. fat)	1 mg	Cholesterol

Cranberry Pudding Cake with Orange Sauce

What better way to celebrate autumn than with this warm cranberry dessert? It needs to be served warm, so put it in the oven at the start of the meal; when you're ready for dessert, the dessert will be ready for you.

Makes 8 servings

Cake
3/4	cup whole wheat flour
3/4	cup all-purpose flour
2/3	cup sugar
1	tablespoon baking powder
3	tablespoons chopped walnuts or pecans
1	cup evaporated skim milk
1	tablespoon vegetable oil
1 1/2	teaspoons vanilla extract
1 1/2	cups cranberries, coarsely chopped

Topping
2	teaspoons sugar
1/4	teaspoon ground cinnamon

Orange Sauce
1	tablespoon plus 1 teaspoon cornstarch
1/4	teaspoon ground cinnamon
2/3	cup orange juice
1/3	cup water
2	tablespoons maple syrup

Preheat oven to 350°.

Lightly oil a 1-quart baking dish or spray with a nonstick cooking spray.

In a large bowl, combine both types of flour, sugar, baking powder, and nuts. Mix well.

In another bowl, combine milk, oil, and vanilla. Add to dry ingredients, along with cranberries. Mix until all ingredients are moistened. Spoon batter into prepared pan.

Combine topping ingredients and sprinkle evenly over cake.

Bake 40 minutes, until firm. Place on a wire rack.

Prepare sauce by combining cornstarch and cinnamon in a small saucepan. Mix well. Add remaining sauce ingredients, stirring until cornstarch is dissolved. Bring mixture to a boil over medium heat, stirring constantly. Continue to cook, stirring, for 1 minute.

To serve, spoon hot cake into individual bowls and top each serving with 2 tablespoons of the sauce.

Each serving provides:			
254	Calories	49 g	Carbohydrate
6 g	Protein	222 mg	Sodium
4 g	Total fat (1 g Sat. fat)	1 mg	Cholesterol

Golden Papaya Cake

Like bits of gold, the chopped papaya and golden raisins sparkle in this jewel of a cake.

Makes 12 servings

Topping
2	teaspoons sugar
1/4	teaspoon ground cinnamon
1/16	teaspoon *each* ground nutmeg and ground ginger

Cake
3/4	cup whole wheat flour
3/4	cup all-purpose flour
1	teaspoon baking soda
1/2	teaspoon baking powder
1/2	teaspoon ground cinnamon
1/4	teaspoon *each* ground nutmeg and ground ginger
1	cup vanilla nonfat yogurt
1/3	cup firmly packed brown sugar
2	egg whites
2	tablespoons vegetable oil
1	teaspoon vanilla extract
1/2	teaspoon lemon extract
1	cup chopped papaya, in 1/4-inch pieces, peeled, seeds discarded
1/3	cup golden raisins

Preheat oven to 350°.

Lightly oil an 8-inch square baking pan or spray with a nonstick cooking spray.

In a small bowl or custard cup, combine all topping ingredients. Mix well and set aside.

To make the cake, in a large bowl, combine both types of flour, baking soda, baking powder, and remaining spices. Mix well.

In another bowl, combine yogurt, brown sugar, egg whites, oil, and extracts. Beat with a fork or wire whisk until blended. Add to dry mixture, mixing until all ingredients are moistened. Fold in papaya and raisins. Spoon mixture into prepared pan, smoothing the top lightly with the back of a spoon. Sprinkle topping evenly over cake.

Bake 30 minutes, until a toothpick inserted in the center of the cake comes out clean.

Place pan on a wire rack to cool slightly. Cut into squares and serve warm for best flavor.

Each serving provides:

142	Calories	26 g	Carbohydrate
4 g	Protein	151 mg	Sodium
3 g	Total fat (0 g Sat. fat)	1 mg	Cholesterol

Maple Apple Cake

A perfect ending to any meal, this cake is best when served warm or at room temperature. It can be made with pears in place of the apples, or a combination of both fruits. Be sure to use pure maple syrup rather than maple-flavored syrup, for a rich maple taste.

Makes 12 servings

3/4	cup whole wheat flour
3/4	cup all-purpose flour
1	teaspoon baking powder
1/2	teaspoon baking soda
1/2	teaspoon ground cinnamon
1/2	cup maple syrup
1/2	cup applesauce (unsweetened)
1/3	cup firmly packed brown sugar
2	egg whites
2	tablespoons vegetable oil
1	teaspoon vanilla extract
2	medium Golden Delicious apples, unpeeled, chopped into 1/4-inch pieces (2 cups)
	Confectioners' sugar

Preheat oven to 350°.

Lightly oil an 8-inch square baking pan or spray with a nonstick cooking spray.

In a large bowl, combine both types of flour, baking powder, baking soda, and cinnamon. Mix well.

In another bowl, combine remaining ingredients, *except* apples and confectioners' sugar. Beat with a fork or wire whisk until blended. Stir in apples, mixing well. Add to dry mixture, mixing until all ingredients are moistened. Spoon into prepared pan.

Bake 40 to 45 minutes, until a toothpick inserted in the center of the cake comes out clean.

Cool in pan on a wire rack.

Just before serving, sprinkle top of cake lightly with confectioners' sugar. Cut into squares.

Each serving provides:

154	Calories	30 g	Carbohydrate
2 g	Protein	106 mg	Sodium
3 g	Total fat (0 g Sat. fat)	0 mg	Cholesterol

California Grape Cake

*Red grapes make a delicious, moist topping for this unusual coffee cake.
There's lots of applesauce in it, making it tender and moist—a perfect dessert
or snack. It looks nice too, as if the cake were topped with bubbles!*

Makes 8 servings

Topping

2	tablespoons sugar
1	teaspoon ground cinnamon
2	cups seedless red grapes, cut in half (measure after cutting)

Cake

3/4	cup whole wheat flour
3/4	cup all-purpose flour
1 1/2	teaspoons baking powder
1/2	teaspoon baking soda
1/2	teaspoon ground cinnamon
1	cup applesauce (unsweetened)
1/4	cup sugar
3	egg whites
1	tablespoon vegetable oil
2	teaspoons vanilla extract

Preheat oven to 350°.

Lightly oil a 9-inch cake pan or spray with a nonstick cooking spray.

To prepare topping, in a small bowl or custard cup, combine sugar and cinnamon. Mix well and set aside. Set grapes aside.

To prepare the cake, in a large bowl, combine both types of flour, baking powder, baking soda, and cinnamon. Mix well.

In another bowl, combine remaining cake ingredients. Beat with a fork or wire whisk until blended. Add to dry mixture, mixing until all ingredients are moistened. Spoon batter into prepared pan.

Sprinkle 2 teaspoons of the sugar and cinnamon mixture evenly over the cake. Spread grapes over cake. Press them down gently into the batter. Top with remaining sugar and cinnamon.

Bake 35 to 40 minutes, until a toothpick inserted in the center of the cake comes out clean. (Make sure you do not stick the toothpick into a grape.)

Cool in pan on a wire rack.

Each serving provides:			
190	Calories	38 g	Carbohydrate
4 g	Protein	193 mg	Sodium
3 g	Total fat (0 g Sat. fat)	0 mg	Cholesterol

Citrus Sunshine Cake

What a great way to add the fiber and good nutrition of vegetables—hide them in a sweet, moist cake!

Makes 12 servings

Cake

3/4	cup whole wheat flour
3/4	cup all-purpose flour
1 1/2	teaspoons baking powder
1	teaspoon ground cinnamon
1/8	teaspoon ground allspice
1/2	cup sugar
1/3	cup frozen orange juice concentrate, thawed
2	egg whites
2	tablespoons vegetable oil
1	teaspoon vanilla extract
1	teaspoon grated fresh orange peel
1	teaspoon grated fresh lemon peel
1	cup (packed) finely shredded yellow summer squash, unpeeled

Topping

2	teaspoons sugar
1/2	teaspoon ground cinnamon

Preheat oven to 350°.

Lightly oil an 8-inch square baking pan or spray with a nonstick cooking spray.

In a large bowl, combine both types of flour, baking powder, cinnamon, and allspice. Mix well.

In another bowl, combine sugar, orange juice concentrate, egg whites, oil, vanilla, orange peel, and lemon peel. Beat with a fork or wire whisk until blended. Stir in squash. Add to dry mixture, mixing until all ingredients are moistened. Spoon batter into prepared pan.

Combine topping ingredients in a small bowl and mix well. Sprinkle evenly over cake.

Bake 35 minutes, until a toothpick inserted in the center of the cake comes out clean.

Cool in pan on a wire rack.

◆*Quick tip:* While you're shredding the orange and lemon peel, shred some extra and freeze it. Next time you need it, you can use it right out of the freezer.

Each serving provides:

132	Calories	24 g	Carbohydrate
3 g	Protein	71 mg	Sodium
3 g	Total fat (0 g Sat. fat)	0 mg	Cholesterol

Spiced Cornmeal Cake
with Creamy Rum Topping

The inspiration for this moist, dense cornmeal cake came from the very popu-
lar Indian pudding. The rum-flavored topping blends perfectly with the aro-
matic spices in the cake.

Makes 8 servings

Cake

1	cup yellow cornmeal (plus a little extra for dusting the pan)
1	cup all-purpose flour
2	teaspoons baking powder
$1^1/_2$	teaspoons ground cinnamon
$1/_2$	teaspoon ground cardamom
$1/_4$	teaspoon *each* ground ginger, nutmeg, and cloves
1	cup skim milk
$3/_4$	cup firmly packed brown sugar
$1/_2$	cup applesauce (unsweetened)
2	tablespoons vegetable oil
2	egg whites
1	teaspoon *each* vanilla extract and rum extract

Rum Topping

1	cup vanilla nonfat yogurt
2	teaspoons firmly packed brown sugar
$1/_2$	teaspoon rum extract

Preheat oven to 375°.

Lightly oil a 9-inch round cake pan or spray with a nonstick cook-ing spray. Dust pan lightly with cornmeal, then shake out any excess.

In a large bowl, combine cornmeal, flour, baking powder, and spices. Mix well.

In another bowl, combine remaining cake ingredients. Beat with a fork or wire whisk until blended. Add to dry mixture, stirring until all ingredients are moistened. Spoon mixture into prepared pan.

Bake 25 to 30 minutes, or until a toothpick inserted in the center of the cake comes out clean.

While cake is baking, combine topping ingredients, mixing well. Chill until serving time.

Place pan on a wire rack. Cut cake into wedges and serve warm for best flavor. Top each serving of cake with 2 tablespoons of the topping.

(If you are not serving the cake right away, you can keep it moist by covering the hot cake with a clean dish towel until serving time.)

Each serving provides:

294	Calories	56 g	Carbohydrate
7 g	Protein	182 mg	Sodium
4 g	Total fat (1 g Sat. fat)	1 mg	Cholesterol

Orange Cake with "Magic" Orange Sauce

I call it "magic" because when the cake is baked, the orange sauce magically appears. The cake is moist, the sauce is sweet, and the dessert is sure to be a winner. For a really special presentation, invert a serving of cake into a bowl, top with a scoop of lowfat or nonfat vanilla ice cream or frozen yogurt, then top with the hot orange sauce.

Makes 9 servings

2/3	cup all-purpose flour
2/3	cup whole wheat flour
1	tablespoon baking powder
1	teaspoon ground cinnamon
1/2	cup plus 2 tablespoons skim milk
1/4	cup firmly packed brown sugar
1/4	cup molasses
2	tablespoons vegetable oil
11/2	cups very hot water
1/4	cup plus 2 tablespoons frozen orange juice concentrate, thawed
3	tablespoons firmly packed brown sugar

Preheat oven to 350°.

In a 9-inch square ungreased baking pan, combine both types of flour, baking powder, and cinnamon. Mix well, right in the pan.

In a small bowl, combine milk, 1/4 cup brown sugar, molasses, and oil. Mix well. Add to dry mixture. Mix with a fork until batter is smooth, then spread evenly in the pan.

Using the same small bowl, combine hot water, orange juice concentrate, and 3 tablespoons of brown sugar. Gently pour over the batter.

Bake 40 minutes. Let stand 15 minutes.

To serve, scoop cake with a large spoon and invert into individual serving bowls. Spoon sauce over each serving.

Serve hot for best flavor.

✧*Serve-again hint:* Serve leftovers cold or heat each serving briefly in the microwave.

Each serving provides:

182	Calories	36 g	Carbohydrate
3 g	Protein	180 mg	Sodium
3 g	Total fat (0 g Sat. fat)	0 mg	Cholesterol

Hot Fudge–Raspberry Pudding Cake

This is a revised version of a luscious cake that was popular in the '70s. It's best served hot and is a delectable way to end a special meal. In place of the raspberries, dark, sweet pitted cherries will also work.

Makes 9 servings

1/2	cup whole wheat flour
1/2	cup all-purpose flour
1/4	cup plus 2 tablespoons sugar
2	tablespoons cocoa (unsweetened)
2	teaspoons baking powder
1/2	cup skim milk
2	tablespoons vegetable oil
1 1/2	teaspoons vanilla extract
3/4	teaspoon almond extract
1	cup raspberries (unsweetened), fresh or frozen (if using frozen berries, thaw them slightly, separate them, and drain on towels to remove ice crystals)
1/2	cup firmly packed brown sugar
3	tablespoons cocoa (unsweetened)
1 3/4	cups very hot water

Preheat oven to 350°.

In a 9-inch square ungreased baking pan, combine both types of flour, sugar, 2 tablespoons cocoa, and baking powder. Mix well, right in the pan. Make a well in the center of the mixture and pour in the milk, oil, and extracts. Mix with a fork until smooth, then spread batter evenly in the pan.

Sprinkle raspberries evenly over batter.

In a small bowl, combine brown sugar with 3 tablespoons cocoa, mixing well. Sprinkle evenly over the batter, then gently pour hot water over it all.

Bake, uncovered, 40 minutes. Let stand 15 minutes.

To serve, scoop with a large spoon and invert into individual serving bowls. Spoon sauce over each serving.

Serve hot for best flavor.

❖*Serve-again hint:* Serve leftovers cold or heat each serving briefly in the microwave.

Each serving provides:

175	Calories	35 g	Carbohydrate
3 g	Protein	122 mg	Sodium
4 g	Total fat (1 g Sat. fat)	0 mg	Cholesterol

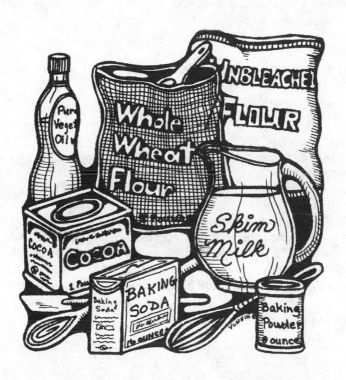

Brownies Deluxe

I call these tender, moist brownies "deluxe" because they taste so rich and chocolatey. They can be made with cocoa or carob powder and are luscious either way.

Makes 12 brownies

Brownies
1/2	cup whole wheat flour
3/4	cup sugar
1/3	cup cocoa (unsweetened)
1/4	teaspoon baking powder
3	egg whites
1/2	cup applesauce (unsweetened)
1	tablespoon vegetable oil
1	teaspoon vanilla extract
1/8	teaspoon almond extract

Icing
2	tablespoons cocoa (unsweetened) or carob powder
2	tablespoons honey
1	tablespoon skim milk
1/8	teaspoon almond extract (optional)

Preheat oven to 350°.

Lightly oil an 8-inch square baking pan or spray with a nonstick cooking spray.

In a medium bowl, combine flour, sugar, cocoa, and baking powder. Mix well.

Place egg whites in a small bowl. Beat with a fork or wire whisk until frothy. Add applesauce, oil, and extracts, mixing well. Add to dry mixture. Mix until all ingredients are moistened. Spoon into prepared pan.

Bake 20 to 25 minutes, until a toothpick inserted in the center of the brownies comes out clean. Do not overbake.

Cool in pan on a wire rack.

In a small bowl, combine icing ingredients. Mix well. Spread on cooled brownies.

❖*Serve-again hint:* Topped with lowfat vanilla ice cream and the Hot Honey-Fudge Sauce on page 439, you have a dessert to die for!

❖*Variation:* Carob powder will work in place of the cocoa, giving a different yet still delicious flavor.

Each serving provides:			
107	Calories	22 g	Carbohydrate
2 g	Protein	26 mg	Sodium
2 g	Total fat (0 g Sat. fat)	0 mg	Cholesterol

Strawberry Jam Bars

Adapted from Oat Cuisine, *these fruity-sweet bars are a perfect dessert, breakfast bar, or anytime snack. They're simply stupendous when served warm and topped with lowfat vanilla ice cream. Any jam will work; however, my family is definitely partial to strawberry.*

Makes 16 bars

1	cup rolled oats
$1/2$	cup all-purpose flour
$1/2$	cup whole wheat flour
$1/2$	teaspoon baking powder
$2/3$	cup skim milk
$1/3$	cup firmly packed brown sugar
2	tablespoons vegetable oil
1	teaspoon vanilla extract
$1/3$	cup fruit-only strawberry jam (or any other favorite flavor)

Preheat oven to 350°.

Lightly oil an 8-inch square baking pan or spray with a nonstick cooking spray.

In a large bowl, combine oats, both types of flour, and baking powder. Mix well.

In a small bowl, stir together milk, brown sugar, oil, and vanilla. Add to dry mixture, mixing until all ingredients are moistened.

Set aside $1/2$ cup of oat mixture. Spread remaining mixture in the bottom of prepared pan.

Spread jam evenly over oat mixture.

Using a ¹/4 teaspoon measuring spoon, drop reserved mixture evenly over jam. Press down lightly into the jam, wetting your fingertips slightly to prevent sticking.

Bake 23 to 25 minutes, until top is firm and edges begin to brown.

Place pan on a wire rack to cool slightly, then cut into squares and serve warm or at room temperature.

Each serving provides:

99	Calories	18 g	Carbohydrate
2 g	Protein	23 mg	Sodium
2 g	Total fat (0 g Sat. fat)	0 mg	Cholesterol

Blueberry Bread Pudding with Lemon Glaze

My Mom came up with this luscious dessert. She combined two of our favorites (bread pudding and lemon sauce) with special results.

Makes 8 servings

Bread Pudding

4	slices whole wheat bread, cubed (4 cups)
1	cup blueberries, fresh or frozen (if using frozen, there's no need to thaw)
2	cups skim milk
3	egg whites
1/3	cup sugar
1	teaspoon vanilla extract
1/4	teaspoon lemon extract
1/4	teaspoon ground cinnamon
1/8	teaspoon almond extract

Lemon Glaze

1	cup water
3	tablespoons sugar
1 1/2	tablespoons lemon juice
1	tablespoon plus 1 teaspoon cornstarch

Preheat oven to 350°.

Lightly oil an 8-inch square baking pan or spray with a nonstick cooking spray.

Place bread cubes in prepared pan. Top with blueberries.

In a medium bowl, combine remaining bread pudding ingredients. Beat with a fork or wire whisk until blended. Pour over bread and blueberries. Let stand 10 minutes.

Bake 45 minutes, until set. Place on a wire rack to cool.

When bread pudding is finished baking, combine glaze ingredients in a small saucepan. Bring to a boil over medium heat, stirring constantly. Continue to cook, stirring, 1 minute.

Spoon glaze over bread pudding. With a long-tined fork, pierce the pudding every inch or so to allow some of the glaze to run down into the pudding.

Chill.

♦ *Variation:* If you want the otherwise clear glaze to have a light pink tint, you can replace 1 tablespoon of the sugar with a red jelly, such as currant or grape. Be sure to use jelly and not jam.

Each serving provides:			
136	Calories	27 g	Carbohydrate
5 g	Protein	129 mg	Sodium
1 g	Total fat (0 g Sat. fat)	1 mg	Cholesterol

Cranberry-Orange Bread Pudding

If you buy lots of cranberries in the fall and keep them in the freezer, you can enjoy them all year long. This pudding is delicious warm or cold and is a natural for Thanksgiving.

Makes 12 servings

Bread Pudding

8	slices (1-ounce each) whole wheat bread, torn into small pieces
2	cups fresh (or frozen, thawed) cranberries
1	large orange, peeled and sectioned (grate peel first, then discard white membrane)
1	teaspoon grated fresh orange peel
3/4	cup sugar
2	12-ounce cans evaporated skim milk (3 cups)
5	egg whites
1	teaspoon vanilla extract
1/4	teaspoon almond extract

Topping

2	teaspoons sugar
1/4	teaspoon ground cinnamon

Lightly oil a 9-inch square baking pan or spray with a nonstick cooking spray.

Place *half* of the bread in prepared pan.

In a blender container, combine cranberries, orange sections, orange peel, and 1/4 cup of the sugar. Blend, turning the blender on and off several times, until cranberries are coarsely chopped but not pureed. Spoon cranberry mixture over bread. Top with remaining bread.

Rinse blender and add remaining sugar, milk, egg whites, and extracts. Blend just until combined. Pour mixture evenly over bread.

Let stand 45 minutes at room temperature.
Combine topping ingredients and sprinkle evenly over bread.
Preheat oven to 325°.
Bake, uncovered, 40 to 45 minutes, until set.
❖*Serve-again hint:* What a delicious breakfast!

Each serving provides:

176	Calories	34 g	Carbohydrate
8 g	Protein	196 mg	Sodium
1 g	Total fat (0 g Sat. fat)	3 mg	Cholesterol

Peach-Nut Pudding Cake

One bowl, one pan, and eight delicious servings of this tender, moist cake.
Serve it warm, either alone or topped with lowfat vanilla ice cream, for a
dessert that you can almost make while your company is coming up the walk.

Makes 8 servings

1/4   cup whole wheat flour
1/4   cup all-purpose flour
1   teaspoon baking powder
1/3   cup firmly packed brown sugar
2   egg whites
1   teaspoon vanilla extract
1/2   teaspoon almond extract
1 1/2 cups chopped, peeled, ripe peaches (choose peaches that are
       very ripe)
2   tablespoons chopped walnuts

Preheat oven to 325°.

Lightly oil a 9-inch pie pan or spray with a nonstick cooking spray.

In a medium bowl, combine both types of flour and baking powder. Mix well, then stir in brown sugar. Add egg whites and extracts
and mix until all ingredients are moistened. Stir in peaches and nuts.

Spoon mixture into prepared pan.

Bake 30 to 35 minutes, until center of cake feels firm.

Serve warm.

Note: For a fancy presentation, you can make a design on the top of
the cake by placing a doily over the cake, sprinkling with confectioners' sugar, then removing the doily. Be sure to do this just before serving, as the sugar will soon disappear into the cake.

	Each serving provides:		
99	Calories	19 g	Carbohydrate
2 g	Protein	79 mg	Sodium
2 g	Total fat (0 g Sat. fat)	0 mg	Cholesterol

Angel Cake Pudding

In this delicious version of the all-American bread pudding, angel food cake replaces the traditional bread cubes. It's a delectable, sweet dessert that is great by itself, and it can also be topped with any flavor fruit-only pancake topping.

Makes 8 servings

Cake Pudding

4	cups angel food cake, cut into small cubes
1/3	cup raisins, preferably golden
2	cups skim milk
3	egg whites
1/4	cup sugar
2	teaspoons vanilla extract

Topping

2	teaspoons sugar
1/4	teaspoon ground cinnamon

Preheat oven to 350°.

Lightly oil an 8-inch square baking pan or spray with a nonstick cooking spray.

Place cake cubes and raisins in prepared pan, making sure the raisins are evenly distributed.

In a medium bowl, combine milk, egg whites, sugar, and vanilla. Beat with a fork or wire whisk until well blended. Pour over cake. Let stand 5 minutes.

In a small bowl or custard cup, combine topping ingredients. Sprinkle evenly over pudding.

Bake, uncovered, 40 to 45 minutes, until pudding is set and top is lightly browned.

Serve warm or cold.

✦*Quick tip:* Stop by your local supermarket and pick up an already baked angel food cake. The rest is easy.

Each serving provides:

150	Calories	5 g	Carbohydrate
5 g	Protein	248 mg	Sodium
1 g	Total fat (0 g Sat. fat)	1 mg	Cholesterol

Strawberry Custard Pie

Filled with luscious fresh strawberries, this crustless pie is so easy, you'll want to make it every time fresh berries appear on the grocery shelf. It's delicious warm or cold and looks pretty when sprinkled with a little confectioners' sugar just before serving.

Makes 8 servings

Strawberries

4	cups strawberries, cut in half lengthwise (measure after cutting)
3	tablespoons sugar
1	tablespoon plus 1 teaspoon cornstarch
1	tablespoon orange juice

Custard

1	cup skim milk
$1/4$	cup whole wheat flour
$1/4$	cup all-purpose flour
3	egg whites
3	tablespoons sugar
2	teaspoons vanilla extract
$1^1/2$	teaspoons grated fresh orange peel
$1/8$	teaspoon ground cinnamon

Preheat oven to 350°.

Lightly oil a 9-inch pie pan or spray with a nonstick cooking spray.

In a large bowl, combine strawberries, sugar, cornstarch, and orange juice. Mix well. Spoon into prepared pan.

In a blender container, combine all of the custard ingredients. Blend until smooth. Pour over berries.

Bake 45 minutes, until golden.

Each serving provides:

118	Calories	24 g	Carbohydrate
4 g	Protein	38 mg	Sodium
1 g	Total fat (0 g Sat. fat)	1 mg	Cholesterol

Spiced Yellow Summer Pie

There's one word missing from the name of this recipe—squash! It's really a yellow squash pie, but no one will ever guess. What a perfectly delicious way to use up an abundant vegetable. It's delicious plain and can also be topped with crushed pineapple and lowfat whipped topping or vanilla nonfat yogurt.

Makes 8 servings

Crust

1¹/₂	tablespoons margarine, melted
1¹/₂	tablespoons honey
³/₄	cup graham cracker crumbs

Filling

4	egg whites
2¹/₂	cups (rounded) yellow summer squash, unpeeled, cut into ¹/₂-inch to 1-inch pieces
1	cup nonfat dry milk
¹/₄	cup sugar
1¹/₂	teaspoons vanilla extract
1¹/₂	teaspoons pumpkin pie spice
1	tablespoon all-purpose flour
1	teaspoon baking powder

Preheat oven to 350°.

Combine margarine and honey in a 9-inch pie pan. Add graham cracker crumbs and mix until crumbs are moistened. Press crumbs onto bottom and sides of pan to form crust. Bake 5 minutes.

In a blender container, combine all filling ingredients. Blend until smooth. Pour into crust. Bake 25 minutes, or until set.

Cool slightly, then chill.

◆*Quick tip:* Eliminate the crust and just bake the filling. Serve it warm, scooped into bowls and topped with lowfat vanilla ice cream or frozen yogurt.

Each serving provides:

155	Calories	25 g	Carbohydrate
6 g	Protein	229 mg	Sodium
3 g	Total fat (0 g Sat. fat)	2 mg	Cholesterol

Winter Fruit Crisp

You don't have to wait for winter to make this delicious dessert. Freeze some cranberries while they are in season and enjoy this treat all winter long.

Makes 8 servings

Fruit
1/3	cup water
1	tablespoon cornstarch
2	cups cranberries (if using frozen cranberries, thaw them slightly before using)
1	medium Golden Delicious apple, unpeeled, thinly sliced
1	medium pear, unpeeled, thinly sliced
1/3	cup sugar
1	cup fresh orange sections, or 1 eight-ounce can mandarin oranges, packed in juice, drained

Topping
1	cup rolled oats
3	tablespoons all-purpose flour
1	teaspoon ground cinnamon
2	tablespoons firmly packed brown sugar
3	tablespoons honey
2	tablespoons vegetable oil

Preheat oven to 350°.

Lightly oil a 9-inch pie pan or spray with a nonstick cooking spray.

In a small bowl, combine water and cornstarch. Stir to dissolve cornstarch.

In a medium saucepan, combine cranberries, apple, pear, sugar, and cornstarch mixture. Cook over medium heat, stirring frequently, 5 to 10 minutes, until cranberries pop. Remove from heat.

Gently stir orange sections into cranberry mixture. Spoon into prepared pan.

To prepare topping, in a medium bowl, combine oats, flour, cinnamon, and brown sugar, mixing well. Add honey and oil. Mix with a fork until all ingredients are moistened. Distribute evenly over cranberry mixture.

Bake, uncovered, 30 to 35 minutes, until lightly browned.

Serve warm or cold.

Each serving provides:			
203	Calories	40 g	Carbohydrate
2 g	Protein	3 mg	Sodium
5 g	Total fat (1 g Sat. fat)	0 mg	Cholesterol

Maple Peach Crisp

*Raisins dot this luscious dessert, with maple syrup adding sweetness and fla-
vor. Although it's a perfect summer dessert, it can be made throughout the
year with frozen unsweetened peaches. (Be sure to thaw and drain them
first.)*

Makes 8 servings

Peaches
6   cups thinly sliced ripe peaches, peeled (about 2 pounds)
1/3   cup raisins
2   teaspoons cornstarch
1   teaspoon ground cinnamon
1/4   cup maple syrup
1   tablespoon lemon juice

Topping
1   cup rolled oats
1/4   cup whole wheat flour
2   tablespoons chopped walnuts
1/2   teaspoon ground cinnamon
3   tablespoons maple syrup
2   tablespoons vegetable oil
1   teaspoon vanilla extract

Preheat oven to 350°.

Lightly oil a 9-inch pie pan or spray with a nonstick cooking spray.

Place peaches and raisins in a large bowl. Combine cornstarch and
cinnamon and sprinkle over peaches. Toss to distribute cornstarch
mixture.

Add maple syrup and lemon juice, mixing well. Spoon into prepared pan.

In a small bowl, combine oats, flour, walnuts, and cinnamon, mixing well. Add remaining ingredients. Mix until all ingredients are
moistened. Distribute topping evenly over peaches.

Bake, uncovered, 35 minutes, until lightly browned.
Serve warm or cold.

❖*Serve-again hint:* Why not enjoy a sweet breakfast? After all, it's really cereal and fruit!

Each serving provides:			
223	Calories	42 g	Carbohydrate
3 g	Protein	4 mg	Sodium
6 g	Total fat (1 g Sat. fat)	0 mg	Cholesterol

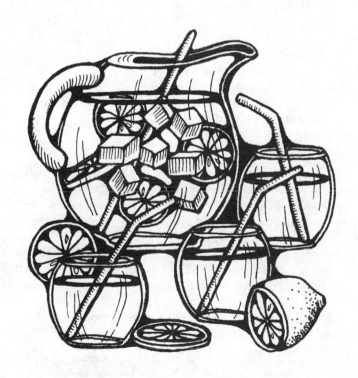

Strawberry-Rhubarb Crisp

This luscious springtime dessert can be served warm or cold and is ideal topped with vanilla nonfat frozen yogurt or ice cream. If you've never tried rhubarb, this is a great place to start. (Rhubarb leaves are toxic, so be sure to discard them.)

Makes 8 servings

Fruit

3	cups quartered fresh strawberries
2	cups fresh rhubarb, cut into 1/2-inch pieces
1/3	cup sugar
2	tablespoons cornstarch
1/4	teaspoon ground cinnamon
1/2	cup orange juice

Topping

1	cup rolled oats
3	tablespoons whole wheat flour
2 1/2	tablespoons sugar
1	teaspoon ground cinnamon
2 1/2	tablespoons orange juice
2	tablespoons vegetable oil

Preheat oven to 350°.

Lightly oil a 9-inch pie pan or spray with a nonstick cooking spray. Toss strawberries and rhubarb together in a large bowl.

In a small bowl, combine sugar, cornstarch, and cinnamon. Gradually stir in orange juice, stirring until cornstarch is dissolved. Pour over fruit and mix well. Place fruit in prepared pan.

To prepare topping, combine oats, flour, sugar, and cinnamon in a medium bowl, mixing well. Add orange juice and oil. Mix with a fork until all ingredients are moistened. Distribute topping evenly over fruit.

Bake 35 minutes, until fruit is bubbly and topping is lightly browned.

✦*Quick tip:* Frozen (thawed) rhubarb will also work. Look for it in the grocery store or freeze your own when rhubarb is in season.

◇*Serve-again hint:* In parfait glasses, alternate layers of fruit and topping with vanilla nonfat frozen yogurt. Serve right away for an elegant dinner finale.

Each serving provides:

172	Calories	31 g	Carbohydrate
3 g	Protein	3 mg	Sodium
5 g	Total fat (1 g Sat. fat)	0 mg	Cholesterol

Pumpkin Crisp

One easy way to cut calories and fat from pies is to eliminate the crust and substitute a crispy topping instead. This version is so sweet and rich, no one will feel anything is missing.

Makes 8 servings

Filling
1	1-pound can pumpkin
3	egg whites
1/2	cup firmly packed brown sugar
1/2	cup evaporated skim milk
2	teaspoons pumpkin pie spice
1	teaspoon vanilla extract
1	teaspoon maple extract

Topping
3/4	cup rolled oats
3	tablespoons whole wheat flour
1/2	teaspoon pumpkin pie spice
2 1/2	tablespoons maple syrup
2	tablespoons vegetable oil

Preheat oven to 350°.

Lightly oil a 9-inch pie pan or spray with a nonstick cooking spray.

In a large bowl, combine all filling ingredients. Beat with a fork or wire whisk until blended. Pour into prepared pan.

To prepare the topping, in a small bowl, combine oats, flour, and pumpkin pie spice, mixing well. Add remaining ingredients. Mix until all ingredients are moistened. Distribute topping evenly over pumpkin filling.

Bake, uncovered, 35 minutes, until filling is set and top is lightly browned.

Serve at room temperature. Refrigerate leftovers.

Each serving provides:

184	Calories	32 g	Carbohydrate
5 g	Protein	48 mg	Sodium
5 g	Total fat (1 g Sat. fat)	1 mg	Cholesterol

Gingered Pear Crisp

Crystallized ginger in the topping adds just the right spark of flavor to this fruity dessert. Served warm or cold, it's delicious topped with nonfat vanilla ice cream or frozen yogurt.

Makes 8 servings

Pears

4	large Bosc pears, unpeeled, cut lengthwise into quarters, cored, and then sliced crosswise into 1/8-inch slices (2 pounds)
1/4	cup firmly packed brown sugar
1	tablespoon lemon juice
1/2	teaspoon ground cinnamon

Topping

1/2	cup whole wheat flour
1/4	cup Grape Nuts cereal
1/4	cup firmly packed brown sugar
1/2	cup finely chopped crystallized ginger (1 ounce)
2	tablespoons vegetable oil
2	tablespoons orange juice

Preheat oven to 375°.

Lightly oil a 9-inch pie pan or spray with a nonstick cooking spray.

Place pears in a large bowl and sprinkle with brown sugar, lemon juice, and cinnamon. Mix well. Transfer pears to prepared pie pan.

To prepare topping, in another bowl, combine flour, Grape Nuts, brown sugar, and ginger. Mix well, using a fork. Add oil and orange juice. Continue to mix until all ingredients are moistened and mixture resembles coarse crumbs.

Sprinkle topping evenly over pears.

Bake, uncovered, 35 to 40 minutes, until lightly browned.

Each serving provides:

201	Calories	41 g	Carbohydrate
2 g	Protein	30 mg	Sodium
5 g	Total fat (1 g Sat. fat)	0 mg	Cholesterol

No-Bake Desserts

Even when you have no time to bake, lots of delectable, sweet desserts can be assembled quickly and easily. They work just as well to satisfy that sweet tooth. Some of the desserts in this section require a little stove-top cooking, while others are simply assembled and chilled. The important principle here is to make sure all of the main building blocks are nutritious, lowfat ingredients, such as reduced-fat or fat-free ice cream and other dairy products, reduced-fat silken tofu, angel food cake, and lots of fruit.

From simple puddings to exotic trifles, they're all here and all made easy and healthful—just for you.

Fabulous Berry Party Trifle

Wow! Can you believe it? A fabulous party dessert with only 1 gram of fat per serving? Whatever you do, don't tell them it's good for them!

Makes 12 servings

Cream Filling
1	12-ounce container lowfat (1%) cottage cheese
2	8-ounce containers fat-free lemon yogurt
1/4	cup plus 2 tablespoons sugar
1	teaspoon vanilla extract
1/4	teaspoon lemon extract

Cake Layer
1	10 to 12-ounce angel food cake

Fruit Layer
4	cups mixed raspberries, blueberries, and sliced strawberries (fresh fruit is best, but frozen unsweetened fruit, thawed and drained, can also be used)
1 1/2	cups strawberry jam

Have a clear, straight-sided 2-quart to 3-quart bowl ready.

Place cottage cheese in a blender container. Blend just until smooth. Spoon into a bowl and add remaining filling ingredients, mixing well. Place in the refrigerator while preparing remaining layers.

Cut cake into 1-inch cubes (6 cups of cubes).

Combine fruit and jam in another bowl, tossing gently. (Because raspberries are so delicate, it is best to toss the other fruits with the jam and then gently fold in the raspberries.)

To assemble, arrange *half* of the cake cubes in the bottom of the bowl. Top with *half* of the fruit, making sure it touches the edges of the bowl so it will look pretty. Spoon *half* of the creme filling (about 1 1/2 cups) evenly over the fruit.

Repeat the three layers.

Cover and chill several hours or overnight.

If desired, before serving, garnish with a few small dollops of strawberry jam.

✧*Serve-again hint:* Pray for leftovers!

Each serving provides:

200	Calories	43 g	Carbohydrate
7 g	Protein	335 mg	Sodium
1 g	Total fat (0 g Sat. fat)	1 mg	Cholesterol

Blueberry Couscous Loaf

In this unusual dessert, couscous is mixed with blueberries, then molded into a loaf. When chilled, the loaf is sliced and topped with a delectable blueberry sauce. This is so different, you really have to try it.

Makes 12 servings

Couscous Loaf

3	cups water
1¹/₂	cups couscous, uncooked
¹/₂	cup orange juice
¹/₄	cup plus 2 tablespoons honey
1	tablespoon plus 2 teaspoons cornstarch
1	tablespoon vanilla extract
¹/₂	teaspoon *each* lemon and orange extract
¹/₂	teaspoon ground cinnamon
1¹/₂	cups fresh or frozen (thawed and drained) blueberries

Blueberry Sauce

1	cup fresh or frozen blueberries (if using frozen berries, there's no need to thaw)
¹/₄	cup orange juice
¹/₄	cup fruit-only blueberry, raspberry, *or* strawberry spread

Line a 4 × 8-inch loaf pan with waxed paper.

Bring water to a boil in a small saucepan. Stir in couscous, cover, remove from heat, and set aside for 5 minutes.

In another small saucepan, combine orange juice, honey, cornstarch, extracts, and cinnamon. Stir to dissolve cornstarch. Bring to a boil over medium heat, stirring constantly. Continue to boil, stirring, for 1 minute, or until mixture has thickened.

Fluff couscous with a fork. Stir couscous into the honey mixture, about a quarter at a time, stirring well after each addition. (You may need to transfer everything to a bowl, if your saucepan is too small to allow enough room for mixing.) Gently fold in blueberries.

Spoon mixture into prepared pan. Press in place with the back of a spoon. Cover and chill thoroughly, preferably overnight.

Prepare sauce up to an hour before serving time: Place blueberries and orange juice in a small saucepan. Bring to a boil over medium heat. Reduce heat slightly and simmer 5 minutes. Remove from heat and stir in fruit spread.

Invert loaf onto a serving plate and gently remove wax paper. Slice loaf and top each serving with a heaping tablespoon of sauce.

Each serving provides:			
167	Calories	37 g	Carbohydrate
3 g	Protein	5 mg	Sodium
0 g	Total fat (0 g Sat. fat)	0 mg	Cholesterol

Tofu and Apple Butter Parfaits

Silken tofu blended with vanilla yogurt makes a smooth, creamy pudding. It can be enjoyed by itself or layered in parfait glasses with apple butter or jam. This nutritious dessert looks as good as it tastes.

Makes 4 servings

1	10-ounce package reduced-fat silken tofu
1	cup vanilla nonfat yogurt
1/4	cup confectioners' sugar
1 1/2	tablespoons frozen orange juice concentrate, thawed
1	teaspoon vanilla extract
1/4	teaspoon ground cinnamon
6	2 1/2-inch graham cracker squares
1/4	cup plus 2 tablespoons apple butter, unsweetened

Have four 8-ounce parfait glasses ready.

Place tofu in a blender container and blend until smooth. Spoon into a medium bowl. Add remaining ingredients, *except* graham crackers and apple butter. Mix well.

To assemble parfaits, place 1/4 cup of the tofu mixture in each parfait glass. Then add one crumbled (not crushed) graham cracker on top of the tofu in each glass. Top each graham cracker with 1 tablespoon of apple butter, spreading the apple butter evenly over the graham cracker pieces, touching the sides of the glass.

Next, add another 1/4 cup of tofu mixture to each, followed by one half of a graham cracker, crumbled, and then 1/2 tablespoon of apple butter. Top with remaining tofu (about 3 tablespoons on each).

Chill thoroughly.

Note: Most parfait glasses are narrow at the top, therefore the second graham cracker-apple butter layer requires smaller amounts than the first layer. However, if your glasses are wide at the top, you will probably need to alter the amounts and make this layer the same as the bottom one, using one graham cracker square and 1 tablespoon of apple butter for each one.

Each serving provides:			
225	Calories	42 g	Carbohydrate
7 g	Protein	108 mg	Sodium
3 g	Total fat (1 g Sat. fat)	2 mg	Cholesterol

Graham-Jam Torte

This is actually a building project, rather than a recipe! The idea came from the little houses I used to build out of cards as a child. The graham crackers will absorb the applesauce and, when the dessert has chilled, it becomes soft and can be cut like cake. The kids will love to help with this one.

Makes 6 servings

9	graham crackers, $2^{1}/_{2} \times 5$ inches (do not break into squares)
3	teaspoons fruit-only peach or apricot jam
3	teaspoons fruit-only raspberry jam
1	cup applesauce (unsweetened)
2	teaspoons chopped walnuts
	Ground cinnamon

Spread 1 teaspoon of the jams on each of 6 graham crackers (half will have peach jam and half will have raspberry). Spread $1^{1}/_{2}$ tablespoons of applesauce on top of the jam on each cracker. Layer the graham crackers on top of each other, jam side up alternating jam types. Then carefully stand them up sideways. Place 1 graham cracker on the opened jam side of the torte.

Spread $1^{1}/_{2}$ tablespoons of applesauce on 1 of the remaining graham crackers and place it, applesauce side down, on top of torte. Break remaining graham cracker in half and spread $1/_{2}$ tablespoon of applesauce on each piece. Use these to make the ends of the torte, placing the applesauce side in. "Frost" the entire torte with remaining applesauce. Sprinkle with chopped nuts and cinnamon.

Chill 5 to 6 hours, or overnight. (Do not cover.)

Slice crosswise to serve.

	Each serving provides:		
126	Calories	24 g	Carbohydrate
2 g	Protein	128 mg	Sodium
3 g	Total fat (1 g Sat. fat)	0 mg	Cholesterol

Layered Lemon Cups

A quick, no-bake, make-ahead dessert, these easy dessert cups combine the flavors of lemon, cocoa, and cinnamon in a treat that tastes like a lemon pie. You'll need to make these a day ahead, because they have to chill overnight in order for the crumb layers to absorb the yogurt. (To make more servings, simply double or triple the recipe.)

Makes 2 servings

1	tablespoon plus 1 teaspoon sugar
1¹/₂	teaspoons cocoa (unsweetened)
¹/₈	teaspoon ground cinnamon
¹/₄	cup graham cracker crumbs
1	8-ounce container nonfat lemon-flavored yogurt

In a small bowl or custard cup, combine sugar, cocoa, cinnamon, and graham cracker crumbs. Mix well. Set aside 4 teaspoons of mixture to use as topping.

In each of 2 custard cups, place 1 rounded tablespoon of the crumb mixture. Spoon 2 tablespoons of yogurt over the crumbs in each cup. Divide remaining crumbs and sprinkle over yogurt.

Divide remaining yogurt evenly and add to each cup. Divide reserved crumb mixture and sprinkle evenly over tops of cups.

Chill overnight, or until crumbs on the top and bottom are completely moistened.

Each serving provides:

196	Calories	41 g	Carbohydrate
5 g	Protein	145 mg	Sodium
1 g	Total fat (0 g Sat. fat)	0 mg	Cholesterol

Peach-Berry Angel Shortcake

Fresh, juicy peaches and ripe, red strawberries are soaked in honey and served atop ice-cold vanilla ice cream and tender angel food cake. What more need I say?

Makes 6 servings

2	cups sliced strawberries
2	cups thinly sliced peaches, peeled (frozen unsweetened peaches will work)
2	tablespoons honey
1	teaspoon lemon juice
1/2	teaspoon vanilla extract
	Angel food cake, sliced 1-inch thick
1/2	cup lowfat vanilla ice cream or frozen yogurt

In a medium bowl, combine strawberries, peaches, honey, lemon juice, and vanilla. Mix well, cover, and chill several hours, or overnight.

To serve, place a slice of cake on each serving plate. Top each slice with 1/2 cup of ice cream. Stir peaches and berries and spoon 1/3 cup over each serving.

Serve right away.

✦*Quick tip:* You can save lots of time by purchasing a ready-baked angel food cake, available in most bakeries and grocery stores.

✧*Serve-again hint:* Add other fruits to make a delicious fruit salad or a multifruit topping. Try crushed pineapple, sliced banana, fresh orange sections, cherries, and/or grapes.

Each serving provides:

227	Calories	47 g	Carbohydrate
5 g	Protein	269 mg	Sodium
3 g	Total fat (2 g Sat. fat)	9 mg	Cholesterol

Fruit-Topped Fruit Toast

Picture a luscious medley of fresh fruit, spooned over toasted cinnamon-raisin bread, and then topped with a sweet fruit puree. The fruit mixture and puree are made ahead and it's an easy last-minute dish to assemble. (Frozen, unsweetened, fruit will also work, but if you make this when fresh fruit is in season, it's a delightful way to celebrate the fruits of summer.)

Makes 8 servings

Fruit

2	oranges, peeled and sectioned (discard white membranes)
3	large plums, peeled and coarsely chopped
3	large apricots, unpeeled, coarsely copped
2	large peaches, peeled and coarsely chopped
15	sweet red cherries, cut in half and pitted
2	to 3 tablespoons sugar, depending on ripeness of fruit

Fruit Puree

1	orange, peeled and sectioned (discard white membranes)
1	large plum, peeled and coarsely chopped
2	large apricots, peeled and coarsely chopped
1	large peach, peeled and coarsely chopped
3	to 4 tablespoons sugar, depending on ripeness of fruit
1	teaspoon grated fresh orange peel
1/4	teaspoon ground cinnamon
1	teaspoon vanilla extract
1/3	cup vanilla nonfat yogurt

Toast

8	slices cinnamon-raisin bread (1-ounce slices)

Prepare fruit by combining all ingredients in a medium bowl and mix well. Chill several hours or overnight.

To prepare the puree, in a medium saucepan, combine all puree ingredients, *except* vanilla and yogurt. Bring to a boil over medium heat. Reduce heat to medium-low and simmer 15 minutes. Place fruit in a blender container and blend until smooth. Pour into a bowl.

In a small bowl, combine vanilla and yogurt. Gradually stir about 1/2 cup of the puree into the yogurt, 1 tablespoon at a time, then add to puree and mix well.

Chill several hours or overnight.

To serve, cut each slice of bread in half diagonally, making 2 tri-angles. Toast the bread and place 2 slices on each individual serving plate. Spoon ¹/2 cup of fruit over the bread. Top with 3 tablespoons of the purée.

Serve right away.

Note: Angel food cake or fat-free pound cake can be used in place of the raisin bread.

❖*Serve-again hint:* The fruit and puréed topping can also be served over lowfat or nonfat ice cream or hot oatmeal.

Each serving provides:

227	Calories	51 g	Carbohydrate
4 g	Protein	118 mg	Sodium
2 g	Total fat (0 g Sat. fat)	0 mg	Cholesterol

Maple-Rum Millet Pudding
with Chocolate Topping

Put hot, cooked millet in the blender, along with a few quick ingredients and presto! You have pudding. It's a delicious, new way to eat whole grains.

Makes 4 servings

Millet Pudding
$3/4$ cup water
$3/4$ cup skim milk
$1/2$ cup millet, uncooked
$1/4$ cup maple syrup
1   tablespoon firmly packed brown sugar
2   tablespoons skim milk
1   tablespoon rum
$1^1/4$ teaspoons vanilla extract

Chocolate Topping
2   tablespoons pure maple syrup
1   tablespoon cocoa (unsweetened)

Combine water and skim milk in a small saucepan. Bring to a boil over medium heat, stirring frequently. Stir in millet, cover, reduce heat to medium-low, and simmer 25 minutes, until most of the liquid has been absorbed.

In a blender container, combine hot millet with remaining pudding ingredients. Blend until smooth. Spoon into a shallow bowl.

Chill.

To prepare the topping, combine maple syrup and cocoa in a small bowl or custard cup. Mix until smooth. Place in the refrigerator until serving time.

Divide pudding evenly into 4 individual serving bowls. Drizzle each serving of pudding with 2 teaspoons of the chocolate topping.

Each serving provides:			
219	Calories	45 g	Carbohydrate
5 g	Protein	33 mg	Sodium
1 g	Total fat (0 g Sat. fat)	1 mg	Cholesterol

Chocolate–Peanut Butter Surprise Pudding

The surprise is the layer of peanut butter "hidden" in the middle of the pudding. This delicious idea came from our creative son-in-law, who is the family authority on both chocolate and peanut butter. Thanks, Larry!

Makes 8 servings

2	tablespoons plus 2 teaspoons peanut butter, creamy or chunky (choose one without added sugar or oil)
8	2¹/₂-inch graham cracker squares
¹/₄	cup cornstarch
¹/₄	cup cocoa, unsweetened
¹/₂	cup sugar
4	cups skim milk
1¹/₂	teaspoons vanilla extract
1	2¹/₂-inch graham cracker, crushed (for garnish)

Have a 7 × 11-inch shallow pan ready.

Spread peanut butter on graham crackers, spreading 1 teaspoon on each graham cracker. Set aside.

In a medium saucepan, combine cornstarch, cocoa, and sugar. Mix well, pressing out any lumps with the back of a spoon. Gradually add milk, stirring to dissolve cornstarch and cocoa. Cook over medium heat, stirring constantly, until mixture comes to a boil. Continue to cook, stirring, 1 minute more. Remove from heat and stir in vanilla.

Spread *half* of the pudding in the bottom of the pan. Place the graham crackers, peanut butter side up, on top of the pudding. Top with remaining pudding.

Sprinkle crushed graham cracker over pudding.

Chill.

Each serving provides:

181	Calories	31 g	Carbohydrate
7 g	Protein	138 mg	Sodium
4 g	Total fat (1 g Sat. fat)	2 mg	Cholesterol

Warm Pineapple-Farina Pudding

*Cream of Wheat (farina) is often used in desserts in Greece and the Middle
East. It makes a rather thick pudding that also doubles as a filling breakfast
and is traditionally served hot and topped with cream. However, nonfat
vanilla or lemon yogurt make delicious substitutes for the high-fat cream.*

Makes 6 servings

1	8-ounce can crushed pineapple (packed in juice), drained (reserve juice) Water
$1/3$	cup sugar
$1^1/_2$	teaspoons vanilla extract
$1/2$	teaspoon lemon extract
$1/4$	teaspoon ground cardamom
$2^1/_2$	tablespoons soft, tub-style margarine (not diet margarine)
$3/4$	cup Quick Cream of Wheat, uncooked

In a small bowl, combine reserved pineapple juice with enough
water to equal $2^1/_2$ cups. Add pineapple, sugar, extracts, and cardamom. Mix well. Set aside.

Melt margarine in a large nonstick skillet over medium heat. Add
Cream of Wheat, then reduce heat to medium-low and cook, stirring
frequently, 10 minutes.

Stir pineapple mixture and gradually add to farina, stirring briskly.
Cook, stirring frequently, 10 to 12 minutes, until mixture is thick and
most of the liquid has been absorbed.

Spoon into individual serving bowls. Top with yogurt, if desired.
Serve right away.

❖*Serve-again hint:* Leftovers can be chilled and served as a delicious
dessert or snack.

Each serving provides:

194	Calories	34 g	Carbohydrate
2 g	Protein	121 mg	Sodium
5 g	Total fat (1 g Sat. fat)	0 mg	Cholesterol

Very Peachy Tapioca

This is a delightful way to enjoy fresh peaches. Be sure to choose very ripe peaches, preferably the ones at the bottom of the basket that are a little too soft to eat out of hand.

Makes 6 servings

1	cup water
3/4	cup orange juice
1/4	cup sugar
3	tablespoons quick-cooking tapioca
6	medium, very ripe peaches (1 1/2 pounds total), peeled, cut in half, seeds removed
1/2	teaspoon almond extract
1/4	teaspoon vanilla extract

In a medium saucepan, combine water, orange juice, sugar, and tapioca. Stir mixture and let stand 5 minutes.

In a medium bowl, mash 4 of the peaches, using a fork or potato masher. Chop remaining peaches and set them aside.

Add mashed peaches to saucepan. Bring mixture to a boil over medium heat, stirring frequently. Continue to cook, stirring, for about 30 seconds. Remove from heat and stir in extracts and reserved chopped peaches.

Spoon into 1 large bowl or 6 individual bowls.

Chill thoroughly.

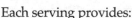

Each serving provides:			
103	Calories	26 g	Carbohydrate
1 g	Protein	23 mg	Sodium
0 g	Total fat (0 g Sat. fat)	0 mg	Cholesterol

Banana-Berry Tapioca

Don't know what to do with those too-ripe bananas? This is a perfect way to use them. The addition of nonfat dry milk to the pudding adds a richer taste without adding fat. This is a quick and easy homestyle dessert.

Makes 8 servings

2	medium, very ripe bananas (the riper the bananas, the sweeter the pudding will be)
1	teaspoon lemon juice
2	cups skim milk
1/3	cup nonfat dry milk
2	tablespoons sugar
3	tablespoons quick-cooking tapioca
2	teaspoons vanilla extract
1 1/2	cups thinly sliced strawberries, fresh or frozen (if using frozen berries, thaw them only enough to allow you to slice them—do not thaw them completely)

In a medium saucepan, thoroughly mash bananas with lemon juice. Stir in skim milk, dry milk, and sugar. Stir in tapioca. Let mixture stand 5 minutes.

Bring mixture to a full boil over medium heat, stirring constantly. Continue to cook and stir for 30 seconds. Remove from heat and stir in vanilla. Let pudding cool for 10 minutes, then stir in strawberries.

Spoon pudding into 1 large bowl or 8 individual bowls.

Chill thoroughly.

Each serving provides:

95	Calories	20 g	Carbohydrate
4 g	Protein	65 mg	Sodium
0 g	Total fat (0 g Sat. fat)	2 mg	Cholesterol

Orange-Rum Rice Cream

Modeled after a very rich dessert that I used to make, this light version has all of the interesting flavors of the original. It's thick and creamy and makes a quick, nutritious dessert.

Makes 5 servings

1	cup reduced-fat ricotta cheese
1/4	cup powdered sugar
1 1/2	teaspoons vanilla extract
1/2	teaspoon rum extract
2	large oranges, peeled and sectioned (discard white membranes)
1 1/2	cups cooked brown rice
1	tablespoon slivered almonds (optional)

In a medium bowl, combine ricotta cheese, sugar, and extracts. Mix well. Add orange sections and rice. Mix gently until well combined. Chill.

To serve, spoon into individual serving bowls (or tall-stemmed sherbet glasses) and, if desired, sprinkle with almonds.

❖*Serve-again hint:* What a delicious breakfast!

Each serving provides:

177	Calories	31 g	Carbohydrate
6 g	Protein	47 mg	Sodium
3 g	Total fat (1 g Sat. fat)	12 mg	Cholesterol

Berry-Berry Pudding

Made from frozen strawberries and raspberries, this luscious pudding allows you to enjoy the fruits of summer all year long. The berries are added while still frozen, so there's no need to even wait for them to thaw.

Makes 4 servings

1	10-ounce package frozen raspberries, in light syrup
1¹/₂	cups frozen strawberries
¹/₄	cup plus 2 tablespoons sugar
¹/₃	cup water
2	tablespoons plus 2 teaspoons cornstarch

In a medium saucepan, combine raspberries, strawberries, sugar, and *half* of the water. Bring to a full boil over medium heat, stirring frequently.

In a small bowl or custard cup, combine cornstarch with remaining water. Stir to dissolve cornstarch. Stir into saucepan. Continue to cook, stirring constantly, 1 minute.

Press berry mixture through a sieve or strainer into a bowl. Using the back of a spoon, press as much of the berry pulp as possible through the strainer. Discard seeds.

Divide pudding into 4 custard cups.

Chill.

◆*Quick tip:* If you don't want to wait for the pudding to chill, you can serve it warm, as a perfect sauce to top lowfat or nonfat ice cream, angel food cake, or fresh fruit.

	Each serving provides:		
186	Calories	47 g	Carbohydrate
1 g	Protein	3 mg	Sodium
0 g	Total fat (0 g Sat. fat)	0 mg	Cholesterol

Molasses-Raisin Pudding

Served hot, this pudding makes a wonderful treat to serve on cold winter nights. Serve it as is or spoon it over lowfat or nonfat vanilla ice cream for a homestyle dessert everyone will rave about. The leftovers (if there are any!) can either be eaten cold or reheated in a microwave.

Makes 4 servings

1²/₃	cups water
¹/₃	cup molasses
3	tablespoons firmly packed brown sugar
¹/₃	cup whole wheat flour
³/₄	teaspoon ground cinnamon
¹/₈	teaspoon ground cloves
1	cup skim milk
¹/₄	cup raisins

In a medium saucepan, combine water, molasses, and brown sugar. Bring mixture to a boil over medium heat, stirring frequently. Boil 10 minutes, reducing heat a little, but keeping mixture boiling.

In a small bowl, combine flour, cinnamon, and cloves. Mix well. Gradually add milk, stirring constantly. Mix until smooth.

Slowly stir flour mixture into saucepan. Cook, stirring constantly, 3 minutes.

Add raisins, reduce heat to low, and continue to cook and stir 5 minutes more.

Remove saucepan from heat and let stand 5 minutes, then stir pudding and spoon into individual serving bowls. Serve warm for best flavor.

Each serving provides:

194	Calories	46 g	Carbohydrate
4 g	Protein	48 mg	Sodium
0 g	Total fat (0 g Sat. fat)	1 mg	Cholesterol

Chocolate-Raspberry Pudding

If chocolate is your favorite flavor, you'll love this rich, creamy pudding. It's delicious plain and also makes a great topping for strawberries or pineapple. If you've been intending to take the "tofu leap" but haven't gotten around to it yet, this is a perfect way to begin!

Makes 4 servings

1   10-ounce package reduced-fat silken tofu
1   10-ounce package frozen raspberries in light syrup, thawed
        slightly and drained
$^1/_3$ cup confectioners' sugar
$^1/_4$ cup cocoa
$^1/_4$ teaspoon vanilla extract

Combine all ingredients in a blender container and blend until smooth.

Chill thoroughly.

❖*Variation:* Frozen unsweetened cherries make a delicious alternative to the raspberries. If you use cherries, add a drop or two of almond extract to really bring out their flavor.

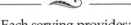

Each serving provides:			
163	Calories	33 g	Carbohydrate
5 g	Protein	6 mg	Sodium
3 g	Total fat (1 g Sat. fat)	0 mg	Cholesterol

Raspberry-Orange Pudding

Serve this thick, creamy pudding in tall-stemmed sherbet glasses for a rich dessert that can take you from family dinners to elegant dinner parties.

Makes 4 servings

1	10-ounce package reduced-fat silken tofu
1	10 ounce package frozen raspberries in light syrup, thawed slightly and drained
1/4	cup confectioners' sugar
1/2	teaspoon grated fresh orange peel

Combine all ingredients in a blender container and blend until smooth.

Chill thoroughly.

✦*Quick tip:* Grate several oranges at a time and store the peel in a small container in the freezer. There's no need to even thaw before using.

Each serving provides:

140	Calories	28 g	Carbohydrate
4 g	Protein	5 mg	Sodium
2 g	Total fat (0 g Sat. fat)	0 mg	Cholesterol

Strawberry Split Sundaes

Hot strawberry sauce spooned over vanilla ice cream makes one of the most luscious "comfort" desserts you can make. And, it's so easy!

Makes 4 servings

2	cups strawberries, fresh or frozen, cut in half (measure after cutting) (thaw frozen berries slightly before cutting)
1/3	cup strawberry jam
1/4	cup orange juice
1/2	teaspoon ground cinnamon
1	tablespoon cornstarch (increase to 1 1/2 tablespoons if using frozen berries)
1	tablespoon water (increase to 1 1/2 tablespoons if using frozen berries)
1	teaspoon grated fresh lemon peel
4	scoops vanilla fat-free ice cream or frozen yogurt (1/2 cup each)

In a small saucepan, combine strawberries, jam, orange juice, and cinnamon. Bring to a boil over medium heat, stirring frequently.

Combine cornstarch and water in a small bowl or custard cup. Stir to dissolve cornstarch. Add to saucepan, along with lemon peel. Cook, stirring constantly, about 30 seconds, or until mixture has thickened.

Spoon hot sauce over ice cream.

Serve right away.

❖*Serve-again hint:* Leftovers can be eaten cold as pudding or briefly heated in a microwave.

Each serving provides:

202	Calories	49 g	Carbohydrate
3 g	Protein	62 mg	Sodium
0 g	Total fat (0 g Sat. fat)	0 mg	Cholesterol

Cinnamon Ice Cream

Inspired by my good friend and fellow food-lover, Cheryl Martin, this flavored ice cream is quick and delicious and can turn even plain angel food cake into the fanciest of desserts.

Makes 16 servings
(1/2 cup each serving)

1/2   gallon fat-free or lowfat vanilla ice cream or frozen yogurt
4   teaspoons ground cinnamon

Let ice cream stand at room temperature until softened slightly. (Do not let it turn to liquid.) Place in a large bowl and add cinnamon. Mix well, making sure cinnamon is evenly distributed throughout the ice cream.

Return ice cream to carton or place it in a plastic container. Place in freezer until firm.

Each serving provides:

101	Calories	23 g	Carbohydrate
2 g	Protein	50 mg	Sodium
0 g	Total fat (0 g Sat. fat)	0 mg	Cholesterol

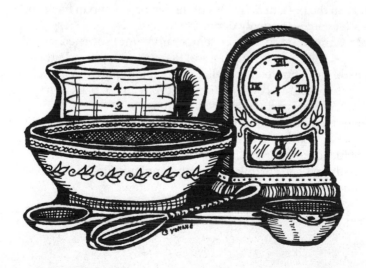

Lemonade Ice Cream Pie with Blueberry Sauce

*There are lots of scrumptious choices with this tantalizing dessert. You can
serve the pie without the sauce, you can spoon the hot sauce over the pie, or
you can chill the sauce and serve it cold. You may want to just make the
sauce without the pie and spoon it over angel food cake, fresh fruit, or lowfat
vanilla ice cream. Any way you do it, you're sure to love it.*

Makes 8 servings

Lemonade Pie
2¹/₂   tablespoons graham cracker crumbs
1   quart fat-free or lowfat vanilla ice cream or frozen yogurt
1   6-ounce can frozen lemonade concentrate, thawed

Blueberry Sauce
¹/₃   cup sugar
¹/₂   cup water
¹/₂   teaspoon ground cinnamon
¹/₄   cup fruit-only raspberry, strawberry, or blackberry spread
1   tablespoon water
1   tablespoon cornstarch
3   cups fresh or frozen (unsweetened) blueberries

Spray a 9-inch pie pan with nonstick cooking spray.

To prepare pie, sprinkle 2 tablespoons of the graham cracker
crumbs on the bottom and sides of the pie pan. Tilt pan back and
forth a few times to evenly distribute the crumbs.

Let ice cream stand at room temperature until softened slightly.
(Do not let ice cream turn to liquid.) Place in a large bowl and add
lemonade concentrate. Mix well, using a folding motion. Spoon ice
cream into prepared pan, swirling the top with the back of a spoon.

Sprinkle evenly with remaining crumbs.

Cover pie with aluminum foil and return to freezer.

To prepare sauce, in a medium saucepan, combine all ingredients,
except blueberries. Stir to dissolve cornstarch. Stir in blueberries. Cook
over medium heat, stirring frequently, until mixture comes to a boil.
Continue to cook, stirring constantly, 1 minute.

To serve pie, let pie stand at room temperature for a few minutes, then cut with a sharp knife. (If pie is too hard to cut, dip the knife in hot water before cutting each slice.) Return remaining pie to freezer. Spoon 2 tablespoons of the sauce over each serving.

Each serving provides:

247	Calories	60 g	Carbohydrate
3 g	Protein	69 mg	Sodium
1 g	Total fat (0 g Sat. fat)	0 mg	Cholesterol

Easy Tortoni

Tortoni is a luscious ice cream-like dessert that is traditionally made from whipped cream. This version is also delicious, and it's just as cold and refreshing, but most of the fat is gone.

Makes 6 servings

1	quart fat-free or lowfat vanilla ice cream or frozen yogurt
1	teaspoon rum extract
1/4	cup coarsely chopped almonds, lightly toasted*

Line 6 muffin cups with paper liners.

Remove ice cream from container and place in a large bowl to soften slightly.

Add rum extract and almonds to ice cream and mix well. (Do not let ice cream turn to liquid.) Spoon ice cream into muffin cups. Cover pan with foil and place in freezer until serving time (at least 1 hour).

Serve in the paper cups.

*Place chopped almonds on an ungreased baking sheet in a single layer. Place in oven or toaster oven at 300° until lightly toasted.

Each serving provides:

168	Calories	32 g	Carbohydrate
4 g	Protein	67 mg	Sodium
3 g	Total fat (0 g Sat. fat)	0 mg	Cholesterol

Hot Honey-Fudge Sauce

Wow! Serve this thick, sweet, and oh-so-wonderful sauce over lowfat or non-fat vanilla ice cream, angel food cake, or both. It also makes a great dipping sauce for fresh apples or pineapple. No one will believe it's fat-free. Refrigerate any leftover sauce and either serve it cold or reheat in a microwave for a few seconds.

Makes 1 cup

Sauce

1/4	cup plus 2 tablespoons cocoa (unsweetened)
1/4	cup firmly packed brown sugar
1	tablespoon plus 1 teaspoon cornstarch
1/2	cup skim milk
1/4	cup honey
1	teaspoon vanilla extract

Optional

A few drops of mint, almond, orange, or coconut extract, or a teaspoon or two of instant coffee granules

In a small saucepan, combine cocoa, brown sugar, and cornstarch. Mix well, pressing out any lumps with the back of a spoon.

Gradually stir in the milk and honey.

Bring mixture to a boil over medium heat, stirring constantly. Continue to cook and stir 1 minute. Remove from heat.

Stir in vanilla and any optional ingredients, if desired.

✦*Quick tip:* If serving this sauce hot for dessert, you can assemble it in the saucepan before dinner, set it aside, and just cook when ready.

Each tablespoon provides:

40	Calories	10 g	Carbohydrate
1 g	Protein	6 mg	Sodium
0 g	Total fat (0 g Sat. fat)	0 mg	Cholesterol

Mandarin Chocolate Cream Topping

Inspired by my kids' love for a similarly flavored ice cream, this scrumptious topping combines the popular flavors of chocolate and orange. For a special dessert, spread it on a slice of angel food cake, then top with fresh orange sections. Or, use it to top cut-up fresh fruit in tall-stemmed sherbet glasses.

Makes 1 cup

1	10-ounce package reduced-fat silken tofu
3	tablespoons confectioners' sugar
2	tablespoons cocoa (unsweetened)
2	tablespoons frozen orange juice concentrate, thawed
1	teaspoon vanilla extract

Combine all ingredients in a blender container. Blend until smooth. Chill.

✧*Serve-again hint:* This makes a delicious fondue-type dip for fresh fruit—a great after-school snack.

Each tablespoon provides:

21	Calories	3 g	Carbohydrate
1 g	Protein	1 mg	Sodium
1 g	Total fat (0 g Sat. fat)	0 mg	Cholesterol

Beverages

Beverages can provide a valuable source of vitamins, minerals, and even fiber (when made with fruit). Homemade drinks made from fruits and fruit juices are far superior to sugar-laden soda. Even many of the commercial juice and water combinations contain high amounts of sugar and very few nutrients.

This section contains lots of ideas for combining fruits and vegetables to make luscious drinks. Be creative and try other variations. Fresh fruits can be blended with fat-free or reduced-fat ice cream to produce the thickest of shakes. Even leftover fruit salad can be blended to become a beverage treat. Fruits can even be combined with vegetables.

Beverages can be made quickly and easily. All you need is a large pitcher or bottle and, in some cases, a blender. If some of these recipes make more than you can consume at one time, consider yourself lucky. You'll have some to enjoy later. Leftover hot drinks can be reheated in a microwave, and cold drinks can be stored in the refrigerator for later servings. Even thick blender drinks can be blended again with a little more ice to make them thicker.

In addition to meal accompaniments, beverages make wonderful snacks. There's nothing more refreshing than a cold drink on a hot day or more satisfying than a hot drink on a cold day. And who doesn't love a milkshake any day?

Ready, set, blend!

Breakfast Dreamsicle Delight

Here's a great way to get the nutrition of both juice and milk in one delicious drink. It's perfect for breakfast and also makes a refreshing pick-me-up at any time of day.

Makes 6 servings
($^3/_4$ cup each serving)

1	6-ounce can frozen orange juice concentrate, thawed
1$^1/_2$	cups cold skim milk
1	cup cold water
$^1/_4$	cup confectioners' sugar
1	teaspoon vanilla extract
2	cups ice cubes

Combine all ingredients in a blender container. Blend on high speed until ice is completely dissolved.

Serve right away.

✦*Quick tip:* Place the orange juice concentrate in the refrigerator at night; it should be thawed and ready to use by morning.

✧*Serve-again hint:* Refrigerate any leftover drink and whirl it in the blender before serving.

Each serving provides:

100	Calories	22 g	Carbohydrate
3 g	Protein	33 mg	Sodium
0 g	Total fat (0 g Sat. fat)	1 mg	Cholesterol

Lemon-Lime Apple Spritzer

Cold, bubbly, and very thirst-quenching, this easy drink is a delicious and healthful substitute for soda. If you have time, be sure to use freshly squeezed lemon and lime juices. They're so much tastier than the bottled varieties.

Makes 6 servings
(1 cup each serving)

3   cups apple juice
3   tablespoons sugar
2^1/$_2$ tablespoons lemon juice
2^1/$_2$ teaspoons lime juice
2^3/$_4$ cups club soda, chilled

Combine apple juice, sugar, lemon juice, and lime juice in a pitcher or bottle. Chill.

At serving time, add club soda. Stir.

Serve in tall glasses over ice.

Each serving provides:

84	Calories	21 g	Carbohydrate
0 g	Protein	28 mg	Sodium
0 g	Total fat (0 g Sat. fat)	0 mg	Cholesterol

Pineapple-Grapefruit Fizzy

So refreshing and thirst-quenching, this delicious mix really hits the spot. It's a great party drink, at home everywhere from a backyard picnic to a fancy dinner party.

Makes 8 servings
(3/4 cup each serving)

1   6-ounce container frozen grapefruit juice concentrate, thawed
1¹/2   cups pineapple juice
1   liter ginger ale (33.8 ounces), chilled

Combine grapefruit juice concentrate and pineapple juice in a large bottle or pitcher. Chill.

Just before serving, add ginger ale.

Fill tall glasses with ice cubes. Pour drink over ice and serve.

◇*Serve-again hint:* Pour it into a tall glass over a half cup of vanilla fat-free or lowfat ice cream.

Each serving provides:

103	Calories	25 g	Carbohydrate
1 g	Protein	10 mg	Sodium
0 g	Total fat (0 g Sat. fat)	0 mg	Cholesterol

Iced Maple Coffee Floats

Here's a perfect use for that leftover morning coffee. Instead of throwing it away, how about a super coffee float for tonight's dessert? For more servings, the recipe doubles or triples easily.

Makes 2 servings

1¹/₂	cups strong coffee
2	tablespoons maple syrup
¹/₄	teaspoon ground cinnamon
¹/₂	teaspoon vanilla extract
¹/₈	teaspoon maple extract
1	cup vanilla fat-free or lowfat ice cream or frozen yogurt

Combine coffee with remaining ingredients, *except* ice cream. Chill thoroughly.

To serve, place ¹/₂ cup of ice cream in each of 2 glasses. Pour chilled coffee over the ice cream.

Serve right away.

Each serving provides:

161	Calories	37 g	Carbohydrate
2 g	Protein	52 mg	Sodium
0 g	Total fat (0 g Sat. fat)	0 mg	Cholesterol

Sober Sangria

This is my favorite nonalcoholic version of the popular Spanish drink. It's bubbly and cold and chock-full of delicious fruit. It makes a great party drink and also a perfect afternoon pick-me-up. I like to serve it in tall glasses, with long-handled iced tea spoons to use for scooping the fruit.

Makes 8 servings
(1 cup each serving)

2	cups grape juice (use the purple grape juice rather than the white)
2	cups cranberry juice cocktail
1/2	cup orange juice
1	tablespoon sugar
1	small, sweet apple, unpeeled, cut into quarters, then sliced 1/4-inch thick
1/2	medium orange, unpeeled, cut in half again, then sliced 1/4-inch thick
1/2	lemon, unpeeled, cut in half again, then sliced 1/4-inch thick
3	cups cold club soda

In a large pitcher, combine all ingredients, *except* club soda. Refrigerate several hours or overnight.

Just before serving, stir in club soda.

Fill tall glasses with ice cubes and spoon some fruit into the glasses. Top with sangria.

Each serving provides:

94	Calories	24 g	Carbohydrate
0 g	Protein	22 mg	Sodium
0 g	Total fat (0 g Sat. fat)	0 g	Cholesterol

Three-Fruit Smoothie

If you don't have a mango, you can use a can of drained, unsweetened apricot halves for this drink. Either way, this is a superb way to get the family to eat more fruit. It makes a perfect breakfast drink or after-school snack.

*Makes 4 servings
(1 cup each serving)*

1	large, ripe mango, peeled, center seed discarded
1	8-ounce can pineapple chunks, packed in juice, undrained
1	large, very ripe banana
1	8-ounce carton fat-free apricot, peach, or pineapple yogurt
1¹/₂	tablespoons sugar
¹/₂	teaspoon vanilla extract
1¹/₂	cups ice cubes

In a blender container, combine mango, pineapple, banana, yogurt, sugar, and vanilla. Blend until smooth. Add ice cubes, a few at a time, and continue to blend until ice is completely dissolved.

Pour into glasses and serve right away.

Each serving provides:

175	Calories	43 g	Carbohydrate
3 g	Protein	30 mg	Sodium
0 g	Total fat (0 g Sat. fat)	0 mg	Cholesterol

Tropical Treat

Fruit drinks such as this one were one of my son Mike's mainstays in college. Armed with his blender and a great imagination, he created this delicious combination.

Makes 2 servings
(1 cup each serving)

1/2	small, ripe banana
1/2	cup crushed pineapple (packed in juice), undrained
1/2	cup frozen strawberries, unthawed
1/3	cup orange juice
1/3	cup skim milk
2	teaspoons sugar
1/8	teaspoon coconut extract
1/2	cup ice cubes

In a blender container, combine all ingredients, *except* ice cubes. Blend, adding ice carefully while blending. Continue to blend until ice is dissolved.

Divide evenly into 2 glasses.

Serve right away.

Each serving provides:

121	Calories		29 g	Carbohydrate
2 g	Protein		23 mg	Sodium
0 g	Total fat (0 g Sat. fat)		1 mg	Cholesterol

Minted Pineapple Lemonade

*I discovered this refreshing combination by accident one day when I thought
I had defrosted two cans of lemonade. When I realized that one was pineapple
juice and the other was lemonade, I decided to make the best of it. The results
were delicious.*

Makes 6 servings
(about 1 cup each serving)

4	cups pineapple juice
2	cups water
1/2	cup frozen lemonade concentrate, thawed
1 1/2	tablespoons sugar or honey
1/4	teaspoon mint extract (make this a scant teaspoon)

Combine all ingredients in a large pitcher and mix well.
Pour over ice cubes in tall glasses.

❖*Serve-again hint:* The well-chilled leftover lemonade makes a
delectable fruit-flavored float. Simply pour it over a scoop of lowfat
or nonfat vanilla ice cream in a tall glass and enjoy.

Each serving provides:

143	Calories	36 g	Carbohydrate
1 g	Protein	3 mg	Sodium
0 g	Total fat (0 g Sat. fat)	0 mg	Cholesterol

Melon-Berry Cooler

One of the "thirst-quenchingest" drinks around, this cooler is a perfect summer treat. There's no better pick-me-up on a hot day.

Makes 2 servings
(1 cup each serving)

2   cups watermelon, cut into small balls or cubes, seeds removed
1   cup (rounded) frozen strawberries (unsweetened)
2   teaspoons lime juice

Combine all ingredients in a blender container. Blend just until smooth.

Serve right away.

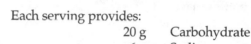

Each serving provides:			
86	Calories	20 g	Carbohydrate
1 g	Protein	6 mg	Sodium
1 g	Total fat (0 g Sat. fat)	0 mg	Cholesterol

Orange Bubbly

More nutritious than soda but with all the fizz, this refreshing, family-pleasing drink is packed with vitamin C. It's best when served right away, but it can be "refizzed" by stirring in a little more tonic water.

Makes 4 servings
(1 cup each serving)

1	6-ounce can frozen orange juice concentrate, thawed
3	cups chilled tonic water or seltzer water
1/2	fresh lime, cut into wedges

Pour orange juice concentrate into a large pitcher. Stir in tonic water.

Serve over ice. Add a lime wedge to each glass.

Store any leftovers, along with a few lime wedges, in a tightly covered bottle or jar.

Each serving provides:

149	Calories	37 g	Carbohydrate
1 g	Protein	9 mg	Sodium
0 g	Total fat (0 g Sat. fat)	0 mg	Cholesterol

Banana-Berry Shake

This creamy shake is cool, smooth, and refreshing, and you can vary the flavor by using lemon yogurt in place of vanilla. Why not try it both ways?

Makes 2 servings
(1¹/4 cups each serving)

1   medium, ripe banana, peeled, cut into chunks
1   cup frozen blueberries, unsweetened
1   tablespoon sugar or honey
5   ice cubes
1   cup vanilla nonfat yogurt (or lemon)

In a blender container, combine banana, blueberries, and sugar. Blend until smooth. Add ice and yogurt. Blend until ice is dissolved. Serve right away.

Each serving provides:

216	Calories	48 g	Carbohydrate
7 g	Protein	81 mg	Sodium
1 g	Total fat (0 g Sat. fat)	3 mg	Cholesterol

Cappuccino Frappé

Coffee lovers will be in ecstasy when they indulge in this cold, delicious, frothy drink. It's sweet and filling enough to count as dessert.

Makes 2 servings
(1 cup each serving)

1	cup reduced-fat or fat-free vanilla ice cream or frozen yogurt
1/2	cup chilled double-strength coffee (or you can use espresso)
1/2	teaspoon vanilla extract
1	teaspoon sugar (optional)
4	large ice cubes

In a blender container, combine ice cream, coffee, and vanilla (and sugar if desired). Turn blender on and carefully add ice cubes, one at a time, while blending. Blend 1 minute, or until ice is gone.

Serve right away.

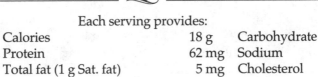

Each serving provides:

96	Calories	18 g	Carbohydrate
3 g	Protein	62 mg	Sodium
2 g	Total fat (1 g Sat. fat)	5 mg	Cholesterol

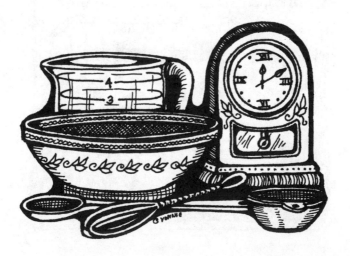

Juicy Tea Combo

There are so many delicious combinations you can try. Let your imagination guide you. Some of my favorites are blackberry tea with pineapple juice, almond tea with apple juice, raspberry tea with cranberry juice, and orange tea with apricot nectar. You can even combine two flavors of tea with the juice and create even more variations.

Makes 6 servings
(1 cup each serving)

4   herbal tea bags, any flavor (or combination of flavors)
4   cups boiling water
2   cups fruit juice, any flavor
1   tablespoon sugar or honey, or to taste

Place tea bags in boiling water and let steep according to package directions. Remove and discard tea bags.

In a pitcher or jar, combine tea with remaining ingredients. Stir to combine.

Chill thoroughly.

Serve over ice.

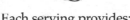

Each serving provides:			
48	Calories	12 g	Carbohydrate
0 g	Protein	2 mg	Sodium
0 g	Total fat (0 g Sat. fat)	0 mg	Cholesterol

Caribbean Party Tea

The combination of fruit juice and tea, lightly laced with rum, makes an island punch so refreshing, you'll think you hear the ocean waves!

Makes 8 servings
(about 1 cup each serving)

1½	cups pineapple juice
1½	cups apricot nectar
½	cup orange juice
⅓	cup rum
1	tablespoon lemon juice
¼	cup sugar or honey
½	teaspoon coconut extract
4	cups freshly brewed tea, regular or decaffeinated

In a large pitcher or jar, combine all ingredients, *except* tea. Mix well. Stir in tea.

Chill thoroughly.

Serve over ice, stirring tea before serving. Garnish with orange or lemon slices, if desired.

Each serving provides:

105	Calories	21 g	Carbohydrate
0 g	Protein	6 mg	Sodium
0 g	Total fat (0 g Sat. fat)	0 mg	Cholesterol

Mangoade

There's lemonade and there's limeade, so why not mangoade? It's cool, refreshing, and downright delicious.

Makes 5 servings
(1 cup each serving)

1   large, ripe mango, peeled and cut into chunks, center seed
        discarded
2   cups orange juice
1/4   cup lime juice
1/4   cup sugar
1/2   teaspoon grated fresh orange peel
2   cups water

In a blender container, combine mango, 1 cup of the orange juice, the lime juice, sugar, and orange peel. Blend until smooth. Pour through a strainer into a pitcher or jar.

Add water and remaining orange juice. Mix well.

Chill.

Stir before serving.

Each serving provides:

120	Calories	30 g	Carbohydrate
1 g	Protein	4 mg	Sodium
0 g	Total fat (0 g Sat. fat)	0 mg	Cholesterol

Carrot-Pineapple Juice

*There are lots of vitamins packed into this refreshing juice. Served ice cold,
it's perfect with snacks or as an accompaniment to any meal.*

Makes 2 servings
(³/₄ cup each serving)

1¹/₂   cups coarsely chopped carrots
1¹/₂   cups pineapple juice

In a blender container, combine carrots with *half* of the pineapple
juice. Blend thoroughly. Pour juice through a strainer into a small
pitcher or jar (reserve pulp—see note below). Stir in remaining juice.
Chill.

Note: Don't throw away the fiber-rich carrot pulp. Use it in breads or
muffins in place of applesauce, shredded carrots, or canned pumpkin.
It also works well in zucchini bread in place of the zucchini and is
great in the Carrot-Raisin Corn Muffins on page 279.

Each serving provides:			
89	Calories	22 g	Carbohydrate
1 g	Protein	19 mg	Sodium
0 g	Total fat (0 g Sat. fat)	0 mg	Cholesterol

Raspberry-Almond Smoothie

This is just one delicious flavor combination for making a thick, cold, refreshing fruit shake. You can create lots of others by simply varying the fruits, sherbet flavors, and extracts.

Makes 2 servings
(1¼ cups each serving)

1	cup raspberry sherbet (¹/₂ pint)
³/₄	cup skim milk
1	cup frozen raspberries (unsweetened or in light syrup), partially thawed (¹/₂ of a 10-ounce package)
¹/₄	teaspoon almond extract
¹/₈	teaspoon vanilla extract

Combine all ingredients in a blender container. Blend until smooth. Serve right away.

Each serving provides:

201	Calories	42 g	Carbohydrate
5 g	Protein	92 mg	Sodium
3 g	Total fat (1 g Sat. fat)	7 mg	Cholesterol

Orange-Berry Smoothie

The flavors of orange and raspberry complement each other so well in this super-sweet drink. Try other combinations, too, and create exciting new flavors by using different flavors of sherbet.

Makes 2 servings
(1¹/₄ cups each serving)

1	cup orange sherbet
³/₄	cup orange juice
1	cup frozen raspberries or strawberries (unsweetened or in light syrup), partially thawed
¹/₄	teaspoon vanilla extract

Combine all ingredients in a blender container. Blend until smooth. Serve right away.

Each serving provides:

210	Calories	48 g	Carbohydrate
2 g	Protein	45 mg	Sodium
3 g	Total fat (1 g Sat. fat)	5 mg	Cholesterol

Apricot-Berry Fruit Floaters

A simple favorite among both kids and adults, these colorful cubes can be added to ice tea or any flavor juice. They also make great warm weather snacks. (A fruit cube in a paper cup can keep a little one happy for quite a while.) And, if you like, you can be creative and make the cubes out of other juice flavors and use other fruits for the centers.

Makes 12 to 14 cubes

12 to 14 assorted strawberries, blueberries, and raspberries (fresh or frozen)

2   cups apricot nectar (this is an approximate amount, since the sizes of ice cube trays varies)

Place a berry in each section of a divided ice cube tray. Pour juice over fruit.

Freeze until cubes are solid.

To serve, place cubes in a tall glass and add ice tea, fruit juice, or iced herbal tea.

Each serving provides:

23	Calories	6 g	Carbohydrate
0 g	Protein	1 mg	Sodium
0 g	Total fat (0 g Sat. fat)	0 mg	Cholesterol

Spiced Lemonade Tea

This versatile, old-fashioned lemonade can be a cool summer refresher or a soothing, cold-weather fireside drink. Pour it over ice cubes in tall glasses or heat it in a saucepan or microwave and pour it into mugs. Why not try it both ways?

Makes 6 servings
(1 cup each serving)

3   cups water
2   cups tea, either regular or decaffeinated
1/2   cup lemon juice
1/2   cup sugar
1/8   teaspoon ground cloves

Combine all ingredients in a pitcher (or saucepan, if serving hot). Stir until sugar is dissolved.

Serve hot or cold.

Each serving provides:			
70	Calories	19 g	Carbohydrate
0 g	Protein	3 mg	Sodium
0 g	Total fat (0 g Sat. fat)	0 mg	Cholesterol

Mocha-Orange-Spice Coffee

*A perfect, sweet ending to any meal, this dessert-type coffee is all you need.
Or, sip it by the fire with a friend. It'll warm your heart.*

Makes 2 servings
(³/₄ cup each serving)

1	tablespoon firmly packed brown sugar
1	tablespoon cocoa (unsweetened)
¹/₈	teaspoon grated fresh orange peel
¹/₁₆	teaspoon ground cinnamon
¹/₁₆	teaspoon ground allspice
1¹/₂	cups strong, hot coffee (regular or decaffeinated)
3	tablespoons nonfat dry milk
¹/₄	cup very hot water

In a blender container, combine brown sugar, cocoa, orange peel,
and spices. Add hot coffee. Blend until smooth, about 5 seconds.

Dissolve dry milk in hot water and add to blender. Blend on high
speed until frothy.

Serve right away.

◆*Quick tip:* The water for the dry milk can be heated in the microwave for a few seconds while the rest is blending. If you prefer,
¹/₄ cup evaporated skim milk (also heated) can be used instead.

\multicolumn{4}{c}{**Each serving provides:**}			
60	Calories	13 g	Carbohydrate
3 g	Protein	43 mg	Sodium
0 g	Total fat (0 g Sat. fat)	1 mg	Cholesterol

Tahitian Tea

A delicate combination of flavors makes this tea a special hot treat. It's a wonderful breakfast drink, especially alongside a steaming bowl of hot cereal. It's also a delicious fireside drink to share with special friends.

Makes 3 servings
(1 cup each serving)

1	cup orange juice
1	cup pineapple juice
1	cup water
1	2¹/₂-inch cinnamon stick
2	nickel-size pieces of fresh ginger root
2	teaspoons firmly packed brown sugar
14	whole cloves
¹/₄	teaspoon anise seeds
1	peppermint-flavored herbal tea bag

In a small saucepan, combine all ingredients, *except* tea bag. Bring to a boil over medium heat, stirring occasionally. Reduce heat to medium-low and simmer, uncovered, 5 minutes.

Add tea bag, cover, remove from heat, and let stand 5 to 10 minutes.

Pour tea through a strainer into mugs.

❖*Serve-again hint:* Leftovers can be served cold or reheated and served hot.

Each serving provides:

96	Calories	24 g	Carbohydrate
1 g	Protein	7 mg	Sodium
0 g	Total fat (0 g Sat. fat)	0 mg	Cholesterol

Hot Spiced Cider with Honey and Lemon

A special autumn treat, apple cider is delicious when simmered with spices and served steaming hot in mugs. For a festive appearance, garnish each mug with a slice of lemon and add a cinnamon stick for stirring.

Makes 4 servings
(1 cup each serving)

1	quart apple cider
$1/3$	cup honey
$1/2$	medium lemon, unpeeled, sliced crosswise into $1/4$-inch slices
2	$2^{1}/2$-inch cinnamon sticks
8	whole cloves

Combine all ingredients in a small saucepan. Bring to a boil over medium heat. Reduce heat to medium-low and simmer 15 minutes.

Pour cider through a strainer into mugs.

Serve right away.

❖*Serve-again hint:* Leftovers can be served cold or reheated in a saucepan or in a microwave. If you have an office microwave, take some along for a unique coffee-break treat.

	Each serving provides:		
206	Calories	54 g	Carbohydrate
0 g	Protein	10 mg	Sodium
0 g	Total fat (0 g Sat. fat)	0 mg	Cholesterol

Cranberry Cider Punch

On a cold winter day, this wonderful, hot punch will really warm your heart. The cranberry juice and spices add just the right amount of zip.

Makes 10 servings
(1 cup each serving)

1	32-ounce bottle apple juice
4	cups water
1	12-ounce can frozen cranberry-raspberry juice concentrate, thawed
1/2	cup orange juice
2	3-inch cinnamon sticks
1/4	cup firmly packed brown sugar
1	teaspoon whole cloves
1	teaspoon whole allspice

In a large saucepan, combine apple juice, water, cranberry-raspberry juice concentrate, orange juice, cinnamon sticks, and brown sugar.

Place cloves and allspice in a tea strainer or tie them in cheesecloth to make a spice bag. Add them to saucepan. Bring to a boil over medium-high heat. Reduce heat to low, cover, and simmer 15 minutes.

Remove and discard spice bag and cinnamon sticks.

Spoon punch into mugs and serve hot.

✧*Serve-again hint:* Serve as a delicious cold beverage or pour into a mug and reheat in a microwave.

Each serving provides:

161	Calories	40 g	Carbohydrate
0 g	Protein	10 mg	Sodium
0 g	Total fat (0 g Sat. fat)	0 mg	Cholesterol

Café Mocha

One of my favorite breakfast drinks, this steamy, hot mixture of coffee and cocoa is a delicious way to start the day. Add a homemade muffin and you have perfection. This recipe is for one serving, but it can easily be multiplied to make more.

Makes 1 serving
(³/4 cup each serving)

3	tablespoons nonfat dry milk
1¹/2	teaspoons sugar
1	teaspoon cocoa (unsweetened)
³/4	cup hot coffee
¹/8	teaspoon vanilla extract

Combine dry milk, sugar, and cocoa in a coffee cup or mug. Mix well. Pour hot coffee into cup, stirring to dissolve cocoa mixture. Stir in vanilla.

Serve right away.

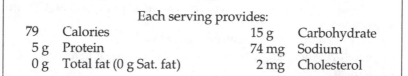

Each serving provides:

79	Calories		15 g	Carbohydrate
5 g	Protein		74 mg	Sodium
0 g	Total fat (0 g Sat. fat)		2 mg	Cholesterol

Warm Indian Milk Punch

A wonderful fragrance and delicate flavor make this tea perfect with snacks at teatime or anytime.

Makes 4 servings
(1 cup each serving)

3¹/₂	cups water
10	whole cloves
¹/₂	teaspoon fennel seeds
¹/₄	teaspoon ground cardamom
3	tablespoons sugar
1	3-inch cinnamon stick
2	nickel-size slices fresh ginger root
4	tea bags (regular or decaffeinated)
1	cup skim milk

In a medium saucepan, combine water with remaining ingredients, *except* tea bags and milk. Bring to a boil over medium heat, stirring occasionally. Reduce heat to medium-low and simmer 10 minutes. Add tea bags, cover, remove pan from heat, and let stand 10 minutes.

Add milk and reheat over medium heat until punch is hot. Discard tea bags.

Pour punch through a small strainer into 4 mugs.

❖*Serve-again hint:* Enjoy the leftovers cold or reheat in a saucepan or in a microwave.

Each serving provides:

63	Calories	14 g	Carbohydrate
2 g	Protein	40 mg	Sodium
0 g	Total fat (0 g Sat. fat)	1 mg	Cholesterol

Glossary of Ingredients

All-purpose flour   The most commonly used flour. It has been milled, so, unlike whole wheat flour, it has been stripped of the bran and the germ. For added fiber and vitamins, it can be used in combination with whole wheat flour.

Arborio rice   A starchy, short-grained Italian rice that creates a thick, creamy sauce as it cooks, yet retains the firmness of the grain. It is available in specialty stores and in many large grocery stores.

Barley   A whole grain available in most grocery stores. Most stores carry "pearled" barley, which is the commonly used form that has had the tough outer hull removed.

Basmati rice   A scented rice with a delicate nut-like flavor and aroma. It is used in Indian and Middle Eastern cooking and is available in health food stores, specialty stores, and many large grocery stores.

Black beans   Also known as turtle beans. They are used extensively in Mexican and Caribbean cooking and are available in grocery stores and health food stores in dry form and also canned and ready to use.

Black-eyed peas   Legumes that are widely used in African and Caribbean cooking. They have an earthy flavor and are available in dry form or in cans in most grocery stores.

Brown rice   Rice with the outer bran remaining. It has been minimally processed and is more nutritious than white rice. It is available in health food and grocery stores.

Bulgur   Whole wheat berries that have been steamed, then dried and cracked. It is similar to cracked wheat, which has not been steamed and therefore takes a little longer to cook. Most recipes use them interchangeably, which is not a problem as long as you read the label and follow the suggested cooking time.

Cannellini   White kidney beans. They are a popular ingredient in Italian cooking. *See* Kidney beans.

Cheddar cheese   A semi-firm cheese that is available as either whole milk, reduced-fat, or fat-free. I prefer the flavor and "meltability" of the reduced-fat over the fat-free.

Chick peas   Also known as garbanzo beans. They are firm-textured legumes that are used extensively in Indian and Middle Eastern cooking. Chick peas are available in health food stores and in most large grocery stores in dry form or canned and ready to use.

Chilies   The most used seasoning in Mexican cuisine. These peppers are available either fresh, canned, or dried.

Cider vinegar   A tangy vinegar made from apple juice. It is available in grocery stores and has a unique, fruity flavor.

Cilantro   The leaf of the coriander plant, also known as Chinese parsley. It is a pungent herb with a slightly musty flavor and is often used in Asian and Latin American cooking.

Cinnamon stick   The dried bark of a certain type of evergreen tree. It is in the form of a rolled-up stick and can be used whole to season liquids. It is available in jars in the spice section of most large grocery stores.

Confectioners' sugar   Also known as powdered sugar. It is ideal for sprinkling on desserts and for making glazes and icings.

Cornmeal   A grain made from finely ground dried corn. It is used in corn breads, corn puddings, and tortillas. Look for stone-ground cornmeal in health food stores and most grocery stores.

Cornstarch   A powdery white thickener. It is derived from corn and gives a transparent sheen to sauces. It is used to thicken soups, stews, puddings, and sauces. It is usually found with the baking ingredients in grocery stores.

Cottage cheese   A soft cheese that is available in varieties from full-fat to fat-free. I prefer the flavor and texture of the lowfat (1% milkfat) variety. For a nondairy substitute, crumbled tofu will work in most recipes.

Couscous   A semolina product, similar to tiny bits of pasta. It cooks very quickly and is a popular ingredient in Middle Eastern and North African cooking. Couscous is found with either the grains or imported products in most grocery stores.

Cracked wheat   *See* Bulgur.

Dates   Glossy, very sweet, oval fruits grown mostly in the Middle East and California. They are usually sold dried and can be eaten as is or chopped and added to baked goods. They are available in health food stores and most grocery stores.

Dijon mustard   A tangy French mustard made with white wine. It is available in most grocery stores.

Egg whites   In all of my recipes I use egg whites in place of whole eggs, because the cholesterol is all in the yolk. (Two egg whites are equivalent to one whole egg.) Commercial egg substitutes can be used, but in many cases it is more economical to buy the whole eggs and just use the whites. In most baked goods, a three-ounce piece of tofu will also work in place of one egg. (Place the tofu in a blender with the liquid ingredients and blend until smooth.)

Farina   Coarse-grained particles of wheat. Packaged under the name Farina or Cream of Wheat, it is available in the cereal section of most large grocery stores. It can be eaten as a hot cereal and is often used to make desserts in Asian and Middle Eastern countries.

Fennel   A plant of Mediterranean origin, also known as finocchio. It has a licorice-like flavor that mellows when the vegetable is cooked. Fennel can be eaten raw or cooked. It is frequently used in Italian and Mediterranean cooking.

Feta cheese   A white cheese made from goat's milk. It has a distinctive tangy flavor and is a common ingredient in Greek cooking. It is high in sodium, but its strong flavor allows it to be used sparingly. Feta is available in most large grocery stores.

Ginger root   A tuber that resembles a thick, knobby root. It has a pungent, hot flavor and plays a prominent role in the cooking of most Asian countries. It is not necessary to peel ginger root before using. Look for it in the produce section of most large grocery stores.

Great Northern beans   White beans with a mild flavor and soft texture. They are available in dry form or canned and ready to use and can be found in most large grocery stores.

Green chilies   Green chili peppers that are available with the foreign foods in most grocery stores. The varieties include mild, medium, or hot, and both chopped or whole. I prefer the quality of the whole ones, and I buy them and chop them myself.

Jalapeño pepper   A small, fiercely hot green chili that is popular in Mexico.

Jicama   A tuber from a tropical plant. It resembles a turnip and has a crunchy texture and sweet flavor. It can be eaten raw or cooked and in Mexico is often used in salads. It also makes a good dipping vegetable.

Kasha   Buckwheat groats, or grits. This grain has a nutty flavor and is a common ingredient in Russian cooking. Kasha is found in health food stores and with either the grains or imported foods in most large grocery stores. Different sizes (granulations) may be available; most recipes use the small or medium sizes.

Kidney beans   Kidney-shaped legumes. Red and white (cannellini) varieties are available in health food stores and most grocery stores in dry form or canned and ready to use. They are most commonly used in soups and stews.

Lemon peel   The outermost yellow part of the lemon. It is usually called "lemon zest" and does not include the white part of the peel.

Lentils   Small, thin legumes that are available in different colors, including yellow, red, and greenish-brown. They are available dried in health food stores and grocery stores and cook more quickly than other legumes.

Mango   A sweet fruit with a soft texture and perfumy flavor. It is extremely popular in India, Mexico, and the Caribbean. Mangoes are available in the produce section of most large grocery stores. When ripe they turn shades of red, yellow and orange, and they must be peeled before eating.

Molasses   A liquid sweetener that is a by-product of sugar cane refining. The darker the molasses, the stronger the flavor. Blackstrap molasses, the darkest, is higher in minerals and is usually found in health food stores, while the lighter varieties are found in grocery stores.

Mozzarella cheese   An indispensable cheese in Italian cooking. It is available as either whole-milk, part-skim, reduced-fat, or nonfat.

I prefer the flavor and "meltability" of the part-skim variety over that of the reduced-fat or nonfat.

Olive oil   The favored oil in Italian, Greek, and Middle Eastern cooking. It is high in monounsaturated fat, a quality many health experts believe can help lower blood cholesterol levels. For the lightest flavor, look for extra-virgin olive oil. It is available in grocery stores and keeps best in a cool, dark place.

Orange peel   The outermost orange part of the orange. It is usually called "orange zest" and does not include the white part of the peel.

Oriental noodles   There are many varieties, however, for the recipes in this book, I prefer either soba (buckwheat) or somen (wheat) noodles. Both are found in health food stores, Asian groceries, and many large grocery stores.

Orzo   A tiny, rice-shaped pasta. It is found in the pasta section of most grocery stores.

Papaya   A tropical fruit popular in Mexico, the Caribbean, and many Asian countries. It turns yellow when ripe and the skin and seeds must be discarded. Papayas are available in the produce section of most large grocery stores.

Parmesan cheese   A hard cheese that is most abundant in Italian cooking. It can be purchased already grated, but tastes so much richer when bought in a chunk and grated just before using. Most health food stores carry a variety made from soy milk.

Peanut butter   Made from ground peanuts. Choose one made without added sugar or fat.

Penne   A tube-shaped pasta. They are about 2 inches long and are cut diagonally on the ends.

Picante sauce   A spicy, tomato-based sauce that is used as a condiment with many Mexican dishes. It is available in jars in most grocery stores and is either mild, medium, or hot.

Pimientos   Sweet red peppers. They are found in jars and are usually alongside the pickles in most large grocery stores.

Pinto beans   Legumes that are popular in Mexican dishes. They are a mottled color in the dry form and turn an even, light brown when cooked. They are also available canned and ready to use and are found in most grocery stores.

Pita bread   Flat breads. They can be opened to form a pocket and filled with a variety of sandwich fillings. They are available in most large grocery stores and are popular in Middle Eastern countries. Choose the whole wheat variety.

Polenta   A cornmeal pudding made by cooking cornmeal in water. It can be thick or thin and can be served as a hot breakfast cereal or as a side dish or entrée.

Portobello mushrooms   Thick and meaty mushrooms available in the produce department of most large grocery stores. (They look like giant mushrooms.) The tough stems are not edible.

Quinoa (pronounced KEEN-wah)   A relatively quick-cooking grain that's very high in protein and is also an excellent source of minerals. It has a fluffy texture and a light, subtle flavor.

Red wine vinegar   *See* Wine vinegar.

Rhubarb   A vegetable with long, red, celery-like stalks. It is considered to be a fruit by most people. It is very tart and is often combined with other fruits to make pies. The leaves are toxic and must be discarded.

Ricotta cheese   A soft, bland cheese. It is available in either whole-milk, part-skim, or nonfat varieties and is used extensively in Italian cooking, especially in lasagne and in cheesecakes. I prefer the texture of the part-skim over that of the nonfat, which tends to be watery. I have had good results by combining both part-skim and nonfat in a recipe.

Rolled oats   Whole oats that have been steamed and flattened into flakes. They are different from quick-cooking oats, which are cut into smaller, thinner pieces. Most grocery stores carry rolled oats in the cereal section. They are often called "old-fashioned oats."

Salsa   Mexican sauces. They are served as dips or spooned over many Mexican bean dishes and tortilla dishes, such as tacos, burritos, and enchiladas. The most familiar are the tomato-based salsas that are found in jars in most grocery stores. They are available either mild, medium, or hot.

Sesame oil An oil that is pressed from sesame seeds and has a strong, toasty flavor. It is generally used in small quantities to flavor Asian and Indian dishes.

Sherry A wine that is excellent for cooking. I buy an inexpensive medium to medium-dry sherry, rather than the more expensive cooking sherry.

Shiitake mushrooms Popular Asian mushrooms. They have a smoky flavor and large, meaty brown caps. The stems are tough and should be discarded. Shiitakes are available dried or fresh in many large grocery stores and also in Asian specialty stores.

Silken tofu Tofu with a smooth, custardy texture. See "All About Tofu" on page 16.

Snow peas Peas with an edible pod. They are used abundantly in Asian cooking and are delicious stir-fried. They are available fresh in most large grocery stores.

Soy sauce A product made from fermented soy beans. It is essential to Chinese and Japanese cooking and is available in regular and reduced-sodium forms in most grocery stores. Asian markets carry a wide variety of imported brands with different ingredients and flavors.

Split peas Small dried peas. They may be green or yellow and are excellent in soups and stews. They are available in dried form in health food stores and most grocery stores.

Sun-dried tomatoes Tomatoes that are dried, giving them a sweet flavor and chewy texture. They are available in most large grocery stores. Buy them dry and reconstitute them in boiling water, rather than buying the ones that are packed in oil.

Tahini Made from ground sesame seeds. It has a texture similar to peanut butter and is often used in sauces in Middle Eastern countries.

Tofu Also called bean curd, it is made from soy beans. See "All About Tofu" on page 16.

Tomato sauce Most grocery stores carry salt-free tomato sauce, which is lower in sodium than regular tomato sauce.

Tomatoes, canned Salt-free canned tomatoes are lower in sodium than regular canned tomatoes and are available in most grocery stores.

Tortillas   Thin, flat breads made of either corn or wheat flour. They are generally available refrigerated or frozen and are staples of Mexican cooking.

Vegetable broth   A meatless soup base made from vegetables, water, and spices. (See page 32.)

Vegetable broth mix   A combination of soup-flavored spices. (See page 34.)

Vegetable oil   When recipes call for vegetable oil, choose canola oil, which is low in saturated fat and high in monounsaturated fat. See page 3.

Wine vinegar   A mild vinegar that is pungent without being harsh. It is available either red or white, with color being the main difference.

Yellow split peas   *See* Split peas.

Yogurt   A cultured milk product. It is available in whole-milk, lowfat, and nonfat forms and can be used to replace sour cream in recipes.

Yolk-free noodles   Noodles that are made with egg whites rather than whole eggs and do not contain cholesterol. They are available in most grocery stores.

Index

International Conversion Chart

These are not exact equivalents: they have been slightly rounded to make measuring easier.

LIQUID MEASUREMENTS

American	Imperial	Metric	Australian
2 tablespoons (1 oz.)	1 fl. oz.	30 ml	1 tablespoon
1/4 cup (2 oz.)	2 fl. oz.	60 ml	2 tablespoons
1/3 cup (3 oz.)	3 fl. oz.	80 ml	1/4 cup
1/2 cup (4 oz.)	4 fl. oz.	125 ml	1/3 cup
2/3 cup (5 oz.)	5 fl. oz.	165 ml	1/2 cup
3/4 cup (6 oz.)	6 fl. oz.	185 ml	2/3 cup
1 cup (8 oz.)	8 fl. oz.	250 ml	3/4 cup

SPOON MEASUREMENTS

American	Metric
1/4 teaspoon	1 ml
1/2 teaspoon	2 ml
1 teaspoon	5 ml
1 tablespoon	15 ml

WEIGHTS

US/UK	Metric
1 oz.	30 grams (g)
2 oz.	60 g
4 oz. (1/4 lb)	125 g
5 oz. (1/3 lb)	155 g
6 oz.	185 g
7 oz.	220 g
8 oz. (1/2 lb)	250 g
10 oz.	315 g
12 oz. (3/4 lb)	375 g
14 oz.	440 g
16 oz. (1 lb)	500 g
2 lbs	1 kg

OVEN TEMPERATURES

Farenheit	Centigrade	Gas
250	120	1/2
300	150	2
325	160	3
350	180	4
375	190	5
400	200	6
450	230	8